Urban Poverty in Britain 1830–1914

James H. Treble

Department of History
University of Strathclyde

Batsford Academic

FOR MY MOTHER AND FATHER

First published 1979
© James H. Treble

ISBN 0 7134 1906 7

Printed and bound in Great Britain by
Redwood Burn Ltd,
Trowbridge & Esher

for the publishers, B.T. Batsford Ltd
4 Fitzhardinge Street, London W1H 0AH

Contents

List of Tables

Preface

This book is primarily concerned with three themes. Firstly, it attempts to delineate the principal causes of poverty. Secondly, it looks at those expedients which were employed to mitigate some of its social consequences. Thirdly, it tries to show what poverty actually meant in terms of food consumption and housing. But since it is devoted to urban society, it largely ignores the equally, or perhaps more, pressing problems posed by rural poverty. Partly the exclusion of the countryside has been dictated by the necessary limitations imposed by word length. But partly also it reflects my view that the rural problem could not be satisfactorily integrated within the thematic framework which has been adopted. In many important respects the experience of the rural worker differs from that of his urban counterpart. Rural society poses the problem of how to evaluate payments in kind at a time when they had largely disappeared in an urban setting. The nature of rural credit differed in certain important respects from that which was available to the town dwellers. There were marked differences between the urban and rural labour markets, although there were equally significant divergences, for at least part of this period, between the markets for agricultural labour in Scotland and England. Again, it would be difficult to discuss social suffering amongst the crofting community in the Scottish Highlands within the approach adopted in this volume. In short, rural poverty requires to be treated in a separate book.

Like most authors, I am indebted to many individuals and institutions. I am indebted, first of all, to Professor Asa Briggs who, at the University of Leeds, introduced me to the works of the nineteenth century social analysts and who showed me, as an undergraduate, that the poverty question was an important subject for academic study in its own right. I am grateful, too, to the late Professor W.H.B. Court who, during my period as Research Assistant at the University of Birmingham, encouraged me to probe into the social literature of the post-1870 period and who helped to shape some of my early thoughts upon the nature of urban poverty. In the preparation and completion of this book, I owe most to Hamish Fraser and Tom Devine, my friends and colleagues at Strathclyde, who have read, and commented critically upon, most of the final draft. I have greatly benefited from their wise counsel. I am also indebted to my friend and colleague John Hume who looked at my section upon technological unemployment and who, in discussion, has increased my understanding of the relationship between economic growth and technical change. Another debt which must be acknowledged is to my former student, Dr. Norman Murray, who generously made available to me his transcripts from the Scottish press for the 1830s and 1840s and who drew to my attention, and translated from the Gaelic, the poem on old age pensions which has been incorporated into Chapter 3. Bette Duncan of the University of Strathclyde gave in invaluable assistance in collecting material on poverty and unemployment in the West of Scotland during the first decade and a half of the twentieth century. I am grateful also to the Staff of the Mitchell Library, Glasgow, the University of Glasgow Library, and the Reading Room and State Paper Room of the British Museum for their assistance in dealing with my queries; to my friend and colleague Tom McAloon, who on occasion kept my flagging spirits going; and to my uncle and aunt, Mr. and Mrs. Adam Manderston, who kindly provided me with a base from which to work when I was in London. I am also greatly indebted to Mrs. David Elder of Dunlop, Ayrshire, who has speedily and expertly produced an excellent typescript from a far from legible manuscript; to the late Rev. W.J. Moffat and Mr. L.V. Wells, successively Senior History Masters at Lawrence Sheriff School, Rugby, for introducing me to social history; and to Professor J.T. Ward for suggesting that I should tackle this topic. Again, I am grateful to my Honours Students, past and present, who have stimulated my interest in, and made me re-examine some of my views on, the nature of urban poverty. Finally, I wish to thank my parents who have profoundly influenced, through their own conversation, the way in which I have come to look upon the poverty question. To them, in gratitude and affection, this book is dedicated.

Department of History,
University of Strathclyde.

Introduction

The attempt made by Henry Mayhew in 1851 to differentiate between 'good and bad wages' presented in an embryonic form the concept of the national minimum. In his own words:

> the test . . . for bare sufficiency of wages is, such a rate of remuneration as will maintain not only the labourer himself while working and also when unable to work, but support his family, and admit of the care and education of his children; and as those wages may be termed good which admit of more than this being done, even so are they bad which admit of less.[1]

How broadly Mayhew's middle-class contemporaries would have subscribed to this definition of the social wage is impossible to determine with any degree of precision. None the less, despite this fundamental drawback, certain generalisations can still be confidently advanced about middle-class attitudes towards the main features of Mayhew's thesis. Many, while acknowledging the reality of below subsistence earnings, revealed in the parochial investigations of the emerging statistical societies' movement and in the 1834-5 and 1835-41 inquiries into the conditions of handloom weavers, would have rejected that part of the argument which sought to attach moral opprobrium to employers whose rates of pay failed to guarantee a modest standard of well-being. Furthermore, this act of rejection was not simply an emotional reaction to unpleasant social facts or a defence mechanism to the 'underconsumptionist' analysis of poverty which was articulated by working-class Chartists and Owenists. For it derived its intellectual justification from the impersonal interaction of market forces and, what was less easily reconcilable with that concept, the 'iron law of wages' — that wildly unfactual, but socially comforting, *apologia* for low pay — whose grasp on the thinking of the middle classes had not yet been broken. A small minority, however, propagators of more heterodox views, would have accepted the essential validity of Mayhew's attack upon the socially irresponsible manufacture or sub-contractor. Among this number would be included Thomas Carlyle whose *Past and Present*, published almost a decade earlier, portrayed starkly the existence of widespread social suffering in the midst of the richest nation in the world, and John Ruskin who, in *Unto This Last* (1861), not merely attacked the 'received' notions of political economy but denounced the spirit of commercialism which sacrificed the working man's best interests to the search for profit. In Ruskin's eyes, what British society required was the adoption of a value system which recognised the worth, and cultivated the development, of the individual. As he expressed it in an evocative passage, in some far-away and yet undreamt-of hour, I can even imagine that England may cast all thoughts of possessive wealth back to the barbaric nations, among whom they first arose; and that, while the sands of the Indus and adamant of Golconda may yet stiffen the housings of the charger, and flash from the turban of the slave, she, as a Christian mother, may at last attain to the virtues and the treasures of a Heathen one, and be able to lead forth her Sons, saying —

'These are MY Jewels'.[2]

Yet while there was this element of debate about the degree of moral responsibility which was attached to the employer who paid his work force badly, there was at the same time a surprising volume of support for Mayhew's definition of 'good wages'. Most middle-class writers who turned their attention to the subject of poverty in the middle decades of the nineteenth century, tended to assume — for relatively few explored the question statistically — that the bulk of the working classes had an income sufficient both to guarantee them reasonable standards of housing and feeding and to enable them to provide cover, through friendly societies and savings banks, for all the ordinary contingencies of life. Rising real wages and shifts from low to better paid jobs in the occupational structure would merely serve to accelerate the rate, and to broaden the dimensions, of working-class advance. But society as a whole, it was accepted, could fulfil a positive role in ensuring the maintenance of this desirable social trend, since it could help to mould a climate of opinion and social institutions conducive to the growth of the spirit of 'improvement'. In one sense the New Poor Law Act of 1834 for England and Wales and the 1845 statute which overhauled the Scottish system of pauper relief can be interpreted as promoting that end. One of the cardinal objectives of the 1834 settlement was, through the twin doctrines of 'less eligibility' and the workhouse test, to wean the able-bodied away for reliance upon 'doles' from the poor rate in areas or occupations where there was a pool of under employed labour. In their stead was to be placed the goal of self-sufficiency which would be achieved either through a rise in the 'natural' rate of wages, once the burden of the poor rate had been lightened, or through migration to towns and cities where labour shortages were reputed to exist. Similarly, the 1845 Scottish measure in its final form disappointed the hopes of those reformers, led by Professor Alison, who had vainly pleaded for the inclusion of the able-bodies as legitimate objects for poor relief. In Scotland, even more than in England and Wales, the social assumption behind poor law reform was that the able-bodied could, through the exercise of foresight and prudence, provide for those periods of unemployment which afflicted over time virtually every household. At a different level the writings of Samuel Smiles and, what was equally important, the simplification of his message for a mass audience at the hands of a host of minor publicists, sought to promulgate the virtues of thrift and self-help as the surest route to working-class independence. Last, but not least, the Charity Organisation Society, which emerged in London in 1869 to advance the cause of 'scientific charity', explicitly subscribed to the view that 'good wages' were the norm in working-class society. As it proclaimed in its Annual Report for 1876, 'the

C.O.S

principle is, that it is good for the poor that they should meet all the *ordinary* contingencies of life, relying not upon public or private charity, but upon their own industry and thrift, and upon the powers of self-help that are to be developed by individual and collective effort.'[3]

According to this analysis, therefore, true poverty was a residual problem, restricted to diminishing pockets of badly paid outworkers, framework knitters, handloom weavers and 'sweated' clothing workers among them, whose occupations would ultimately be extinguished as industry underwent the process of organisational and structural change. But alongside this type of poverty which was the product of exogenous forces at work in the economy was a pervasive indigence which stemmed from the unwise management of 'good wages'. In this context, drink, bad housekeeping and the continuing celebration of 'St. Monday' loomed large in the catalogue of offences which were laid at the door of the undeserving poor. Outwardly this line of reasoning was attractive since it coincided with, and reinforced, many of the most deeply held prejudices of early Victorian society about the nature and causes of working-class poverty. Furthermore, it was in certain respects accurate. Drink and drinking customs played a prominent part in working-class life for most of the period with which this study is concerned. As G.R. Porter commented in 1850, although with much exaggeration,

> among the working classes, so very large a portion of the earnings of the male head of the family is devoted by him to his personal and sensual gratification. It has been computed that among those whose earnings are from 10s to 15s. weekly, at least one-half is spent upon objects in which the other members of the family have no share. among artisans earning from 20s. to 30s. weekly, it can be said that at least one-third of the amount is in many cases thus selfishly devoted.[4]

This pattern of heavy drinking already firmly established by the time that Porter was making his observations, was not to change fundamentally for the better until after 1875-6 when the peak *per capita* consumption figures for beer and spirits were recorded. Yet when due acknowledgement has been made of the significance of these self-inflicted wounds — and this theme will be examined in depth in a subsequent chapter, — the explanation, considered as a whole, is unconvincing. And it is unconvincing basically because its whole emphasis is wrong. Poverty in urban society was much more a produce of specifically economic forces and the social environment which those economic pressures helped to create, and much less the product of moral failings on the part of the individual, than the majority of early victorian thinkers were prepared to allow. For as the pioneering investigations of Charles Booth in London, Seebohm Rowntree in York, Eleanor Rathbone in Liverpool, R.H. Tawney in Glasgow and A.L. Bowley and A.R. Burnett-Hurst in Stanley, Northampton, Reading and Warrington were to demonstrate, urban poverty in the closing years of the nineteenth, and the early years of the twentieth, centuries stemmed principally from low earnings, under employment and unemployment and those questions of family circumstance — illness, widowhood, old age — over which the individual had no control, — and this at a period when the average real income of the working classes was almost fifty per cent higher, at its lowest point, than when Mayhew wrote.[5]

While, therefore, the 'good wage' remained a highly desirable social objective at which the working classes should aim, it has to be abandoned as an analytical tool for drawing the parameters of the poverty problem in the Victorian and Edwardian eras. Its drawbacks are threefold. Firstly, the vagueness of the term itself as to what margin of income was necessary, once subsistence had been obtained, to secure additional social benefits and its failure to take into account the important consideration as to whether the social aims of thrift might alter in the post-1851 world, deprive it of any reasonable degree of precision in measuring the changing incidence of poverty over time. Secondly, 'good wages', in Mayhew's sense, only accrued to a small minority of the working classes throughout the nineteenth century. According to Thomas Wright, writing in 1873,

> it is making a liberal allowance on the favourable side of the matter, to say that not more than one in twenty of the working class get within the standard of comfort we have sketched — who have always a sufficiency of food and clothing, and a decent and healthy home; and who, when too old to find employment in a market in which employers have a choice of younger men, can maintain themselves without having to seek public charity, or becoming dependent upon relatives who, being themselves in straitened circumstances, generally regard such dependence as a burden, and make it very bitter.[6]

Much the same point was made in 1902-3 by A. M'Gillivray and T. Fraser of the Central Glasgow Lodge of the United Operative Masons when they argued that 'to ask a member of the working class if he could save money is . . . impertinence . . . there is no man who is a member of the working class who is able to live and enjoy the luxuries of life, and every one has the right to enjoy the luxuries of life as another.'[7] What these testimonies indicated in unmistakable terms was that the earnings of a substantial proportion of the aristocracy of labour — for M'Gillivray and Fraser were earning, on a yearly basis, 30s. per week,[8] a figure well above Rowntree's primary poverty line of 21/8d. for a moderately sized family — failed to conform to the basic criteria of 'good' remuneration which Mayhew had enunciated half a century earlier. But in relation to the social phenomenon of poverty itself, the vast majority of the working classes would not have equated it with a level of income which made the practice of the Smilesian virtues difficult; rather it represented a more basic social experience in which a considerable proportion of working men and women found themselves unable, even in conditions of full employment, to earn enough to guarantee their families a subsistence diet. In its extreme form, this kind of deprivation was perhaps most marked, at the start of our period, among coarse-grade cotton weavers. 'They are', wrote one commentator, 'in a state of extreme suffering, and when their wages are advanced, and when they have full employment, it is comparative misery; it is not comparative comfort, for they do not think

that, upon the average, they can earn more than a penny an hour'.[9] Nevertheless, long after the powerloom had destroyed the livelihood of these home-
based workers, the same pattern could be discerned among a vast range of
occupations which constituted the unskilled labour market. As the wife of
a member of the labouring class expressed it to Rowntree in 1899, 'if there's
anythink [sic] extra to buy, such as a pair of boots for one of the children . . .
me and the children goes without dinner — or mebbe only 'as a cup o' tea, but
Jim (her husband) ollers takes 'is dinner to work and I give it 'im as usual; 'e
never knows we go without and I never tells 'im.'[10] For those held so firmly
in the grip of poverty it was scarcely surprising that they resented bitterly the
cramping restraints placed upon their consumption of food, measured in terms
of both quality and quantity. Many wives of unskilled labourers must have
echoed the pathetic cry of one of their number in York when she complained
during the relative prosperity of the Boer War, of being 'dead sick of bread
and butter — nothing but bread and butter, until I hate the sight of it.'[11] Yet
escape from such poverty was rarely to be effected by entering the ranks of
those who earned 'good wages'. If its shadow were to be lifted, the event itself
would be marked, in less spectacular fashion, by the emergence of a more
varied and plentiful diet, in itself usually an indication that hitherto dependent
members of the family had entered the labour market. Simply put, poverty,
for the working classes, was primarily about inadequate feeding problems.
Where, in George Julian Harney's words, 'bread and beef and beer' — and that
would be a minimum — graced the table, poverty would be considered to be
absent from the domestic hearth.[12]

Finally, even as the working classes adopted a stringent definition of what
constituted the poverty line, so also did those social scientists who sought to
express, in statistical as well as qualitative form, both the causes, and extent,
of poverty in the late Victorian and Edwardian worlds. Charles Booth, for
example, in dividing those who lived in a state of poverty into two groupings,
made it clear that few concessions had been made in the direction of allowing
for any margin of income for savings:

> by the word 'poor' I mean to describe those who have a sufficiently regular though
> bare income, such as 18s. to 21s. per week for a moderate family, and by 'very poor'
> those who from any cause fall much below this standard. The 'poor' are those whose
> means may be sufficient, but are barely sufficient, for decent independent life; the
> 'very poor' those whose means are insufficient for this according to the usual standard
> of life in this country. My 'poor' may be described as living under a struggle to obtain
> the necessiries of life and make both ends meet; while the 'very poor' live in a state
> of chronic want.[13]

Similarly, while Seebohm Rowntree, in his 1899 survey of York, was to modify
in several important respects Booth's methodology, he still described the state
of primary poverty in starkly uncompromising terms. Those who were to be
classified under this heading consisted of 'families whose total earnings are
insufficient to obtain the minimum necessaries for the maintenance of merely

physical efficiency.'[14] But many of those who were placed in Rowntree's category of secondary poverty — 'families whose total earnings would be sufficient for the maintenance of merely physical efficiency were it not that a portion of them is absorbed by other expenditure, either useful or wasteful'[15] — received an income which left them in any case precariously poised above the level of mere subsistence. Furthermore, although adjustments were subsequently to be made to Rowntree's poverty scale, notably by A.L. Bowley, no major writer in the pre-1914 period endeavoured to liberalise the principal features of his definition of indigence. There was thus a striking degree of accord between the social scientist, those sections of the working classes who felt the pressure of want in their lives, and the considerable numbers of semi-skilled and un-skilled workers 'whose wages only suffice for the necessities and the barest decencies of existence, and for whom . . . any mischance means punery, passing swiftly into pauperism',[16] about the nature and the contours of the poverty problem in society. It began at the point at which aggregate family income failed to yield, or barely yielded, a subsistence standard of living for the family unit as a whole. It is in this sense that poverty will be treated in this book.

In upholding this definition, it is perhaps necessary to say a few words about the approach to the subject that will be adopted. My main aim is to delineate the principal routes to poverty in an urban context; to examine its principal socio-economic characteristics; and to chart its course over time. On the other hand no attempt will be made to deal, in a comprehensive fashion, with the institutional infra-structure — the Poor Laws, private charities, 'make work' projects and *ad hoc* unemployment funds — which was designed to alleviate its worst effects. For such treatment would not merely extend this volume much beyond its allotted length; it would also fail to do justice to the considerable amount of research, published and unpublished, which has been devoted to pauperism at the local level. Institutional response to different aspects of the poverty question will therefore be considered in so far as it sheds light upon how some of the basic requirements of the poor were met; it will not be treated as an object of study *per se*. Finally, although the volume is concerned with a theme which recognises no national boundaries, it concentrates its attention largely upon England and Scotland. If Wales appears only spasmodically in the text, that is more a reflection of my ignorance of Welsh social history than indifference to the extent of social suffering in the Principality.

Chapter 1
Poverty and the Urban Labour Market 1830-1914: Low Pay

Throughout these decades poverty amongst the urban able-bodied was primarily the product of a volatile, highly imperfect, and in certain areas, glutted labour market. Yet to many contemporaries this would have appeared to be a harsh verdict, for the operation of Adam Smith's 'invisible hand', despite the social strains generated by significant structural changes in industry, had yielded substantial benefits to the working classes. New processes and growth points during the course of these years had widened significantly the spectrum of occupations available to the working man and facilitated his transference from the relatively poorly rewarded sectors of the economy, agriculture among them, to more highly remunerated urban outlets. Tangible indicators of this process of change were, to the trained eye of the social observer, everywhere apparent. At their most spectacular they were represented by the creation of new settlements whose fortunes were often linked to a single industry. Crewe, Wolverton and Swindon were essentially the creation of the railway industry, while the transformation of Jarrow and Barrow-in-Furness in the post-1860 era owed much to their ability to exploit the burgeoning iron shipbuilding market. Similarly Coatbridge in Lanarkshire and Middlesborough in the North Riding were to develop, in the post-1830 world, from humble rural origins into mature industrial communities upon foundations of coal, iron and steel. But of perhaps greater significance than this kind of striking discontinuity in social experience was the impact of economic growth upon areas with traditional industrial backgrounds. For example, Coventry's prosperity had in the 1830s and 1840s, been intimately bound up woth the silk-ribbon industry. But after 1870, beginning with the manufacturing of sewing machines, it was to undergo a second industrial revolution as an engineering city. By 1901 cycle and motor car production was the largest single source of employment for its male labour force. In like manner Dundee's virtual monopoly of the jute trade began only in the 1860s, while Glasgow, dominated by cotton in the 1830s, was, by the closing years of the nineteenth century, a centre of excellence in the spheres of steel shipbuilding and marine and general engineering. Internal migration and/or a high natural rate of population increase could also, however, be generated by the growth in the volume of commodities and goods handled in Britain's ports. Liverpool's numbers were in large measure sustained by the growing scale of its commercial operations. In like manner the virtual trebling of Cardiff's population between 1871 and 1911 was a reflection of its emergence as the principal port for exports from the South Wales coalfield.[1] If, therefore, there were several occupations which were destroyed by technological advance in this period — handloom weaving and wool-combing among them, — contemporary middle-class opinion still believed that economic change had produced over time a balance-sheet favourable to the progress of the working classes.

Reinforcing this trend was the fact that the inevitable concomitant of industrialisation was urbanisation. As the work of Saville has demonstrated, between 1851 and 1911 many predominantly rural counties in England and Wales, including Rutland, Cornwall, Huntingdonshire, Radnor, Anglesey and Montgomeryshire, experience an actual decline in their populations. Yet others, with small elements of industry and commerce within their boundaries, lost part of their natural rate of increase to the towns. Into this last category came Oxfordshire, Lincolnshire, Dorset and Shropshire.[2] In Scotland an identical pattern was to emerge. The researches of Malcolm Gray have shown that whole areas of the rural South-East of Scotland were strongly affected by migration in the post-1851 decades. In the rural parishes of East Lothian and Berwickshire there was a net migration rate of between ten and twenty per cent between 1861 and 1871. Again, in the Central District the largely rural county of Perthshire suffered an even more severe drain in numbers in the same decade.[3] These trends, once begun, were not to be reversed. Indeed, between 1851 and 1891 Perthshire's population declined in unbroken fashion, while the subsequent rise was of the most modest proportions. But as their stationary and/or falling numbers indicate, it was in some areas of the Highlands and more particularly the Borders that the pressures of rural migration were most strongly felt in the 1851-1911 period.[4]

The social impact of this movement was twofold. Firstly, most of these migrants helped to accelerate the already high rates of growth of Britain's urban communities. Equally important, they were bound to shift over time the distribution of population in British society. Whereas 48.3 per cent of the population of England and Wales was described as urban-based in 1841, that figure had soared to seventy per cent four decades later.[5] As with England and Wales, so with Scotland; for by the early 1870s the industrial pre-eminence of its West-Central belt was already assured, with Glasgow alone housing 16.5 per cent of the country's people. Secondly, the very fact that the rural dweller had changed his domicile, automatically meant, in many people's eyes, that he had increased his chances of securing improved money wages and of benefiting from some measure of upward social mobility. In this analysis urbanisation and industrialisation were thus the twin pillars upon which working-class improvement was based.

Many of the more optimistic writers in the late Victorian period tirelessly emphasised the massive dimensions of this advance. Leone Levi was to argue that between 1857 and 1884 great benefits had accrued to working classes:

> In a large number of instances working men of 1857 have become middle-class men of 1884. Many a work man of that day has now a shop or an hotel, has money in the bank or shares in shipping or mills. Cases of rising from the ranks are by no means as rare as we might imagine. But working men of the present day are much better off than they were twenty-seven years ago, for all wages are higher. In 1857 the wages of common labourers were 15s. to 17s. a week; now they are from 20s. to 22s., showing an increase of 30 per cent.

More specifically, after trying to calculate how the national income was distributed between the various classes, he claimed that the average income of the families of 'the labouring classes' had risen by fifty-nine per cent between 1851 and 1880.[6] Surveying a slightly longer time-span, Levi's fellow social statistician, Robert Giffen, arrived at much the same verdict. According to Giffen, when account had been taken of occupational shifts, 'there is . . . nothing to be astonished at in an average improvement of the money wages of "working classes" in the last fifty years [1837-1886] amounting to 100 per cent. When the facts are considered, such an improvement is, in reality, antecedently probable.'[7] Finally — although this list could be considerably extended — Sir Thomas Brassey concluded in 1885 that the consensus amongst economists lent 'no support to the vague impression which prevails that the rich are growing richer and the poor poorer than before. Progress — real progress — has been made towards a more satisfactory social order.' By way of qualification, however, he conceded that 'we are very far from having attained to an ideal state of perfection.'[8]

Few of these claims would be accepted uncritically today. Harold Perkin, in a comprehensive *critique* of Levi's and Giffen's methodology, has argued that, when allowance is made for unemployment and changes in occupational structure, the rise in average money wages was restricted to a more modest thirty-nine per cent.[9] But even this estimate might err on the side of generosity since our knowledge of unemployment is largely confined to those cyclical crises which periodically afflicted the economy. What social historians tend to play down is the impact of casuality, seasonality and technological unemployment upon living standards, although there are good grounds for arguing that these forms of unemployment and underemployment actually increased between 1840 and 1890. (See Chapter 2). Nevertheless, when all these caveats have been entered and when Levi's impressionistic evidence of social mobility on the heroic scale has been qualified, the reality of working-class advance remains. For one thing, from the 1850s onwards the friendly societies, those bastions of working-class thrift, experienced an almost uninterrupted increase in their membership until the outbreak of the First World War. Furthermore, there was increasing participation of the working classes in the savings' bank movement, although, if the Greenock returns for 1905-6 were at all representative of the West of

Scotland — 32.5 per cent of the deposits made in that year were for under £1 and 83.6 per cent for under £5 — the level of annual savings remained on the small scale.[10] Other pointers to rising real income, particularly in the last four decades of our period, included the growth of industrial assurance, catering for death and funeral benefits, and the gains which accrued to whole elements of 'the labouring classes' from the retailing revolution, a revolution which was distinguished not only by the proliferation of privately owned multiple and departmental stores but also by the expansion of the co-operative movement in England, Wales and Scotland. Yet these landmarks to social betterment encapsulate only one aspect of the social history of the working classes. Ranged alongside them was the existence of a pervasive and widespread urban poverty problem, whose incidence fluctuated over time according to the state of trade and secular trends at work in the economy, but whose dimensions were scarcely hinted at in the published statistics relating to able-bodied pauperism in England and Wales. Most deeply entrenched amongst the unskilled, although its boundaries were by no means coterminous with the market for unskilled labour, its two salient characteristics — low pay and an irregular pattern of employment — remained unchanged throughout the period under review. It is with the first of these facets of the poverty question that the remainder of this chapter is concerned.

I

Inadequate earnings were highlighted by both Charles Booth and Seebohm Rowntree as a fundamental cause of urban poverty. Among a substantial segment of Booth's Class D, for example, — a class which he defined as being engaged in a perpetual struggle to attain subsistence, — the head of the household was employed in work which in the late 1880s was rarely subject to 'broken time' but which was consistently badly paid. In like manner Rowntree discovered that 640 out of the 1465 families — or 51.95 per cent of the total — who lived in a state of primary poverty in York during 1899-1900, were thus placed because the chief wage-earner, although regularly employed, was poorly remunerated.[11] This situation was not to alter in any significant respect during the business boom which preceded the outbreak of the First World War. As late as 1912-13 low pay was singled out by A.L. Bowley and A.R. Burnett-Hurst as the principal route to primary poverty amongst the population sample which they had analysed in four towns of markedly divergent socio-economic structures. As they pointed out, 'actually on-half of the households below the poverty line at Warrington and Reading, nearly one-half at York, and one-third at Northampton were living in poverty because the wages of the head of the household were so low that he could not support a family of three children or less.' Such poverty was thus 'not intermittent but permanent, not accidental or due to exceptional misfortune, but a regular feature of the towns concerned.'[12] But if this was the position at the beginning of the twentieth century, there can be no doubt that social deprivation existed on a much more formidable scale in the earlier part of our period, particularly in the pre-1870 era, when food and commodity prices — rent excepted — were on trend certainly higher and money earnings appreciably lower than subsequently.

Qualitative evidence to support this thesis can be found in several quarters. Leon Faucher, for instance, after a cursory discussion of the *mores* of Manchester's Irish community, concluded that 'the rate of wages for unskilled labourer (although higher in a large town like Manchester then elsewhere) is yet so low [in 1844] as to require almost constant labour to secure a living, even upon their low standard.[13] Frederich Engels, in his contemporaneous survey of the same geographical area but written from a very different ideological perspective, was not seriously to dissent from these findings. Moreover, these views of outside observers were graphically underlined by the personal testimonies of the recipients of low pay. To John White, an Irish weaver domiciled in the 'cotton capital' of Lancashire, low pay had meant systematic privation:

> for thirteen years he had toiled for a large, a young and helpless family that never could assist him. He had worked early and late, until on three separate occasions through mere exhaustion he had fainted and fallen out of his loom . . . it was well known to many who were present, that during that time he had not spent twelvepence in malt liquor or anything else of the kind.[14]

To a female shoebinder in the London 'slop' shoe trade, earning 3/1½d. per week in the late 1840s, insufficient supplies of foodstuffs — 'the way in which I take my meals generally is what I call worrying the victuals' — were accompanied by a perpetual fear of homelessness: 'my work wouldn't allow me to pay rent . . . I live with this good woman and her husband. The rent is half-a-crown a week, and they allow me to live with them rent free . . . If it wasn't for them I must go to the workhouse; out of what little I earn I couldn't possibly pay rent.'[15] To Irish rag-collectors, earning in and around Bradford 1s. to 1/6d. per day in 1849, an inadequate income meant cramped, and spartanly furnished living accommodation.[16] For all it entailed a reduced expectation of life.

More recently there has been an attempt to transmute the level of poverty which prevailed amongst the lowly paid in the pre-1860 world into statistical form. John Foster, for example, using in a modified form Bowley's revision of Rowntree's primary poverty scale and making appropriate adjustments for the movement of prices, has argued that in 1849, a buoyant year in the national economy, fifteen per cent of Oldham's, twenty-eight per cent of Northampton's, and twenty-three per cent of South Shields's, families were inadequately nourished.[17] But within his sample, it was the households of the unskilled who fared worst, for whereas only fourteen per cent of the households of Oldham's skilled factory workers experienced the devastating effects of underfeeding in their daily lives, the total for those of the labouring class was thirty-five per cent.[18] Again, Anderson, employing as his 'consumption standard . . . the original Rowntree primary poverty line based on York data for 1898-1900', has concluded that approximately twenty per cent of the families included in his sample of Preston's population in 1851, lived in a state of grinding poverty.[19] Finally, Norman Murray, in a most exhaustive analysis of the living standards of the handloom weavers, has calculated that half of Scotland's weaving population – and this includes all fabrics and all grades – fell below the primary poverty line in 1834.[20] In the context of this discussion, however, these findings must be subject to certain qualifications. Firstly, while Foster and Anderson are assuming the existence of conditions of full employment for all the wage-earning members of their samples, Murray has taken into account the reality of broken time in whatever guise it appeared within the weaving community. Secondly, whereas Anderson excluded income derived from lodgers from his inquiry, Foster believed that all lodgers who were not related to the families with whom they were staying, contributed '1s. profit on their keep' to the households concerned.[21] Thirdly, Anderson's sample was to some extent biased against the low paid since handloom weavers and certain female 'sweated' occupations – pre-eminently dressmakers and laundresses – were excluded from his remit.[22] In addition, all three authors are concerned with aggregate family income and not the earnings of the male heads of households. None the less, despite the validity of these points, these data, considered as a whole, serve to provide further proof of the deleterious effect of poorly remunerated labour upon working-class living standards.

There remains, however, formidable methodological problems when an attempt is made to draw the parameters of those areas of the labour market which yielded scant financial returns to their employees. One basic difficulty is the imprecision which surrounds so much of the extant records of wages and earnings. As A.L. Bowley pointed out, the concept of the average wage was often loosely applied to widely divergent situations.

> Sometimes [the term was] taken to mean the average wage of an employee one week with another throughout a year, or a series of years, and at other times to mean the average wage of all those of a given occupation at a particular date, assuming full work. From this cause alone a discrepancy of 50 per cent between two estimates, both given in good faith, is not at all uncommon.[23]

Yet, even within outwardly homogeneous occupations amongst the low paid, global calculations could effectively conceal significant variations in the returns accruing to individual members of the workforce. To some extent such variations were a reflection of age and sex differences. In handloom weaving, domestic-based tailoring and chairmaking, male labour was always much more highly rewarded than its female counterpart. In like manner child workers, engaged in the production of hand-woven goods, received only a small percentage – sometimes less than one-third – of the wages of the adult male. Underlining this kind of distinction, but completely hidden by average figures, there were substantial differentials, both among those who wove different kinds of fabric and between the skilled fancy weavers and those who worked upon the coarser grades of cloth, within the same type of fabric. Lastly, averages obscure the real distinctions which existed between the same occupation in different parts of the country — Glasgow cotton weavers in the 1830s and 1840s fared better than those in rural Ayrshire, while the Coventry silk weaver was more prosperous than his Macclesfield rival[24] — and in certain instances even within the same town. Where the last situation existed, it was invariably associated with the sweated industries, in which, as late as the 1880s small masters, often themselves the victims of the sub-contracting system, would reduce in competitive fashion the piece rates they offered to their hands. Inter-regional wage variations on the other hand, if they were to narrow between 1850 and 1914, affected the broad spectrum of skilled and unskilled trades. Whereas, for example, Glasgow members of the Associated Carpenters and Joiners of Scotland averaged 36/1½d. for a fifty-one hours' week in 1892, their Aberdeen counterparts only received 27/7½d., or almost twenty-five per cent less. Again, while masons in Blackburn, Bolton and Liverpool worked, in the early 1890s, for between 48.5 and 49.5 hours weekly in the summer at an hourly rate of 8d. to 8½d., their colleagues in a small town such as Dorchester were paid 6d. per hour for a 60 hours' working week.[25] Similarly, unskilled labour within the building industry was invariably better paid, in money terms, in London than any other major city.[26]

But quite apart from drawbacks of this nature, there are several other substantial problems still to be faced. In the first place it is sometimes not clear whether certain kinds of wage data have made any allowance for unemployment which might be encountered during the course of the year. In addition, are we dealing with gross or net figures, for gross income in the outwork trades could be drastically reduced by arbitrary stoppages and unavoidable expenses, ranging from the frame rents which were the first charge upon the income of framework knitters to the cost of trimmings met by sweated needlewomen? Furthermore if the figures for earnings in a particular district are, in chronological terms, widely spaced, what was the state of trade at the time these returns were made and how confidently can they be used to outline trends in the intervening years? More specifically, how far can piece-rates be employed to chart the course of earnings, when the nature of the task and the amount of work exacted could alter over time? Finally, when the historian refers to low pay as a cause of poverty, how do the contours of money income among the unskilled relate to the changing movement of retail prices? For the time-span with which this study is concerned is marked by two periods of rising prises — from the early 1850s to the mid-1870s and from the late 1890s to 1914 — one period, from the mid-1870s to the late 1890s, when a secular decline occurred, and one period, from 1830 to the early 1850s, when there were very sharp, short-term fluctuations in the price levels of grainstuffs. But not even this generalised picture reveals the whole truth, since there existed significant regional price differentials in the pre-1850 era which have, until recent years, been obscured by over-concentration upon London price indices. Again it sheds no light upon the higher prices which many of the working classes had to pay, either because their financial circumstances compelled them both to buy 'dear' in small quantities and to avail themselves, where facilities were available, of a weekly credit account, or because they were exposed to the inflationary effects of 'the truck system' which, if of diminishing significance after 1850, still meant that basic commodities could cost twenty-five per cent more than in other local retail outlets.[27] Nevertheless, notwithstanding these formidable obstacles to exact measurement, it is still possible to delineate roughly those occupations which yielded scanty financial returns to the worker during times of full employment.

Undoubtedly the major such area for adult males throughout these years was that which was covered by the imprecise term of labouring. Rowntree, for example, showed that the average wages of unskilled labour in York in 1899-1900 were insufficient, once an allowance was made for broken time, to preserve a family from primary poverty.[28] Much the same held true in 1912-13 in Northampton where twenty-seven per cent of Bowley's and Burnett-Hurst's sample of the adult male population earned less than 24s. per week, and in Warrington and Reading where the comparable statistic was thirty-two per cent and 50.5 per cent respectively.[29] A parallel trend can be discerned in Glasgow in 1902-3 where an investigation into the wage returns of 1680 labourers revealed that their earnings, when in work, had averaged 19s. per week, which 'supposing they did not spend a penny . . . in drink, . . . [was] not sufficient to provide themselves with either a proper home or the proper necessities'.[30] G.S. Barnsby has painted an even more lugubrious picture of their plight in the Black Country, concluding that twenty per cent of the population, largely comprising the families of ill-remunerated labourers, tended to live below his own definition of subsistence until virtually the end of the nineteenth century.[31] But their position was even more precarious outside the major conurbations. As late as 1912 unskilled male labour could only expect to earn 18s. per week in Cambridge without taking account of the seasonal contraction in the demand for hands which afflicted a town heavily dependent upon the university.[32]

Yet while this evidence highlights the reality of sizable divergencies in the returns accruing to general labour in widely different socio-economic communities, it is a less convincing guide to the movement of earnings within the range of occupations which were sometimes covered by this amorphous label. Convincing answers to this last point cannot of course be given because of the absence of systematic runs of wage data. Instead it is only possible to deal, in broad terms, with the more important groups. Briefly, it can be argued that if there were an elite within the ranks of unskilled labour it was to be found amongst these labourers who serviced bricklayers, builders and masons in the construction industry. In the boom conditions of the mid-1830s, for instance, bricklayers' labourers in Liverpool and Manchester were receiving 18s. during the summer months and 16s. in winter-time. In Edinburgh on the other hand they could only expect, in the spring of 1834, little more than 9s.

per week, and in Birmingham approximately 12s.[33] In the closing years of the decade these rates were to come under pressure — although the Manchester figure still held firm at 18s. in 1839 — and almost certainly declined *pari passu* with the downturns in trade of 1839-42 and 1847-8. By the late 1840s and early 1850s onwards, however, when reliable figures once more beome available, there had taken place a considerable narrowing of the gap between the earnings of builders' labourers in Scotland and the North of England. Whereas Manchester's unskilled building workers obtained 18s. for a 57.5 hours' working week in 1849 and 21s. for a 55.5 hours' week in 1859 — and these were the summer *maxima* — their Glasgow counterparts had experienced an increase from 12s. for 57 hours in 1850-2 to 17s. in 1854-6. Slackness in the economy during 1857-8 was to bring a halt, in the latter case, to this upward movement, when summer earnings fell to 15/9d. amidst gloomy prognostications of a rising volume of unemployment.[34]

Such checks to income had of course always operated; but they were to make their influence felt with greater force in the post-1850 decades when a distinctive building cycle, with its long twenty years' swings, can be clearly distinguished from the shorter seven to ten years' swings of the conventional trade cycle. This meant that the labourer could expect to enjoy rising hourly rates and wages during the intense upsurge in building activity which was encapsulated within the years 1868-76, and in the equally powerful boom of 1895-1903. Conversely earnings and work outlets were reduced in the late 1870s and early 1880s, while in many, but not all, of the major towns, slackness in the industry for much of the decade which preceded the First World War, again acted against the best interests of the labourer. Looking, however, at the secular trend, the gains which were made in the post-1850 era were unmistable. In Glasgow builders' and plasterers' labourers were capable by 1902 of earning 24s. for a 51 hours' week in the summer season; in Birmingham they could hope to secure between 27/7½d. and 31/6½d. according to the length of their working day; in Leeds their wages fluctuated between 26/10d. and 28/10½d. On the whole, as the data indicate, earnings were still higher in the principal English centres of population than in their Scottish equivalents — building labourers' wages in Aberdeen were only 21/3d. in 1905, in Paisley 25/6d. — the highest of all in the London area.[35] But, what is of supreme importance in the context of the poverty question, these figures show that *in times of full employment* certain families of the unskilled could live without any supplementary income above the primary line in the early years of this century.

On the other hand this was not true of the shipbuilding, foundry, and engineering labourers who, over time, fared much worse than the building worker. Engineering labourers' wages were not really collected in a systematic fashion until relatively late in our period, although Bowley's isolated returns for the Manchester district show levels of 16s., in 1834, 15s. in 1849, with thereafter little change until 1872 when 18s. was reached, a figure which accords well with the 18s. to 20s. paid to fitters' labourers in Leeds in the same year. From the 1880s to late 1890s, there was relatively little movement in cash payments to these grades of worker if the data relating to Manchester and Leeds are to be relied upon. In the case of Manchester, the nadir, in money terms, of the engineering labourer's fortune was reached in 1888 when he received 17s., the high point in 1893 when he secured 21s. By 1905 there were relatively few areas which diverged sharply from these levels. In Birmingham weekly earnings were 20s., in Bolton 18s. to 20s., in Manchester and Salford 18s. to 22s., while in Glasgow in 1902 it was thought that the average wage of workshop labourers was 18s., for a 54 hours' week. Among shipyard labourers, Tyneside seems to have paid its unskilled workforce marginally better than elsewhere. In 1887-8 completely unskilled workers could expect to obtain there 18s. for a full week's work; in the Boer War 'boom' of 1899-1901, 21s.; in 1905, 19s. to 23/6. But in the Clyde yards, where the bulk of the labouring class were, as late as 1902, paid at 4½d. or less per hour, average wages tended to fall below 20s. per week. Finally, it must be stated that the returns to foundry labourers conformed in most points of detail to the pattern which has just been described.[36] Without supplementation, therefore, there was little hope of families of this element of the workforce, even when the head of the household was fully engaged, escaping from the grip of primary poverty.

Completely divorced from general labouring, low pay was also a dominant feature of a multitude of outwork trades, some of which provided work for both sexes and others of which — as with needlework and box making — were the preserve of female, and child labour. The bewildering variety of these trades, coupled with the fact that the numerical strength and the composition of this group altered drastically over time, makes generalisation difficult. Some occupations were to disappear completely and relatively speedily under the twin impact of organisational and technological change; others were to crumble more slowly; and yet others — as with 'slop' tailoring — were to receive a new lease of life in the late 1850s and early 1860s with the advent of the sewing machine. Again, it is within this sector that problems about wage data arise in their most acute form, since the 'putting out' system led to different piece-rates being offered to sweated workers, especially in the needlework trades, within the same locality. It was for this reason that Margaret Irwin, Secretary of the Scottish Council of Women's Trades, confessed, as late as 1907-8, that it was impossible to gauge trends in the earnings of Glasgow's home-based, and exclusively female, shirt-finisheres, since 'there is absolutely no standard or uniform rate of pay for work of the same kind in these trades.'[37] Moreover, it was within this segment of the labour market that seasonality and casuality of employment wrought their maximum destruction. This makes it particularly hard, for two reasons, to explore, in a meaningful fashion, the correlation between poverty on the one hand and low pay when in full work on the other. Firstly, in the lives of many of these workers regularity of employment was not the norm. Secondly, it overlooks the point that some elements would switch their jobs, on a systematic, annual basis, in an endeavour to raise slightly, or even to maintain, lowly income levels. But there are other considerations which need to be borne in mind, among them the fact that the earnings of females and children engaged in this type of work were often designed to supplement the income of unskilled adult male labour rather than to support a whole household. None the less since there were sizable numbers of women who through widowhood, desertion, chronic sickness of their husbands or because they remained single, were in effective charge of their own homes, it is vital to devote some space to the course of female earnings in those parts of the labour market which were likely to attract this kind of recruit. To circumvent some of these problems, it is the intention here to examine the wages of certain of the more important occupations at these periods, no matter how short-lived, when the individual was fully employed and, using qualitative as well as quantitative material, to underline the conclusion that primary poverty must have been the inevitable lot of the worker's family unless supplementary earnings existed on a significant scale.

Within the domestic system it has long been accepted that searing distress afflicted the majority of textile workers from the early years of the nineteenth century until the demise of their occupations in the post-1840 decades. Such poverty was the product of a diverse range of economic forces, including unemployment, underemployment, arbitrary deductions by employers and, in some districts, the operation of the truck system. Yet, as the weavers' own complaints make abundantly clear, it also sprang from the inadequacy of their earnings when fully engaged at the loom and working fourteen hours daily for six days per week. In 1818, for example, Macclesfield silk weavers, confronted by 'the unprecedented reduction of our wages and the alarming increase of pauperism' demanded 'a living price' for their labours, although they were better placed than coarse grade calico weavers in Manchester who in the same year had to 'weave very hard' and work 'very long hours to make seven shillings a week.'[38] By the 1830s and 1840s tales of woe of this nature had spread to cover almost all areas and virtually all fabrics. During 1835, a relatively prosperous year for trade, worsted weavers in Leeds maintained that 'with our present wages, when in full employment, we can scarcely get the necessaries let alone the comforts of domestic life.'[39] Identical sentiments were uttered by John Scott, a Manchester silk weaver, who claimed that even with supplementary income from loom rents he did 'not get a sufficiency of the commonest of the necessaries of life' and by James Brennan who argued that the inability of cotton weavers to form viable trade unions stemmed primarily from 'their extreme poverty . . . they are so impoverished, that if they give a halfpenny out of their pockets, they must work for it again.'[40] In the commercial crisis of 1839-42, however, their situation deteriorated. From the West of Scotland in 1840 came the assertion that Kirkintilloch cotton weavers, 'in consequence of the high price of bread, and the low rate of wages, [were] compelled to labour at a rate totally inconsistent with either health or comfort; that after toiling fourteen long hours a day, and exercising the strictest economy . . . [they remained] in a very low state of privation and distress.'[41] In the following year, when Manchester's male domestic workers were receiving on average 'not more than 1s. a day when fully employed', the demand was made, in terms which foreshadowed General William Booth's formulation of the 'cab horse charter' in 1890, for 'food, shelter and clothing' in return for 'our labour.'[42] But if these were broadly the conditions obtaining amongst the urban-based workforce, rural weavers fared worse, for they were more poorly paid and the first victims of any downturn, whether seasonal or cyclical, in the demand for hands. In mitigation of course it can be accepted that many rural domestic workers in England and Scotland were females and children who, as in the mining villages around Coventry, were supplementing the wage of the head of the household who might have no contact himself with the weaving industry. But when full weighting has been given to this qualification, there remained particularly in the South and East of Scotland where in the 1830s two-thirds of the labour force was rural-based,[43] substantial bodies of adult male weavers, widely scattered in the countryside, who were unable, in conditions of full work, to lift the veil of primary poverty.

Nor did framework knitters in the hosiery trade of the East Midlands and woolcombers, heavily concentrated in and around Bradford, fare noticeably better. Stockingers who had already been partly pressurised by hunger into the Luddite risings of 1811-12, looked back, by the 1820s, to a departed 'golden age' of relative plenty. In the words of one of their number in 1822,

> Times are very different now from what they were when you and I were shopmates Ben. We used to club together then and get a comfortable tit-bit two or three nights a week and Saturday night never passed without a general meeting of all the shopmates somewhere or other when the foaming tankard cheered our spirits . . . Now we are all half starved.

And while it might be possible to argue that in this case the witness had exaggerated the prosperity of an earlier, but unspecified, era, there can be little doubt about the reliability of the concluding sentence. Low levels of earnings, when fully engaged at the knitting frame, perpetuated chronic undernourishment. As one Nottingham doctor was moved to observe, by the 1830s a stockinger could easily be identified by his physical appearance: almost without exception 'there is a paleness and a certain degree of emaciation and thinness about them.'[44] On the other hand the turning-point in the economic fortunes of Bradford's wool-combing community did not occur until its defeat in a major trial of strength with the employers in 1826. Thereafter, however, even if money earnings when in full employment did not consistently fall, they were rarely sufficient, as the *Morning Chronicle*'s investigation into the combers' plight in 1849 revealed, to guarantee a subsistence standard of existence.[45]

But it is still a difficult task to chart the secular trend in earnings, even when the scattered statistical evidence is supplemented by qualitative assessments of this kind. Nevertheless, from the admittedly imperfect extant data, certain limited conclusions can be confidently drawn. In the first place the bulk of the weaving population suffered a decline in money and real wages which began at or around the end of the Napoleonic Wars and which continued well into our period. One authority asserted in 1835 that if 'the necessaries of life are . . . lower now than in 1815', weavers' wages 'have fallen much more in proportion.' Whereas food prices had been 'reduced only about 30 per cent', their wages 'declined 60 per cent.'[46] This claim cannot, of course, be indiscriminately applied to all fabrics or all districts. But after due allowance has been made for this fact, it can still be taken as a rough guide to the contours of the general pattern.

Secondly, those who initially bore the brunt of this heavy social burden were located in those less skilled sectors of the labour market which were largely preoccupied with the manufacture of plain goods. In Manchester, for instance, a workman producing coarse grade calicoes could not expect to receive more than 6s. to 8s. gross in the mid-1830s for a full week's work.[47] This figure, which fluctuated relatively little thereafter, was probably typical of the level of earnings for this type of work in all the major cotton towns of the North of England and the West of Scotland. In one sense this is what one would expect, since calico weavers were both operating in a chronically glutted section of the labour market and were the first group to have their livelihood threatened by the inexorable growth of competition from the powerloom. None the less they were by no means unique in the 1830s in being poorly rewarded at the end of a long working week. Linen weavers of the West Riding shared with them this common experience. By the late 1830s domestic workers in the linen town of Barnsley secured 10s. gross and 7/6½d. net for six days' regular employment and their colleagues in Leeds 8/4d. net, 'when in full work, which is seldom the case'.[48] Even then they were marginally better paid than two-thirds of Scotland's linen weaving community who in 1838 obtained between 5/6d. to 7/6d. gross per week.[49] But the 1830s were also to prove a critical decade for the households of many worsted, silk and woollen weavers. Silk weavers of both Manchester and Macclesfield suffered a substantial drop in their earnings when, in the wake of tariff changes in 1826, the superior French product succeeded in capturing a sizable portion of the British market. One Macclesfield employer believed that in the ensuing six years — 1825-31 — the average income of domestic worker in his own town had fallen by more than 100 per cent. In 1825 a fully employed weaver could anticipate gross earnings of 19/7d. per week, by 1831, 9s.[50] Nor were these inflated claims, since corroborative evidence of the dimensions of this fall was supplied by the voluminous data presented to the 1831-2 Select Committee on the Silk Trade and by John Scott who thought that the domestic labour force engaged upon an assorted range of silk goods in Manchester in 1834 could earn no more, on average, than 8/4d. gross when constantly engaged.[51] A very modest degree of recovery from these low points was to set in during the second half of the 1830s — by 1838 the weaving of Jacquard handkerchiefs yielded a weekly return of 9/4d. net in

Macclesfield,[52] — but it never proceeded far enough to enable a weaver to support his family by his labour alone. The fortunes of the Spitalfields silk weavers, in the plainer grades of the ribbon trade, followed roughly the same pattern, although Coventry appears to have enjoyed what measure of prosperity existed in the craft. According to Prest 'first hand' journeymen in Coventry could expect in the 1830s to obtain 10s. weekly from one loom and many had two or more looms at work. Furthermore, even with the rise of the steam silk factory in the city from the late 1840s, the outdoor workers cushioned themselves to some extent from this competition by combining together to establish cottage factories, driven by a steam engine placed at the end of rows of weavers' houses. Ultimately, however, their living standards were to decline in the 1860s, a joint product of the Cobden Treaty of 1860, the obsolescence of the cottage factory as a form of production, and of changing consumer demand.[53] In the worsted industry of the West Riding wages had been falling since 1815. Nevertheless, in most localities, the time-span running from 1830 to 1838 saw a marked acceleration of this trend, although as late as the summer of 1835, adult male worsted weavers in Leeds could still earn 13s. gross and 11/3d. net from large manufacturers and 10s. gross and 8/6d. net from their smaller rivals. Badly hit in this crisis were the plainback weavers who, before the thirty-three per cent reduction in wages which took place between 1831 and 1838, had had no margin of income left for any form of saving. But victims of equally savage cuts were the best paid grades of workers who in Bradford had been capable of obtaining 15/6d. gross in 1830 but who were reduced to 10/6d. in 1838.[54] Furthermore, as with cotton, the advent of the powerloom in the late 1830s and early 1840s effectively excluded any hope of reversing this trend.

Finally, there remains the question of returns accruing to woollen weavers. In some respects they were less hard pressed than most of the other sections of the domestic textile workforce since they were operating in an industry whose organisational conservation meant that it succumbed relatively slowly to the factory system. Furthermore, employers made less use than in other branches of textile production of female and child labour. Earnings, therefore, when fully employed, tended to be somewhat higher than those obtaining elsewhere. H.S. Chapman was one of the several writers who sought to test the validity of this point during the 1830s and 1840s. Comparing the wages of worsted and woollen weavers in the West Riding, he unhesitatingly concluded that the latter group fared much better from the unfettered play of market forces.[55] Again, it is clear that in 1835-9 the best paid elements among the woollen weavers of Leeds could earn from 15s. to 17s. gross per week by working long hours in the summer season.[56] In Scotland also the woollen weaving communities fared on the whole much better than the majority of their colleagues employed upon other fabrics. Galashiels woollen weavers received 12s. gross in 1829, a year of dull trade; 10/4d. in 1849; and 20s. or more as late as 1866-8.[57] Yet it is unlikely that these returns, particularly those which relate to the late 1830s, convey a completely accurate picture of the economic position of the bulk of the workforce. According to Bowley, for example, Leeds woollen weavers averaged 12s. net 'for a week's full work in 1837' whereas the comparable statistic for 1830 had been 'probably 60 per cent higher.'[58] But Leeds wages were always greater than those in the surrounding districts. In Armley and Bramley domestic workers could not earn more than 9s. to 10/6d. gross in 1837, while in some of the smaller centres of the industry full employment produced even more lowly figures, with 6/3d. gross and 4/10d. net being paid in Horsforth.[59] On the other hand woollen weavers in the towns of the Scottish Borders, with their concentration upon the quality sector of the market, were somewhat better rewarded during this key decade, average gross weekly earnings of 16/6. being recorded during 1830-3 and 14/6d. in 1836-8. Even by the late 1840s there had been relatively little deviation from this last figure.[60] Assessed overall, however, there is nothing to suggest that without financial contributions from other members of the household, primary poverty was an infrequent visitor to the hearths of those who plied the loom in the woollen trade.

But the gloom was not completely unrelieved. Among fancy weavers and those engaged in branches of the craft where considerable physical strength was required, wages were consistently higher and more resistant to downward pressures than among workers employed in the plainer lines. In Bolton in 1838 the average gross earnings of bed-quilt weavers — 'the best paid work in the handloom weaving line' — amounted to 15s., although this branch was closed to most because of its physically exacting nature. In the words of one manufacturer, 'they must be stout, able-bodied men, to do the work.'[61] In the same year the gross income of fully employed brocade weavers in Macclesfield came to 16/3d., although the inevitable deductions could reduce this figure by almost one-third to 11/3d. net.[62] In the West of Scotland weavers of the best class of Paisley shawls were still able to secure net weekly earnings of 15/6d. in 1834-5 and 13/2d. in 1837-8.[63] Furthermore, there were brief periods when most weavers benefited from a sudden upsurge in the demand for their labour. Wage advantages were secured in the majority of the Scottish weaving centres in 1825, 1832-5, 1843 and 1845-7, while in Lancashire cotton weavers' spokesmen spoke nostalgically about 1835-6 when 'there was certainly a dawn of life . . . we expected from the sudden change that then took place, that our condition was likely to be improved, because our food got cheaper and our wages increased.'[64]

Real as it was, however, the scale of these improvements has to be kept in perspective. For, as Murray has shown for Scotland, any wage increases which were recorded during the upswing phase of the trade cycle rarely reached the levels attained in the preceding boom. Again, only a very small minority could ever, in the post 1830 years, expect to emulate the earnings of the weavers of Paisley shawls. Indeed, by the late 1840s when coarse grade calico weaving had been almost totally destroyed by the powerloom, the bulk of fancy cotton weavers in the West of Scotland obtained, when in full work, between 5s. and

7s. net weekly.[65] Moreover, to be offset against these ephemeral gains were the increasing incidence of underemployment and the dire plight of the adult male in the country districts who, in the coarser fabrics, could not even reach the low levels of pay of his town-based cousin. While in the early 1830s calico weavers in Manchester and Preston earned 6s. to 7s. weekly, the rural labour force located around Burnley had to be content with 4/6d. or less. The inevitable consequence of such earnings, even after taking into account a wage subsidy from the poor law, was that country workers lived 'usually in a state of great destitution; their houses bare of furniture; their children half clad . . . The weavers themselves have a lean and hungry look', frequently asserting 'that they do not get victuals enough.'[66] Here was hopeless, debilitating and deep-seated poverty. But it was a poverty which differed in degree, not in kind, from that which was present in the households of many of their urban colleagues at the high point of their work cycle — when fully employed — and which would only cease when the process, already launched by 1830, of replacing the handloom by power-driven machinery was finally complete.

During the next three decades the rapid spread of the powerloom factory heralded the final phase of that process, although the numerical decline of the domestic workforce was by no means uninterrupted in every district. While the numbers of handloom weavers fell in Airdrie and Glasgow between 1828 and 1838, they actually rose in some of the ill-paid rural weaving areas of Lanarkshire and Ayrshire.[67] Similarly, many cotton weavers met the initial challenge of mechanisation by transferring to other fabrics rather than by abandoning their craft for other forms of employment. Nevertheless these were short-lived exceptions to an overall pattern of a dwindling labour force. Whereas it was estimated that there were from 200,000 to 250,000 cotton handloom weavers in Britain in the early 1830s, a relatively small percentage of this total remained twenty years later when, in the graphic phrase of a Lancastrian contemporary, the hand trade was 'almost exploded.'[68] Again, at the end of the 1850s only a few isolated pockets of worsted weavers and domestic combers in the West Riding had survived the twin threats of the powerloom and Lister's combing machine, while by the 1860s outworkers in Coventry were in danger of being reduced to the position of a sweated and casual workforce because of their inability to compete against the factory system. Even where — as with wool — the pace of change was slower, there was little to modify a picture of decay which can be most precisely illustrated from Scottish data. While there were approximately 85,000 looms engaged in the manufacture of every type of fabric in Scotland in 1838, there were a mere 10,000 left by 1860.[69]

Amongst the major domestic trades, however, this pattern was, before 1850, exclusively confined to weaving, for even the numbers of poorly paid framework knitters, earning 11/7d. gross in Nottingham in 1836 when in full work, did not contract significantly until the 1870s.[70] Indeed, at the very time that handloom weaving had started its irreversible decline — the 1830s and 1840s, — whole sectors of the domestic labour market, including tailoring, shirtmaking, dressmaking and cabinetmaking, witnessed a considerable increase in their labour supply. Furthermore, the most rapid expansion in the supply of hands occurred in those area of the market which were unmistakably associated with low pay, irregularity of employment and lengthy working hours — in short, with the sweating system.

The evolution of that system was essentially determined by the interaction of three forces. In the first place it was relatively easy to obtain sufficient skill to practise one part of a given occupation. Shirt-finishing, shirtmaking and general needlework were often taken up by widows who were compelled to re-enter the labour market after the death of their spouses, by spinsters who had left domestic service, and by married women who sought to supplement the casual earnings of their husbands. Again, it was thought that young girls could be taught the rudiments of 'slop' tailoring work in a limited busy season of three or four months. Among male outlets too, there was always a substantial invasion of the 'dishonourable' trades by individuals who had hitherto had little contact with such work. The most regularly quoted example of this trend was the influx of Jewish immigrants of East European origin into the sweated tailoring workshops of the East Ends of London and Glasgow and the Leylands district of Leeds during the 1880s and 1890s.[71] Nonetheless, when placed against the broad spectrum of the sweated industries, the Jewish 'greener' represented only a minor element in a continuing infusion of untrained labour from a wide variety of backgrounds. In the London of the 1850s silk weavers from Spital-fields and Bethnal Green and costermongers were known to set up as self-employed 'garret masters' in cabinetmaking and as 'little masters' in the badly paid 'slop' hatting trade.[72] On the other hand there was also a small segment of the labour force which was drawn from skilled workers who, because of irregular habits or failing physical powers, were the victims of downward social mobility.

Secondly, particularly between 1860 and 1890, the growth of sweating was abetted by increasing subdivision of tasks. In some cases subdivision sprang primarily from technical advance. In the clothing and shoemaking industries the advent of the sewing machine in the 1850s and 1860s meant that the degree of specialisation in the work executed by the individual could be considerably refined. Thus in tailoring workshops catering for the wholesale ready-made market, cutting-out, basting, machining, button-holing and pressing would be carried out by different employees, while among the largely female home workers there was a corresponding concentration upon one kind of garment. Subdivision was of course ultimately to proceed furthest in clothing and shoe-making factories. But until the 1890s technical change tended to lead to a proliferation of small workshops and the expansion of the female labour force rather than the development of a fully integrated factory system. The growth of female employment was most clearly observed in tailoring and its ancillary trades. In Greater London, for instance, tailoring and needlework provided employment in 1861 for 98,000 women and only 22,000 men. In Leeds there

were 935 males and 29 females returned as tailors at the 1851 Census; by 1881
the respective totals were 2148 and 2740 respectively. But these returns merely
mirrored a national pattern, for while between 1871 and 1891 the number of
men following tailoring in England and Wales rose by only seven per cent —
from 111,860 to 119,496, — the female workforce grew by no less than 134
per cent, or, expressed in numerical form, from 38,043 to 89,224.[73] Technology,
therefore, initially strengthened a domestic system of production which, at its
lowest level, generated incomes which by themselves were quite inadequate,
when fully employed, to keep the worker's family above the poverty line.

Finally, as already indicated, the sweating system led to the emergence of
'little masters', often dependent for an uncertain livelihood upon short-term
credit and prepared to hawk their goods to potential customers when they
lacked, or were temporarily deprived of, a good connection with a wholesale
house. In the East End of London 'garret masters', a little known group until
the 1820s, quickly became a distinctive part of the 'slop' furniture trade in the
subsequent decades. Usually linked to a large warehouse and assisted either by
their own children or two or three workmen, they tended to specialise in only
one line of furniture since the rate of turnover in their output — they 'must
work very rapidly' claimed one commentator — largely determined their profits.[74] Identical processes were at work in hatmaking where 'the small master',
having completed the bodies of silk hats, sought to sell them to wholesale
workshops for finishing; in tailoring and dressmaking; and in bootmaking where
the 'champer master' applied the principle of sub-division of labour within his
own family to eke out a miserable existence. Of these groups, however, only the
'garret master' in the furniture trade was to survive intact until 1914, although
in London his equivalents in tailoring and dressmaking were much more resistant to the factory system than in other major provincial centres during the
post-1890 period. But in boot and shoemaking, as L.P. Gartner has shown for
Stepney and C.B. Hawkins for Norwich, the self-employed small master from
the 1890s onwards found himself gradually squeezed out of existence by large,
mechanised units of production.[75]

The kaleidoscopic nature of these changes alone makes the task of charting
the course of fully employed workers' earnings formidable. But this is by no
means the sole obstacle. For even if the earnings received from a major employer
of labour are known, how confidently can they be applied, in such a highly
imperfect labour market, to even the individual town in which he operated?
Most writers in the late nineteenth and early twentieth centuries abandoned
hope, because of the profusion of piece and time rates, of doing more than
drawing roughly the parameters within which the wages of those unorganised
groups moved. Examining this question in a Scottish context in 1893, Elizabeth
Orme was content to list examples on the grounds that 'there is no uniform
rate of wages throughout the [clothing] trade for women workers. Every shop
has its own rate, which is chiefly determined by the will or the circumstances
of the employer.'[76] Much the same point was made at the conclusion of the

investigation of the Women's Industrial Council into female domestic workers in Liverpool in 1909 and the contemporaneous inquiry, conducted by Mrs. Carl Meyer and Miss Clementina Black, in Longdon.[77] Furthermore, confronted by data for women's 'usual weekly earnings' which differed, in the case of Liverpool's vestmakers, by 900 per cent, what light do such vast disparities shed upon the poverty question?[78] Where female outworkers in the early years of this century were earning as little as 2/6d. to 5s. per week, the lowest figures mentioned in the Liverpool survey, they consisted usually of two quite separate groups: they were either widowed and elderly who were partly dependent upon the poor-rate for their support or married women who, operating on a casual basis, saw domestic work as a means of contributing to the family budget. In the latter instance, their pattern of income can only be taken as an indirect indicator of a family under economic pressure, in the former as a tangible sign of distress. But in neither case can the data be legitimately interpreted as 'weekly earnings when fully employed'. Again, because we are dealing with seasonal trades, with considerable fluctuations in the size of weekly incomes between the slack and busy months and a rising volume of unemployment in the dull season, should we largely concentrate on the period of peak activity? And if the seasonal peak is selected as our measurement of a working week, should our focus of attention be switched to aggregate family income rather than the earnings of the head of the household since in tailoring, cabinetmaking and, above all, shoemaking, 'little masters' and home-based workers often operated as a family unit? For example, in the late 1840s in London it was argued that 'the only means of escape from the inevitable poverty which sooner or later overwhelms those in connection with the cheap shoe trade is, by the employment of the whole Family of children as soon as they are able to be put to the trade.'[79] Much the same was true of Northampton where one shoemaker wrote in 1852 that

> no single-handed man can live; he must have a whole family at work, because a single-handed man is so badly paid he can scarce provide the necessaries of life ... As soon as they [the children] are big enough to handle an awl, they are obliged to come downstairs and work.[80]

Little had changed by the early 1860s when Dr. Edward Smith, analysing the diets of 'third class' shoemakers in Staffordshire and Northamptonshire, acknowledged the existence of this form of supplementation, even if it 'was ill paid for and uncertain in quantity.'[81]

In the light of these methodological difficulties, it is necessary to make three points about how low pay will be treated in the ensuing discussion. Firstly, it is intended, wherever possible, to examine the earnings of fully employed workers, male and female, in those sectors of the domestic system which were inextricably linked with the sweated workshop and the domestic hearth. Secondly, where the data permit, attention will be focused upon 'typical wages', or, as more than one survey put it, upon earnings which were most representative of a given group of outworkers. Thirdly, because of the acknowledged imperfections in the data, use will also be made of qualitative statements which provide some insight into the correlation between low pay and poverty.

Among the most poorly rewarded of these elements were those females who were compelled to rely upon their proficiency as needlewomen and tailoresses to support themselves and perhaps a family. For unlike the female workforce in handloom weaving, the women who were employed as outworkers in the clothing trades were very often the principal, or sole, wage-earners in a household, a point which was forcibly underlined by Peter Fyfe's examination of 660 registered domestic workers in Glasgow in 1907. Of this total twenty-eight per cent were spinsters, twenty-seven per cent widows and less than half — forty-five per cent — married women.[82] Within this group needlewomen who worked in their own homes, either because of growing infirmity or the need to look after children, fared worst of all. In Edinburgh, for instance, it was thought that in the mid-1840s their daily returns fluctuated between 8d. and 1s. Translated into a weekly sum 'a woman, neat handed, might make 4s. or 5s.,' but it was not unknown 'for a shop that keeps them in good work' to pay them 'not more than 2s. 6d.'[83] Mayhew's evidence for London in 1848-9 was broadly in accord with these findings. Of fifty-one needlewomen that he interviewed, none had earned more than 5s. in the previous week, although with thirty-four of this number claiming to have received 2s. or less, it is clear that an element suffered from serious underemployment. Moreover, even in better paid sectors of the London 'slop' trades, returns to female labour were totally inadequate for their own subsistence, with 6/8d. gross and 2/5d. net going to trouser hands and 4/6d. to 5s. gross and 2/3d. to 2/6d. net to shirtmakers.[84] Inevitably, of course, there were exceptions. Fifty-four widows with children averaged, in St. George's in the East Parish, London, 9/8d. from needlework in the 1840s. But within that area they stood out in stark contrast for three shirtmakers and four 'slop' workers who, with similar family responsibilities, earned respectively 4/8d. and 3/2d., gross per week, and from thirty-three single women and 'unincumbered' widows who secured only 5/9d. gross on average for a week's work.[85] Viewed against this sombre backcloth, it was small wonder that unmarried females living on their own and widows complained of being 'very poor indeed . . . There is a great deal of want, and there is a great deal of suffering amongst them'.[86] And want in this context could be described in the most basic terms. As one waistcoat worker put it,

> I've been short — very short indeed, sir; in want of common necessaries to keep my strength and life together. I don't find that I get by my labour sufficient to keep me. I've no money anywhere, not a farthing in the house; yes, I tell a story, I've got a penny . . . For my old age there is nothing but the workhouse.[87]

For home-based needleworkers there was to be little change for the better in the post-1850 world. J. Strang, for example, arguing that the sewing machine produced returns to workshop machinists in Glasgow of between 7s. and 10s.

per week in 1857, contrasted their position with that of 'a mere sempstress' who 'can scarcely earn half this sum, that, too, through long protracted labour.'[88] Similarly, Dr. E. Smith's sample of thirty-one needlewomen only averaged 3/11½d. gross per week at the time of his investigation in 1863. Making the maximum allowance for the fact that this figure had been depressed by including individuals who were subject to broken time, there can be few doubts that full employment did little to mitigate the harsh burden of poverty to which they were subjected. 'They are,' wrote Smith, 'exceedingly ill fed and show a feeble state of health.'[89] Nor, where appropriate, was the application of the sewing machine to make much alteration to the money income of this category of worker, for the major investigations of the late 1880s and early 1890s were couched in identical language. The House of Lords' inquiry into the sweating system concluded in 1890 that the earnings of the home-based shirtmakers of the East End of London were 'very low', although in reaching its verdict, it tended to concentrate its attention upon the considerable numbers of married women whose husbands were both unskilled and irregularly employed.[90] Charles Booth on the other hand emphasised in 1893 that the typical London shirt-finisher tended to be elderly and widowed, who was compelled to accept work at whatever price that it was offered. Most, unable to earn more than 8d. during a lengthy working day, were unable to live by their earnings alone: 'nearly all receive allowances from relatives, friends, and charitable societies, and many of them receive outdoor relief.'[91]

During the last twenty-five years of our period the adverse pressures against 'slop' needlework and related occupations intensified as traditional tasks such as button-holing, shirt-finishing, shirtmaking, the production of underwear, and capmaking became increasingly the preserve of large workshops and factories. As a result, many outworkers, outside the seasonal peaks, were reduced to the status of a casual labour force, with little scope for any improvement in earnings. Indeed, Margaret Irwin in her evidence to the 1907 Select Committee on Home Work argued that the wages of females working in the outwork clothing industries of Scotland had actually deteriorated since 1890. In her words, 'during the last year we made several supplementary investigations, and we found that the wage figures were quite as low, in fact, in some cases they were rather lower than what we had met with before.' By 1906 full work for Glasgow's home-based shirtmakers meant a gross income, in exceptional circumstances, of 8s., but more usually of 4s. to 5s.[92] These statistics matched almost exactly the earnings of an anonymous London machinist of shirts, nightdresses and underwear in the same year, who, as a single woman, 'had 7s. per week on an average, sometimes less, and paid 5s. for rent; I worked from six a.m. in the morning till ten at night, only taking about one hour for my meals.'[93] In some respects those last data were only representative of those females who were placed at the bottom of the home work hierarchy, for of thirty-six shirtmakers whose cases were examined in London in 1907 by the Women's Industrial Council, the 'most frequent average weekly earnings' ranged between 7s. and

12s. while the corresponding result for makers of underclothing and blouses was between 10s. to 15s. and from 12s. to 15s. respectively.[94] Nevertheless, if these returns accrued exclusively to single women with only themselves to support, they left, at the bottom end, little or no margin for hard times. As S.J. Chapman noted 'a woman cannot live decently on much less than 10s. a week in the provinces, and 11s. in London. This means that for a reasonable day's work earnings should be at a higher rate than 2d. an hour in the provinces; and undoubtedly large numbers of home-workers throughout the country are earning less than 2d. an hour.'[95] For widows, with dependent children, such earnings were palpably insufficient for subsistence. Indeed, it was only in those households where they represented the contribution of married women to the family budget, that they could make the difference between poverty and a modest degree of comfort.

In tailoring on the other hand the pattern is more complex if only because of those changes in the sexual composition of the workforce which have already been mentioned. Even so, certain developments which had an important bearing on rates of remuneration can be easily identified. For one thing, as soon as the industry began to develop, in the 1830s and 1840s, a distinctive sweated, or dishonourable sector, it drew part of its labour supply from the ranks of the adult male population. From the outset such recruits could expect, when fully occupied, a lengthy working day under cramped conditions in the workshop of a small master, often for a meagre reward. One 'slop' coat-hand, working and living with his employer in the East End of London, claimed in 1849 that after toiling from 7 a.m. to 11 p.m. for all seven days of the week, his earnings amounted to 13s. gross. But deductions of 4s. for bed, tea and coffee and 1/9d. for trimmings reduced his income to 7/3d. net. Allowing for broken time, his net weekly wage on a yearly basis was no more than 5/9d. At these levels of remuneration there was little left to buy adequate supplies of food — 'I'm harder worked and worse fed than a cab-horse' — and no prospect of getting 'a coat to our backs.'[96] But working on coats still paid men very much better than trousers which, in the brisk season, could produce as little as 8s. gross and 4/5d. net, with ahead the fearsome prospect of 'weeks and weeks' when 'the work isn't to be had.'[97] Looking at male 'slop' workers, in the aggregate, a full week in the 1840s probably yielded around 13s. gross and, for those who did not live in, perhaps 10s. net. Expressed in another form, these were, for married men, poverty rates of pay.

Yet neither this fact nor the increasing tendency to sub-divide work after 1860 discouraged men from seeking employment in this sector of the market. Indeed, sub-division actually facilitated this process, for, as one Glasgow observer commented in 1890, the sewing machine

allowed these people to introduce themselves into the trade who knew nothing at all about the work; and there are parties at the present time, men that have served their time, working with a machine, that is to say working where a machine is employed, who if they go into a place where handwork is done, cannot do it.[98]

Furthermore, better wages could now be obtained from this form of work than had ever occurred in the pre-1860 era. Francis Gallacher, for example, computed that he had earned, when employed by a Glasgow 'sweater' in the brisk season of 1888, between 17s. and 18s. gross for a 72 hours' week.[99] And if Gallagher's income, without supplementation, would still have left his family in primary poverty, it is at the same time clear that some of his colleagues secured substantially greater rewards. One Jewish employer of male labour believed — although his claims were challenged — that in Glasgow in the late 1880s plain machinists, working on coats, could secure 4/6d., and pressers 7s. to 8s., daily, while a thoroughly competent tailor could expect '6s. to 9s. day of 11 hours'.[100] These figures closely mirrored those of the East End of London where, in the 'slop' workshops examined by Beatrice Potter in the early 1890s, the best paid male machinists and pressers were offered 6s. to 8s. for a full working day.[101] During the busy season of the year, therefore, the families of those who were receiving these rewards could legitimately anticipate rising above the poverty line, although, with the return of dull trade, when under-employment was endemic amongst most grades of the labour force, the spectre of poverty inevitably returned to darken their doors.

How broadly or how narrowly based this process of improvement was in the 1880s and 1890s cannot be established with any degree of precision, although Charles Booth's poverty data can serve as a rough guide to the social and economic status of sweated workers in home industries, particularly in the tailoring and shoemaking trades. Looking at such occupations in the aggregate, Booth discovered that they were well represented among the poverty-stricken population of the East End of London, with 9.5 per cent of their number belonging to his 'very poor', and twenty-six per cent to his 'poor' categories.[102] What is altogether most certain is that from the late 1890s onwards sweating masters, operating from their own workshops, were engaged in a struggle for survival against the encroaching factory system. And among the first casualties of that struggle were the wages and employment prospects of their workforce, a point forcibly underlined by the Jewish Board of Guardians when it discovered that 30.6 per cent of the applicants it relieved in London in 1907-8 came from a tailoring background.[103]

Of sweated female tailoring workers in the post-1850 era the worst paid element comprised those women who followed the trade in their own homes. Beatrice Potter spoke feelingly of 'wives and daughters of the irregularly em-ployed and of the purely parasitic population of East London' who 'slave night and day for a pittance which even a greener would despise, except as apprenticeship to better things.' Elsewhere she was to refer to homeworkers 'women and girls straining every nerve, who cannot earn [making vests and trousers] more than 2d., and must frequently content themselves with ¾d., for an hour's labour.'[104] But within this group there was a 'lowest rank', con-sisting of 'those married women who, without any previous training, take it up under pressure of want. Theirs is the poorest pay and the most irregular work. Here we find "truly starvation" wages.'[105] In Scotland, too, earnings of homeworkers were described in the 1890s as 'slavery in summer and starvation in winter,' although this in part reflected the fact that many of the home-based tailoresses interviewed by Elizabeth Orme were either ill or ageing and whose productivity, therefore, was correspondingly low.[106] Again, in Liverpool in the early 1900s where outworkers toiled long hours to secure 6s. or 7s. gross weekly,

> one widow, who has supported herself and one boy for four years by trouser finishing for one of the chief employers of outworkers in the city, said she could only do so by working from 6 a.m. to 10 p.m. The rate of pay she received was from 1 ¾d. to 3½d. per pair, and she could do one dozen of the lower price in one day. [107]

If, however, the norm, low pay was not the invariable lot of the homeworker. During the busy season in the 1890s, a small minority of vest-makers in London could earn as much as 20s. gross weekly, while in Scotland at least one of Elizabeth Orme's case-studies, working on the same kind of garment, made 15s. But such earnings were denied to the vast majority whose lowly incomes at the seasonal peak could support neither widow nor spinster. Nor, in those areas of the major cities 'where casual labour for men predominates' and where 'the women are frequently the chief wage earners', was the wife's earnings when fully employed, capable, when added to her husband's, of shielding the family from the debilitating effects of primary poverty. Thus, A.D. Steel-Maitland and Rose E. Squire found that in Liverpool female pauperism in the 1900s was overwhelmingly the result of inadequate wages when in full work. The same undoubtedly held true of many home-based tailoresses and clothing workers not merely in that port but throughout Britain.

On the other hand the wages of female labour in tailoring workshops and factories are less easy to determine since the pattern of earnings was powerfully shaped by three factors. In the first place it was affected by the size of the production unit, with the larger shops on the whole paying their employees better than those smaller establishments which dominated the sweated sector. Secondly, the section of the clothing market for which the particular employer was catering had a crucial bearing upon levels of earnings. Those who worked in 'bespoke and stock' workshops received substantially greater incomes than those engaged in the manufacture of 'slop' garments. Thirdly, in establishments where sub-division of work was a prominent feature of their organisational structure, the individual's weekly income would depend in large measure upon the nature of the job that she executed. General hands, machinists, fellers, button-holers and finishers were all differently rewarded, with the learner, usually straight from school and initially paid at most from 2s. to 3s. weekly, at the bottom of the hierarchy.

Nonetheless, good wages could be made within the workship and the factory. In those workshops of East London which in the 1890s produced 'bespoke and stock' clothing, young girls could rise in time from the position of apprentice feller, earning under 9s. for a full week, to that of general hand where they 'will receive in that capacity 2/6d. to 5s. a day, according to the quality of work they are equal to.' Female machinists could also expect a daily income of between 2/6d. and 4s., although they tended to be more concentrated in the 'common' and 'slop' lines. Button-holers on the other hand were worse situated, with an income of 1/6d. to 3/6d. per day being quite common.[108] Such earnings, moreover, were not the exclusive preserve of the East End. Sherwell, in his analysis of sweating in the West End, wrote, in 1897, of 'clever girls' under 'fair conditions' receiving 12s. to 20s., and skilled workers 18s. to 30s., weekly in the busy season, although in the slack period 'even a good workwoman would probably not earn more than seven, eight, or, perhaps, ten shillings per week, while for several weeks together she may earn absolutely nothing.'[109] Similarly, in Glasgow in 1893, female tailoresses, employed by 'second class' and non-union shops upon trousers and vests, could secure 18s. to 20s. per week during the months of peak activity.[110] But there were significant areas of the industry where earnings were much lower than these statistics suggest. In small 'slop' workshops — and the typical sweater of the East End hired fewer than ten workers — poverty wages were paid to a sizable section of the female workforce. Beatrice Potter spoke of the hopelessness of 'the general hand of the small slop-shop' who 'will be expected to "convenience" her master, and her maximum pay will be 1s.6d. a day. And the saving needed in this class of garment [coats] is in no sense a training for better work; indeed it unfits her for it. Therefore we have a limited class of women working in the Jewish coat trade whose earnings can never exceed 1s.6d., and frequently fall below 1s. for twelve hours' work.' Moreover, it was precisely this type of worker who was most exposed to broken time, for whereas those who were in the employ of large contractors would average a 4.5 days' week over the course of a year, 'the great majority of permanently unskilled or imperfectly trained workers' could expect to be occupied, on an annual basis, a mere 2.5 days per week.[111] Similar conditions obtained in the 'slop' shops of Glasgow in 1893 where, if a select number of machinists could earn 16s. weekly at the seasonal peak, most could expect little more than 9s. to 12s. at such times and 7s. or less during the months of dull trade.[112]

This lugubrious picture should of course be modified in certain important respects. For one thing the majority of females engaged in the workshops were single. Outside the 'slop' sector, therefore, they earned, when fully employed, an income, in the brisk season, sufficient to raise them above the poverty line. Similarly where they still lived with their parents, their wages could again have guaranteed an above subsistence standard of living for the family unit. Furthermore, the trend, rapid after 1900, towards clothing factories in the provinces — but not in London — increased regularity of work and raised earnings. And yet, despite the benign influence of these forces, much poverty remained, since 'improvement' did not touch all with an even hand. For some the advent of the factory meant the disappearance of an already precarious livelihood, while for others low pay continued to be a depressing reality. Significantly enough, twenty per cent of the females engaged in shirtmaking in 1906 earned under 10s. per week, and this excluded all home-based workers, while, when the Tailoring Trade Board, set up under the 1909 Trades Board Act, fixed in 1913 its minimum rate for tailoresses, it opted for the lowly figure of 3¼d. per hour.[113]

In shoemaking an identical course of economic change can be traced. As in tailoring, a 'dishonourable' sector had emerged by the 1830s, which from the start made considerable use of child and female labour to reduce costs. Initially, therefore, the rewards it guaranteed to adult male workers were likely to be low. In Northampton it was thought that the shoemaker who worked upon cheap products for the ready-made market could rarely command, in the 1830s and 1840s, much above 10s. per week, a sum which might be raised to 15s. with assistance from his family.[114] In Edinburgh in 1853 the 'second class' hand could earn 12s. gross when in full employment. But the incomes of the main body of that city's labour force — the 1000 workers, or sixty-five per cent of the total, who constituted the 'third class' — fell well short of this modest figure.[115] Finally, in London the adult male outworker, making ready-made boots and shoes, could rarely exceed 13s. in a full week in the late 1840s, while the families of chamber-masters could not exploit their nominal independence to secure an aggregate income which would shield them from poverty.[116] By the early 1860s, however, some improvement had taken place in the condition of several of these groups of workers. In 1863 'third class' shoemakers in the towns and villages of Northamptonshire and Staffordshire earned 12s. weekly, although supplementary income from wives and children was seldom on such a scale as to remove completely the burden of poverty.[117] In Edinburgh the signs of betterment were also the subject of favourable comments when *The North Briton* contrasted the situation of the labour force with the position a decade earlier when 'the trade was proverbial for what appeared to be hopeless poverty.'[118]

By the 1860s, however, technological and organisational change had started to make its presence felt within the trade. The slow but sure trend towards the large workshop and, after 1890, towards the factory was paralleled by the adoption of machinery and the emergence of new growth points such as Leicester and Norwich. Indeed the spread of the sewing machine from the 1860s onwards and the later introduction of machinery for cutting out leather and riveting shoes were outward signs of an industry in a state of flux. Taken together, these developments were to affect the socio-economic standing of the workforce in profoundly different ways. On the one hand, they were bound to create a measure of technological unemployment or underemployment amongst skilled craftsmen who had hitherto had little contact with poverty. Thus, while in the high-class bespoke trade of East London, the clicker who was responsible for cutting out the leather for the uppers of boots and shoes, could still earn 30s. to 35s. per week in the early 1890s, his craft was already under pressure from factories 'carried on upon a wholesale scale', which executed this work more expeditiously. Again, the makers of hand-sewn bespoke shoes were increasingly aware that the demand for their product was falling as the consumer turned towards the cheaper, machine-sewn product from the provinces. But there were also points of gain. In the small ready-made factories of London, clickers could anticipate good rates of wages and fairly regular employment, while first-class female machinists might earn in the busy season 18s. to 22s. per week. Yet, notwithstanding these more socially beneficial features of change, significant areas of poverty continued to exist.

For adult male lasters in the ready-made factories, the 1880s and 1890s represented decades of considerable hardship. In the East End perhaps one-third of their number would be dismissed in the slack period when 'with little or no employment', they 'frequently suffer great privations.' Again, if good wages could still be secured by the few in the 'sew round', or fancy slipper trade of East London, most workers in this branch of the industry were poorly remunerated. Even during the six busy months of each year, its machinists in the 1890s could still only secure 2s. per day compared with 2/6d. a few years earlier, while females sewing felt and carpet uppers by hand obtained a mere 1/3d. for a day's work. As D.F. Schloss observed, this last group consisted largely of married women 'partially supported by their husbands' since 'no one could get a living out of this work.'[119] Finally, there were dwindling numbers of outworkers whose plight was exacerbated by technical change. In some cases age was a barrier to occupational mobility, as with the seventy-six years old children's bookmaker who had formerly earned 12s. to 14s. per week but who, reduced to 5s. by 1907, was compelled at last to resort, with his wife, to the workhouse having 'resisted [that institution] as long as they could.'[120] In other cases — as in Norwich which in the opening years of the twentieth century became an important centre for the factory-based production of ladies' and children's shoes, — small numbers of 'garret masters' clung to their trade because of their unwillingness to break with 'the old ways'. But the price that they and their workers were required to pay for such conservation was high. Operating in a sector of the labour market 'characterised by low wage and great uncertainty of employment', they depended for their survival upon such factory orders as were placed with them at the busy season. At these peak periods female hands could earn 9s. to 10s. per week and male workers much higher. But such incomes were not typical of the level of earnings throughout the rest of the year, for average female income, assessed on an annual basis, was as low as 3s. weekly. The corresponding statistic for the adult male worker was 12s. As these results make abundantly plain, 'garret' workers, remunerated at a rate which left them permanently impoverished, had by the early 1900s been reduced to the status of a reserve pool of labour.[121]

II

If, within the confines of the domestic system, these trades were the principal sources of employment for men and women, there were other more narrowly circumscribed areas of outwork which faithfully conformed to the pattern of low earnings which has just been described. Box-making, although challenged by the rise of the factory, continued to employ a diminishing body of largely female outworkers at very inadequate rates of pay. Charles Booth, for example, drew attention to one East London employer who in 1893 paid 28.2 per cent of his domestic labour force between 2s. and 4s. per week, 43.8 per cent 4s. to 6s., and 15.6 per cent from 6s. to 8s.[122] Yet despite such meagre earnings, all such hands — making plain boxes — could be classified as semi-skilled, having received some training within the factory before marriage. This was not, however, true of home-based match-box makers who, in the same period, could expect little more than 2¼d. to 2½d. per gross. Almost inevitably, therefore, this category of worker most frequently enlisted the help of her children to raise marginally family income, although over time the efficacy of this strategy was largely frustrated by a sharp reduction in the amount of outwork available. For the increasing concentration upon factory production was to mean that whereas London's match-box makers had obtained sufficient work to keep them employed in their own homes for five days per week in the late 1880s, they were fortunate to be fully occupied for more than two days by 1907.[123]

Yet another part of the domestic system which, in general terms, paid badly was the East End fur trade. Here, as elsewhere, there was a small elite of hand sewers who, at the seasonal peak, could occasionally earn as much as 18s. or 19s. in a full week in the 1890s. But more typical of the fortunes of the industry's labour force were those females, frequently elderly and widowed, who, employed upon 'the commonest work', would never receive more than 9s. per week 'in season' and who, in the dull months, were either unemployed or content with the miserable figure of 3s. or 4s. For single women thus situated, as for their colleagues working for 'starvation wages' at sack and carpet slipper making, the stark choice confronting them was either an unending, and frequently unsuccessful, struggle 'to support themselves or to fall back upon charity or the workhouse'.[124] In much the same situation were those married women who in 1906 worked in the principal unskilled domestic trade of Birmingham, the carding of hooks and eyes. According to the findings of Cadbury, Matheson and Shann, such employment yielded on average no more than 3/3½d. per week, a sum, which, when added to the average weekly income of 19/6d. of their husbands, must, in the absence of other wage-earners in the household, have left many families at or below the poverty line.[125]

The final group of outworkers whose socio-economic status must be analysed consists of those who sought their living in the metallic trades. In most branches of these industries the existence of a sweated sector can be easily discerned, although the point in time at which it emerged differed from trade to trade and locality to locality. In the light metal crafts of Sheffield and district, a sweating system was already fully developed by the 1840s. It was mainly rural-based; marked, as always, by a long working day, and dependent upon female and child, as well as male, labour in the manufacture of the more common types of goods. But until the 1860s the light metal trades of South Yorkshire generally prospered within the framework of the small workshop. Thereafter foreign competition and the application of machinery were to have wider repercussions upon the workforce. By the 1880s the impact of these forces upon living standards can be most clearly observed amongst Sheffield's file-cutters who could be effectively divided into two distinct groups. On the one hand, factory workers, using newly installed machinery, had good wages; on the other, there were hand-cutters operating within the domestic system, who, if solely dependent upon their own earnings, were inadequately nourished. The female component in this last category was always badly rewarded, unable to earn more than 7s. to 10s. in 1893; but its male counterpart was also under pressure, with a father and son of fourteen years of age obtaining in 1890 an aggregate income of 18/4d. net for a 70 hours' week. Furthermore, these problems were exacerbated by falling price-rated, a fall which was markedly steeper among sweated hands for whom, between 1883 and 1890, it could range from fifteen per cent to twenty-five per cent.[126] But file-cutters were by no means isolated in their poverty, since the domestic labour force in the spring knife trade could only average 12/9d. to 14/6d. weekly in the late 1880s. Looking, therefore, at these outworkers generally, it is impossible not to endorse the verdict of W.J. Davis, the Factory Inspector of the Sheffield District, when, in 1890, he commented upon the extent of their destitution in trenchant terms.

> How they live I do not know. Some of them say they see meat, so far as they are concerned, about once a week, that is on the Sundays. A man said to me, 'Well, sometimes I do get a little bit of sausage in the middle of the week, but beyond that I get no meat; I cannot afford it.'[127]

After 1893 there was no hope of any sustained improvement since the light metal trades encountered economic problems of formidable dimensions. From 1893 to 1914 little real growth in the output of tools, cutlery and files took place. In social terms the period was distinguished by heavy unemployment in the mid-1890s and a secular decline in real wages.[128] But during these two decades, certain sections of the trades suffered more severely than others. Among them were Sheffield's cutlers — in number roughly 2500 in 1907 — who complained that their 'chief evil . . . is the low wage'. As the Secretary of the Cutlers' Union expressed it in 1907,

> the prices have decreased of late years, and a man can now make only a miserable wage. There is no standard rate of pay, and individual employers are always pulling them down. The union has laid it down that a cutler should make 35s. a week, but the actual average is not over 20s.

Full work meant an income of 25s. gross, but from this figure from 6d. to 1/6d. had to be deducted for shop rent and, in winter, another 4d. for gas. Even then, such earnings were hard to maintain over any lengthy period because of chronic irregularity in employment. 'There is no slack season, but the orders fluctuate very much, so that often a man gets only two or three days' work a week.'[129] Other elements afflicted by a poverty that could be casually related to low pay when in full work included the dwindling army of domestic file-cutters and that portion of hafters and setters-in in the table-knife, spring knife and razor trades who in 1910 earned less than 20s. net per week.[130] But for the majority by that date, income could more than meet basic needs as long as employment held, a reflection in itself of increasing mechanisation which both undermined the *raison d'etre* of the domestic system and produced better returns to the workforce.

The other main element of outworkers in the metallic trades comprised nailmakers and chainmakers, the latter group heavily concentrated in and around Cradley Heath. In both cases the numbers following these occupations declined in the second half of the nineteenth century. Whereas, for example, there were 29,000 nailers in Britain in 1851, this total subsequently fell sharply, with the female component having shrunk from perhaps 10,000 in 1851 to 1700 by 1911.[131] Similarly, by 1890 when the House of Lords drew the attention of the nation to the scale of sweating in the chainmaking industry of the Black Country, the domestic base of that industry had started to be eroded, with, at most, 3000 female and male outworkers still practising the craft. By 1911 only around 2100 chainmakers remained.[132] As with outwork generally, there-fore, innovation and the move towards larger units of production threatened these branches of the domestic system with extinction. But before that point had been reached, below-subsistence earnings were already a prominent feature of each of these trades. The wage data assembled by E. Hopkins for the Stour-bridge area suggest that this conclusion held true for married adult male nailers for virtually the whole of the period running from 1842 to 1897. In the 'black' year of 1842 their earnings were little more than 11s. to 12s. per week, although some recovery had set in by the early and mid-1860s when full work produced a weekly income which fluctuated between 12s. and 15s. gross. After a temporary reverse in 1867 when they fell to 10s. to 12s. per week, nailers' earnings, in the exceptional trade boom of the late 1860s and early 1870s, rose spectacularly to reach 22/6d. in 1872. It is only in this short-lived period that it is possible to speak of returns to the adult male being capable, without supplementation, of keeping a medium-sized family above the poverty line. By the mid-1870s, however, earnings had again started to fall, averaging 7s. to 12s. gross in the 1880s. After this point no lasting recovery was to occur, for if nailers' incomes stood at 14s. gross in 1897, they collapsed in 1894 when, in the wake of massive reductions, they reached little more than 4s. to 5s. per week. But the plight of Stourbridge's female labour force was even more grim, with wages of 3/6d. to 6s. being recorded in 1889, an average which accords closely with the earnings of 4/6d. obtained by women hands in Coventry in the mid-1890s.[133]

In chainmaking, on the other hand, averages are not particularly illuminating since wages varied according to sex, the nature of the task executed, and whether or not the place of employment was the home or a large workshop. Some men, capable of making three hundred-weight of chain in a week, could earn 15s. gross in 1890. But a full week for female hands in the 1890s produced little more than 4/6d. to 6/6d. gross, while child apprentices, drawn from both sexes, would start at 2/6d. [134] In many homes, of course, husband and wife would pool their income, which could raise family earnings above those of the unaided male by as much as twenty-five per cent. R. Sherard, for instance, quoted an example of a husband and wife team who, in Cradley Heath in 1897, received 20s. gross — or 15/4d. net — for converting 'into spikes a ton of iron'.[135] But, equally, a married woman might also have to support the entire house-hold because of the unemployment, sickness, or death of her husband. Yet whichever of these circumstances obtained, the usual issue was not whether the earnings derived from full work could raise the family out of a state of poverty, but the degree of social deprivation to which the house-hold was exposed.[136] As the House of Lords' inquiry concluded, if chainmaking and nailmaking did not employ great numbers, they were unique in one respect: 'in scarcely any [trade] that have come under our notice is so much poverty to be found, com-bined with such severe work and so many hardships. [137]

In any exploration, however, of the relationship between low pay and poverty it is essential to broaden the field of vision from the outwork trades, particularly in the post-1880 period when the domestic system in most spheres of economic activity was in retreat, to embrace the labour market as a whole. In particular it is necessary to examine those unskilled occupations, largely the preserve of women, which yielded scanty rewards. In this respect the two inter-related jobs of washing and charing stand out. Both were heavily dependent upon women who, after marriage, were compelled to seek employment, either be-cause, as at Birmingham, their husbands earned insufficient to support their families, or because the death of their partners deprived the family of its prin-ciapl wage-earner.[138] Indeed, there was a definite tendency, remarked upon by contemporaries, for females who, before they had married, had been in domestic service and who were untrained for any other form of work, to turn automatically at widow-hood to charing and washing as a means of obtaining a livelihood. In most areas, however, neither occupation in the 1840s generated a level of income which would have enabled female heads of households, with-out outside assistance on a generous scale, to preserve themselves and/or their dependants from searing distress. In the early 1840s, for example, able-bodied widows and single women in Edinburgh did not receive more than 1s. to 1/6d. per shop per week for charing. Furthermore, there were, in view of an abundant supply of female labour, limited opportunities of adding greatly to this sum by working for more than two or three employers. Similarly placed were washer-women who, usually hired at the rate of 1s. per day, also had difficulty in procuring more than three of four days' work in a week.[139] Rates of remuneration were somewhat higher in London if the data collected in the 1840s in St. George's in the East can be accepted as representative of the capital. That survey revealed that single women and widows living by themselves averaged 5/9d. per week from charing, widows with dependants, 7/10d. Mangle keepers, widowed and single, did marginally better, with average weekly incomes of between 8/2d. and 8/6d. But it was only the thirteen laundresses, widowed but with children, earning an average of 14/4d. per week, who had any hope of easing slightly the pressures of want in the lives of their families.[140]

After 1850 evidence relating to the movement of their earnings is fragmentary in the extreme. Nevertheless it seems probable that the marked post-1871 decline in the proportion of the female population under twenty-five years of age entering indoor domestic service — in itself a poorly paid occupation whose workforce was frequently cushioned against poverty by 'in kind' payments.[141] — and the slowly broadening spectrum of occupational outlets for women, gradually exercised a positive influence upon day rates. By the early 1900s a competent charwoman, working for a 'good household' in London would get 2/6d. to 3s. per day and reasonable continuity of employment.[142] In Liverpool, Edinburgh, Greenock and Aberdeen the comparable rewards were 2/6d. daily together with meals, while in Glasgow a distinctive group of comparatively young charwomen and washerwomen, some of them single, with 'a good-doing connection among well-to-do people', secured between 14s. to 18s. per week and additional perquisites in the form of food and clothing.[143] In this last instance, however, the work itself was often of a seasonal nature since it was exactly this type of middle-class employer who would choose to spend the summer in one of the Clyde resorts.[144]

Yet if some gains had been won, there are grounds for believing that they were unevenly distributed. Firstly, there were growing numbers of charwomen, cleaning the homes of the better paid sections of the working classes, whose daily remuneration varied from 1s. to 1/6d. — plus their dinner — in Liverpool and from 9d. to 1s. in London. Worst paid of all were the clusters of elderly women, of limited mobility and facing physical powers, who earned as little as 6d. per day from Jewish householders in the East End, who were themselves not far removed from the poverty line.[145] In Glasgow, too, a section of the labour force — 'the older, weaker, and frequently "feckless" person who washes, chars, and minds children for neighbours' — was often underemployed and miserably rewarded. Secondly, the traditional function of the washerwoman was being undermined in some areas by the 'belated industrial revolution' in the laundry trade.[146] Collet has argued that this crucial development took place between 1871 and 1891 when the falling off in the number of females who were engaged in 'washing and bathing services' in England and Wales, underlined the extent to which 'young women between 15 and 25 working full time in steam and other large laundries, displaced the elderly and casual washerwoman.'[147] In one sense, however, this argument is misleading, for the 1870s and 1880s marked the formative phase, rather than the completion, of this revolution. Certainly, in London the rate of change accelerated enormously from the mid-1890s onwards. As one authority wrote in 1900,

the trade is at its present stage of development peculiarly interesting to the student of industrial questions. It is in process of rapid transformation from a domestic into a regular factory system, in which machinery and division of labour plays an important part in the organisation. In the last eight years the development in this direction has been extraordinary. At one time it was only in a few large steam laundries that machinery was to be met with, now it is not an uncommon thing to find a row of houses in separate occupation, the backyards of each of which is roofed in and packed with laundry machinery, all driven by an engine at one end of the row. The old-fashioned 'washerwoman' is fast disappearing, and is superseded by the enterprising . . . 'laundry proprietor', who, turning the tubs out of the back kitchen, fills their place with 'washing machines', and connecting them with a little gas-engine . . . blossoms forth as the owner of a 'factory laundry', ready to deal with six times the amount of work his predecessor could hope to cope with, and to compete fearlessly with scores of similarly equipped rivals.[148]

Not every major city of course proceeded as far as London. In Glasgow as late as 1908 the small domestic laundry still remained, unmechanised, and employing as few as two married hands.[149] Again, in smaller towns and villages, married washerwomen were relatively unaffected by the rise of the steam laundry and able to earn 2s. to 2/6d. per day in the years immediately before 1914. This was true of the female hands in Headington Quarry and, at a more personal level, of both my grandmothers who worked from their own homes at Rugby in Warwickshire and Moulin, near Pitlochry, in Perthshire.[150] But the trend in the major urban centres cannot be disputed. Nor can its social consequences. As the prominent position of aged and widowed washerwomen in the poor relief rolls in the cities of England and Scotland established beyond doubt,[151] these two elements came to occupy the role of an increasingly casual reserve of labour, poorly paid, erratically employed, and deeply impoverished. In the last analysis, therefore, any attempt to produce a social balance sheet of the impact of technical change upon the labour force can only succeed if it recognised the existence of two fundamentally different groups. While those who worked full-time in the larger, mechanised laundries were the true beneficiaries of such change, its casualties included many pauperised female heads of households and a proportion of married women, operating in the traditional manner, who found it progressively more difficult to contribute, in a meaningful fashion, to the budgets of families never far removed from a state of primary poverty.

Yet it would be mistaken to argue that the factory system guaranteed subsistence wages for all. Charles Booth, although treating London's laundresses in 1890 as a 'fairly well paid' group, showed that their earnings varied considerably, with shirt and collar ironers getting from 8s. to 15s. weekly and four to six days' employment, and tub women 2s. to 3s. daily with three to five days' work in a given week.[152] At these rates, therefore, the status of the woman — whether she was single and living alone, single and lodging with her parents, widowed with dependants to support, or married with a wage-earning husband — and the extent to which she was regularly employed, would in large measure govern her relationship to the poverty line. But such a conclusion was equally valid, in the post-1880 era, for a whole host of factory-type or factory-based jobs. Cadbury, Matheson and Shann showed that low wages were the outstanding characteristic of unskilled women's work in Birmingham where, in 1901, twenty per cent of the occupied female population was engaged in the factories of the metal industries. Adopting a more generous scale than Rowntree, they believed that the single girl who still resided in the family home and who paid 7s. per week in board, required 14s. 'to keep herself healthy and respectable'. Included in the latter figure were allowances for amusements and clothing as well as a margin for saving to meet the twin threats of sickness and broken time. Yet 'the average wage in Birmingham for unskilled women over seventeen is barely 10s.' The social sequel, therefore, to 'the present system of payment' was, for many females psychological strain and considerable hardship.

> There is first a waste of nerve and spirit, a continual temptation to overwork, in order to maintain a standard that ought to be maintained, and hence much ill-health and elderly deterioration of physique; lower in the scale we find an acquiescence in conditions which are, to say the least, not conducive to progress; and lower still there is no possibility of escape from physical deterioration. It is not a hopeful prospect for the mothers of the coming generation.[153]

This verdict of course applied not to any specific group of occupations but to the unskilled female labour market as a whole. But that it had relevance for a section of the factory labour force was conclusively proved both by the authors' investigation into the living standards of girls working upon presses in the metallic industries and by their conclusion that average weekly earnings of women over twenty-one years of age in Birmingham's cycle and bedstead trades amounted, in 1905, to 10/6d. and 11/6d. respectively.[154]

Similar findings were reported from other major industrial centres. It was alleged in 1907 that the female contingent in Manchester's india-rubber industry was 'shockingly paid'. In the terse words of the local secretary of the Amalgamated Society of India-Rubber Workers, 'girls, aged 20, get 7s. a week. Is that subsistence?'[155] Again, 'very low' wages were recorded in that city's rag and paper-sorting warehouses where girls obtained 5s. to 8s., and adult female labour, paid on a piece-work basis, 7s. to 10s. weekly. In part these low levels of remuneration were a reflection of the casual nature of such work. Nontheless, since the majority of these workers were the wives or daughters of unemployed men, such earnings had still to serve as 'the chief mainstay of the family'.[156] No better placed were those widows in Liverpool who secured 9s. per week in cotton warehouses[157] and a considerable section of the female workforce engaged in the manufacture of lemonade, jam and confectionery in the 1890s and early 1900s. At the seasonal peak it was possible to earn between 11s. and 15s. weekly in this last group of trades, although, as Olive Malvery discovered, the lowly bottle-washer could expect as little as 3s. But the slack periods brought in their wake the dismissal of casual hands and, for a proportion of those who remained, short-time earnings which could fall to roughly 8s. per week.[158]

An altogether more traditional area of economic activity which on the whole also rewarded its female followers badly, was retailing. I say 'on the whole' because the multiplicity of forms which retailing assumed makes generalisation in this field notoriously difficult. At one level in the pre-1870 decades the possession of a small shop or beerhouse and the attainment of the status of a self-employed person represented a tangible sign of social mobility within working-class society. As one writer expressed it in 1862, 'to rent the whole of a small house for the purpose of letting it in apartments to lodgers, to establish a greengrocer's shop, or a small retail shop for provisions, appear to be the most common mode of investments among those [Irish in the East End of London] who are fortunate enough to be able to economise.'[159] And even after the retailing revolution had been launched in the 1870s and 1880s, these more humble aspirations continued to colour the thinking of a significant element of the working classes. Robert Roberts has shown, in his profound insight into working-class life in early twentieth-century Salford, that artisans who set up their wives as shopkeepers, automatically enhanced their standing in the local community and, hopefully, if the venture were managed with prudence, increased aggregate family income.[160] Nevertheless, as Roberts' mother discovered when confronted by a trader's bill for £5-2-0 in 1911, heavy unemployment among customers meant that mobility on this modest scale[159] uld always be threatened by bad debt and, in the last analysis, by bankruptcy.[161]

In the pre-1870 period, however, many women operated upon a much narrower credit base. Among them were numbers of widows in Edinburgh in the 1840s who 'keep small shops and sell potatoes and greens etc.' as a means of supplementing the sums which they received in outdoor relief from the parochial authorities.[162] Similarly situated were the six shopkeepers, returned as 'widows with incumbrances' in the St. George in the East inquiry, who averaged 9/5d. per week at the time that the survey was made.[163] But not all females whose profits from retailing were rarely adequate unaided to support a family, were widowed or shopkeepers. In parts of Lancashire in the 1830s and 1840s Irish wives, assisted by their children, became hawkers and street sellers of mops, mats, vegetables, fruit and illicitly distilled whisky in an attempt to boost the income of irregularly employed husbands.[164] Fulfilling an identical role were many married women and girls among Mayhew's 'street people' who, selling a wide variety of products — watercress, vegetables, oranges, matches — were often in the late 1840s and early 1850s wretchedly rewarded at the end of a week's work.

Yet it would be inaccurate to treat the lowest rungs of the retailing ladder in the pre-1870 era as the exclusive preserve of female and child labour. In many cases the dominant elements among small shopkeepers, hawkers, pedlars, costermongers and stallholders were either adult males or families who worked as a single unit. In Manchester, for example, in the 1840s 'the lowest kind of shops' — cellars let at rents of 5s. to 7s. per week — seemed mainly to have been in the hands of men whose customers were drawn 'principally [from] . . . the poorer classes of people.'[165] Again, the 400 Irish stallholders in Manchester's markets in the mid-1830s appear to have largely consisted of adult males who operated upon very low profit margins and with few prospects of social betterment. As Howarth, the local toll-collector observed 'the Irish [stall-holders] live in much worse lodgings and on worse food than the English, and are thus able to sell their goods at a lower price; they are contented with less profit. They set up their concern gradually, and carry on their trade with £2; very few get on and rise to be small shopkeepers.'[166] But the initial capital requirements in a whole range of retailing outlets were even lower than this. In London in the early 1850s the would-be itinerant seller of fried fish needed 10s. 'to start properly in the business', although one individual claimed to have 'gone into the trade . . . with 1s., which he expended in fish and oil, borrowed a frying-pan, borrowed an old tea-board, and so started on his venture.'[167] The lack, however, of any savings was not in itself an insurmountable barrier to entry since credit on a small scale was always freely available. Costermongers in London in the 1850s could hire hand-barrows for 3d. per day or 1s. per week during the six months of winter, and, for the rest of the year, at the slightly higher daily rate of 4d. Furthermore, short-term loans, bearing interest at 2d. per day upon 2/6d. and 3d. per day upon 5s., could be raised with which to acquire stock.[168]

The inescapable sequel to this system was to create a spectrum of employment which was literally open to any section of the able-bodied workforce that chose to enter it. Not surprisingly, craftsmen and labourers frequently resorted to hawking, on a casual basis, at times of cyclical unemployment.[169] Not surprisingly, either, the adverse pressures generated by a labour market which was periodically glutted and by a credit structure which pressed harshly upon the nominally independent retailer, meant that incomes from this kind of activity were frequently incapable of ensuring that the individual and/or his family were reasonably fed and decently housed. This was true among others of Irish rag and bone hawkers in the major towns of the West Riding whose average earnings in the late 1840s could fluctuate between less than 6s. to 9s. per week; of the Irish besom-makers and hawkers of Oldham who 'in a good week [in 1849] . . . could only make about 4s.'; and of the 'typical' London costermonger in the 1840s and 1850s who, if he could expect to obtain 30s. to 35s. in the high summer season, was reduced to a 'starvation' income of 4s. to 6s. weekly during a period which was roughly from January to April.[170]

This basic structure, although affected by changes in the retailing industry, underwent no major upheaval in the post-1870 decades. Nonetheless, there were two trends at work which must be acknowledged. Firstly, there was a sustained growth in the number of small general shops, although the origins of this process can be traced back to the pre-1850 period. Secondly, itinerant pedlars began to assume a role of diminishing significance in the retailing world. This development, first discernible in London, was to spread slowly to other parts of the country after 1880.[171] Yet, despite these alterations in the character of the workforce, the social continuities with the past remained strong. Above all, widespread poverty continued to be a major feature in the lives of those who tried to secure a living at this lowly level. As Charles Booth revealed in the late 1880s, no less than 44.25 per cent of street sellers in the East End of London belonged to 'the poor' — his Classes C and D — and a further twenty-five per cent to his Classes A and B, or 'the very poor' who were chronically underfed. Only a minority, comprising coffee stall owners, successful general dealers and those costermongers who had acquired their own donkeys and barrows, earned incomes which lifted them well clear of the poverty line. But among the lowest rank of shopkeepers in East London were 'people in the greatest poverty attempting to pay rent and obtain a living out of the sale of things of hardly any value to customers with hardly any money.'[172]

These conclusions still held good for the opening years of the twentieth century. Hawking in particular produced very uncertain benefits for its followers, even if few were worse rewarded than those females who 'may almost be called "submerged" ', who resorted to wood-chopping and selling in the city of Birmingham. Women, it was noted, who 'make a regular trade of it' could obtain around 6s. per week, although this might in itself be just sufficient to preserve their families from primary poverty since 'their husbands are men who earn about one pound per week if they are willing to work and can get jobs as labourers.' But this occupation, as with general hawking among married women in Liverpool, attracted a casual element as well; 'many people turn to the trade for a few months to tide over a bad time. We find again representatives of the lowest social classes mixed with many who, through the illness or death of the breadwinner, have been driven to it as a last resort.'[173] Until the very end of our period, therefore, there existed an indeterminate, but sizable, number of dealers and traders whose transactions were largely with the poorest sections of the working classes; who knew the presence of penury in their own homes; and who, with only the slenderest of resources to protect them, depended upon the continuation of good trade for their very livelihood.

Finally, there were whole areas of the labour market which were frequently visited by poverty but where it is impossible to chart the course of earnings. In the female sector the long hours and low pay of shop assistants and waitresses were the frequent subject of informed comment from the 1890s onwards, while male workers who were wretchedly remunerated after a full week included carmen, messengers, warehouse labourers and porters. Indeed, as Charles Booth pointed out in the late 1880s, since these jobs yielded a wage of less than 21s. per week to their regularly employed hands, it was impossible in the absence of financial contributions from other members of the household, for the families of such individuals to rise above the poverty line.[174] The same point had equal relevance for the majority of surfacemen and platelayers who in the first decade of this century could only expect between 18s. and 20s. per week.[175] But there were yet other occupations in which a division grew up between those who received for part, or all, of the period under review, above subsistence earnings, and those who, perhaps attracted by high day rates, were exposed to the erratic rhythms of casual employment and the more systematic movement of a seasonal cycle, with its peak and troughs in the demand for hands. Some of the industries which conformed to this pattern have, of course, already been touched upon at an earlier point in this discussion. Among them were building, tailoring, handloom weaving, shoemaking, lemonade and jam production, fur sewing, charing and washing. This list, however, is far from exhaustive, since it omits those dock labourers, fruit porters, carters, barbers, bakers and coalwhippers whose poverty stemmed from the pervasive influence of broken time in their lives rather than any other cause. In other words, it is necessary, in any comprehensive survey of poverty amongst the urban able-bodied, not to confine our analysis to questions of low pay but to extend our field of vision to examine how underemployment and unemployment depressed the living standards of the working classes. It is to this broad theme that we now turn our attention.

Chapter 2
Poverty and the Urban Labour Market 1830-1914: Underemployment and Unemployment

Society only turned belatedly in the 1890s to debate, in a coherent and systematic fashion, the causes of, and solutions to, unemployment within the general context of the British economy. This of course, does not mean that little interest in the topic had been displayed before this point in time. The classical school of political economy, writers on social questions such as the Rev. Thomas Chalmers and Professor W.P. Alison, and successive government inquiries in the 1830s and 1840s, had all attempted to shed light upon low unemployment adversely affected the well-being of the working classes. Furthermore, the best of this work showed an ability to discriminate between the different forms which unemployment assumed. Alison drew attention, in 1840, to the economic phenomenon of overbuilding, with its deleterious social consequences for the subsequent employment prospects of Edinburgh's building workers. Moreover, in addition to highlighting the reality of a substantial seasonal fluctuation in the demand for hands, he dimly discerned the existence of a casual labour problem which in his view represented in part a vindication of the gloomy prognostications of Malthus.[1] At a more parochial level but stripped of all Malthusian overtones, John Stewart sought to delineate the presence of casuality of employment in Liverpool's unskilled labour market in the early 1830s: 'in a town like Liverpool there are always a great many struggling sort of men that cannot get regular employment, but take up with any promiscuous employment they can get.'[2] Again, the problem of cyclical unemployment, if not described in those terms, produced voluminous, and frequently well-informed, comment in the local press. Nonetheless, despite the insights which some of these commentators afforded into what was a highly complex problem, it is impossible to argue that unemployment itself was, before the 1890s, analysed within a framework which would have enabled contemporary observers to have understood, and defined, it in all its manifold forms. Instead society was at most presented with a series of static, and often unconnected, snapshots of some of the issues involved, with the result that it was largely content to focus its attention upon cyclical unemployment and, at other times, to speak about

the unemployed as a morally unregenerate element which was primarily responsible for its own plight.

This idea of the self-inflicted wound was not to disappear very speedily in
the post-1890 era. Geoffrey Drage, writing in 1895, argued that an important
factor in the creation of a labour reserve of erratically employed men was
'faults of character — habits of intemperance, idleness or dishonesty — which
constitute their inferiority. In the opinion of many persons of experience in
the East End, "the public-house" lies at the root of want of employment in
that district.'[3] Nor were these isolated beliefs. They were to receive an intellectual justification from the sturdy individualist philosophy which fortified
many members of the Charity Organisation Society and the frequent appro-
bation of those who were entrusted with the task of attending to the needs of
the poor, either through the Scottish and English Poor Laws or, later, through
the 'make work' schemes associated with the Local Government Circular of
1886 and the 1905 Unemployed Workmen Act. Expressed in an extreme form,
it was believed that 'the contest [for full employment] is not with industrial
conditions, but with original sin.'[4] Nor was the work of Charles Booth entirely
immune from such preconceptions.[5] In particular Booth analysed his Class B
in moralistic, as much as in economic terms:

> the labourers of class B do not, on the average, get as much as three days' work a week,
> but it is doubtful if many of them could or would work full time for long together
> if they had the opportunity.
> . . . . The ideal of such persons is to work when they like and play when they like; these
> it is who are rightly called the 'leisure class' amongst the poor — leisure bounded very
> closely by the pressure of want, but habitual to the extent of second nature.[6]

Yet notwithstanding the strong intellectual ties which bound together the
pre- and post-1890 worlds, it is the discontinuities in social thought between
the two periods which are more striking. For the years after 1890 were distinguished by a willingness to acknowledge the multicausal nature of unemployment and to break the problem down into its component parts. This development in its turn implied the formulation of a more sophisticated methodology
to grapple with many of the basic questions which recurrent, or chronic, unemployment and underemployment posed for politicians, civil servants and social
scientists. Perhaps the most fundamental of these advances was simply the
conceptualisation of the term itself. Seasonality and casuality of employment
were recognised as separate social phenomena; the role of changes in fashion
and technological innovation in altering the demand for labour was defined;
and the devastating nature of cyclical unemployment re-emphasised.[7] Furthermore, as a result of the researches of H. Llewellyn Smith, Charles Booth, Beatrice
Potter, J.A. Hobson and Geoffrey Drage, it was widely accepted by the end of
the 1890s that much of the hardship produced by broken time could be attributed to exogenous variables at work in the national and regional economies.
It was upon these foundations that writers in the post-1900 era were to build.
Beveridge, for example, with the publication of his *Unemployment: a Problem*

of Industry (1909), was greatly to assist his contemporaries' understanding of the parameters of the casual problem and of the social dislocation which followed in its wake. Similarly, Seebohm Rowntree's and Bruno Lasker's joint study, conducted in York in the summer of 1910, was one of the first attempts at expressing, in a statistical form, the relative importance of the different causes of unemployment in a medium-sized community.[8]

Nevertheless this new work did not remove all of the shadows which surrounded major aspects of the topic. Above all it left largely untouched the vital question of how to measure the incidence of unemployment over time, even though Beveridge held out the hope that labour exchanges might ultimately be entrusted with the collection of this kind of information. Writers were thus compelled for the most part to rely upon the 'All Union' returns as general indicators of the amount of broken time amongst the working-classes, although such data were of limited application since they were almost exclusively confined to craft unions which paid idle benefit and which always represented a minor part of the total occupied population. By very definition they ignored female and unskilled male unemployment and provided no insights into the casual, and few into the seasonal, labour markets. Individuals, therefore, periodically sought to supplement these statistics with their own estimates of the dimensions of the problem, although such estimates were more often based upon intuition fortified by personal prejudice than upon any readily apparent sets of rational criteria. For instance, Keir Hardie, supported by Will Thorne, argued that during 1895 unemployment in the United Kingdom affected, at its peak, 1.7 million members of the labour force. The Rev. W. Tozer, on the other hand, surveying the social scene from a different ideological viewpoint, put the total unemployed for all classes at 280,000. Indeed, if 'the old, the infirm, the physically and mentally handicapped, and the idle and the intemperate' were deducted from this figure, the number of 'capable, willing, sober and industrious unemployed' amounted to less than 140,000.[9] Such massive differences echoed those which had formed the basis of the debate in the late 1860s between Dudley Baxter and Leone Levi about the degree to which the average worker was exposed to lost time in a given year. According to Levi, the gainfully employed person below the age of sixty could expect to be idle for four weeks in a calendar year, whereas his opponent, repudiating this optimistic message in its entirety, concluded that 'for loss of work from every cause, and for the non-effective up to 65 years of age, who are included in the census, *we ought to deduct fully 20 per cent from the nominal full-time wages.*'[10] In both controversies, however, the outcome was bound to be inconclusive because the necessary research to produce convincing answers had not been carried out.

But if these facets had still to be explored, social investigators had at least made a start in trying to measure the correlation between unemployment and poverty. In this field much of the pioneering work was again undertaken by Charles Booth. In his survey of East London in the late 1880s he had strongly underlined the paramountcy of economic forces in keeping families at, or below, the poverty line. Fifty-five per cent of the poverty among householders in his Classes A and B and sixty-eight per cent among their counterparts in Classes C and D stemmed directly from 'questions of employment'. This term of course covered much more than unemployment. It applied also to groups within these classes who, although in regular work, were badly paid. Assessed overall, however, broken time emerged as a much more potent cause of working class impoverishment than low pay, with casuality of employment alone accounting for forty-three per cent of the poverty of Classes A and B and 'irregular earnings' a comparable proportion among families in Classes C and D.[11] On the other hand the reverse was true of York a decade later where Seebohm Rowntree found that only 5.14 per cent of those householders living in primary poverty were thus situated because of the impact of unemployment in all its guises as against 51.96 per cent who were regularly employed but miserably remunerated.[12]

Yet the size of these differences should occasion no surprise. In part it was a reflection of the state of the economy at the time at which the respective investigations were mounted. While Booth collected his data at a period when the trade cycle was only slowly moving in an upwards direction after the protracted trough of 1884-7, Rowntree had selected as his starting-point a year — 1899 — of considerable buoyancy in the economic life of the nation. But in another sense these differences are also an indication of the existence of two distinctive labour markets. In York casual, and, outside the building trades, seasonal, unemployment posed few threats to the living standard of the bulk of the working-classes who were principally located in occupational outlets which guaranteed 'very stable' employment under normal trading conditions.[13] In contrast there existed within the East End a seasonal and casual workforce of impressive dimensions. For those who belonged to this reserve — and they included dockers, porters, carters, cabmen, barbers, bakers, domestic servants, all kinds of outworkers in a wide range of consumer trades, building workers and certain grades of factory workers — the pervasive nature of underemployment was as significant in determining their relationship to the poverty line as the admittedly acute, but chronologically limited, social suffering generated by cyclical unemployment.

While the supply of casual labour probably loomed larger in the industrial life of the East End than elsewhere in Britain in the post-1850 period, each major industrial centre possessed identical pools of underemployed men and women. Furthermore, those who constituted this labour reserve could only hope to escape briefly during their lives from the toils of poverty. As Williams and Jones expressed it, 'interposed between the legal pauper and the completely independent workman are layers of under-employed and under-fed semi-dependants who can be drawn upon to depress wages before the pauper supply is reached.'[14] Simply put, the social sequal to casualisation was initially a low standard of living and ultimately pauperism.[15] But since these social aspects cannot be fully understood unless they are related to those specifically economic forces which shaped the contours, and influenced the rate of development, of every local market for casual labour, it is essential to begin this study of unemployment by examining the salient characteristics of casualisation itself.

I

If the casual market was related to, and grew out of, the general market for unskilled labour, the lot of its workers diverged in one crucial respect from that of the majority of unskilled hands. For the distinguishing hallmark of casualisation was the irregular patterns of employment to which the individual was always subjected. In some industries, as in the docks, hands might be hired on an hourly or shift basis, in others by the day or the week. Nevertheless, whatever the length of a particular period of employment, the overall pattern was starkly simple. Viewed over the course of a year, casual labour meant sharp and quite arbitrary fluctuations in the length of the working week:

> the main feature of casual employment is that instead of either being completely in work or completely out of work, the workman gets only two, three, or four days' work a week. The evil is too familiar to require proof; and among certain classes of labourers it is the rule, and not the exception. It results in the maintenance of a large number of families in a condition which will prevent them ever leading an independent and civilised existence, and is more disastrous than complete unemployment, since it tends to perpetuate itself.[16]

Yet despite the fact that it was exposed to the poverty-inducing pressures of chronic underemployment, the casual workforce remained, in geographical terms, remarkably immobile. Stedman Jones has convincingly shown that the casual labourer in London, instead of venturing forth to other parts of the capital in search of work, rarely strayed beyond his immediate locality.[17] The same held true in other areas. In Glasgow, where R.H. Tawney drew attention to a 'very immobile' pool of unskilled building labour, it was widely recognised that the casual hand was reluctant to move far in his bid to secure employment.[18] In Liverpool casual dockers were heavily concentrated in common lodging houses and mean streets adjacent to the waterfront, while in Manchester, as late as 1904, whole groups of casual workers still clung tenaciously to decaying but centrally situated property.[19] 'Opposed [therefore] to the popular notion of a restless, shifting population, ready to turn its hand to anything, the results show dull apathetic men whose passive resistance to all outside influence constitutes their most hopeless feature.'[20] Equally important, the geographical horizons of the female casual hand were often more limited than those of her male equivalent. In particular 'the work of women in the [sweated] trades revealing the greatest surplusage of labour and consequent distress is generally held on a very precarious tenure, is always poorly paid, and does not possess even that limited mobility of which at least unskilled labour is capable.'[21]

To some extent such behaviour can be explained in social terms, for the ties of kinship which bound the casual worker to his or her neighbourhood were always strong. Nevertheless, after giving due weighting to these bonds, it is clear that its real *raison d'etre* was economic in origin and stemmed from the nature of the casual market itself. In the first place the very fact that the individual needed to live near the major outlets for casual employment and to be known by the agents and foremen who did the hiring, if he were to have a reasonable chance of obtaining a fair share of casual work, alone placed an effective brake upon mobility on the heroic scale. In the words of Dr. A.K. Chalmers, speaking in 1904, 'if a man is in regular work he may travel to the outskirts to his home; but if he is dependent upon work at docks or casual work at railway stations, then he lives pretty near where he is employed frequently, and he would not always have the halfpenny to pay the tram.'[22] This factor would of course operate less powerfully in the pre-1870 era when the geographical boundaries of the principal towns were more narrowly circumscribed and when the question of transport costs was scarcely raised. Even so, it was generally agreed that the casual hand would in most circumstances require to live within three-quarters of a mile of his potential place of work.[23] Secondly, the close relationship between the female and male casual markets further reduced the opportunity of seeking employment outside a relatively limited area, since the warehouses and workshops which hired women workers on a casual basis were often located in the same districts as those in which their casually employed husbands worked. In some places this might mean that a disproportionate element of the casual labour force lived in or near the city centre which, despite the accelerating pace of urban renewal and reconstruction after 1870, still continued to be a significant focal point for the irregularly employed. Indeed, from the casual's own viewpoint, residence and work in such a locality were warmly welcomed because of the range of casual jobs which were open to his children. Casual employment as messengers, match, trinket, and newspaper sellers or the possibility of a milk round might enable a boy to contribute 2/6d. to 3s. per week to family income in the early 1900s, 'and that is a very grave consideration, because every shilling is a serious thing for them.'[24] Thirdly, the lack of any rational system for disseminating information about unskilled work outlets generally in the major cities must, for some casual hands, have made a decision not to venture into an adjacent district seem to be a counsel of prudence. Finally, there was widespread acceptance of the futility of such movement which arose not merely from the casual's need to cultivate good contacts with local employers but also from his recognition of the fact that in every area there existed a surplus supply of unskilled labour which would never be fully employed even on the busiest day.

As the work of Beatrice Potter, Booth, Beveridge and Eleanor Rathbone has shown, these features appeared in a deep-seated form in the docks of Britain's ports during the age of steam. Nevertheless, if the data are less profuse for the pre-1880 years, there is sufficient evidence to indicate that the antecedents of the casual problem can be traced back to the era of the sailing ship. In Liverpool in the mid-1830s whole elements of the dock labour force, hired at a daily rate of 2/6d., could anticipate, in the busy season, enormous fluctuations – from two to six days per week according to one source – in their levels of employment in consecutive weeks.[25] Similarly a labour reserve of substantial proportions had emerged, by the start of our period, in London's docks. Mayhew, writing in the 1850s, concluded that whereas full-time work in the capital required roughly 4000 hands, there were no fewer than 12,000 dockers who offered their services to waterside employers.[26] At a more parochial level Pollard-Urquhart confirmed the accuracy of Mayhew's diagnosis when he examined the position of the Irish dock labourer in the East End of London in 1862. For while the Irish docker could expect to obtain 15s. in a full week 'the vacissitudes of wind and trade', or expressed in another form, the impact of seasonality and casuality, reduced his average weekly rate, assessed on an annual basis, to between 10s. and 12s.[27] Indeed, as these comments suggest, the role of the weather was crucial in determining the frequency with which the casual hand was hired. Where adverse climatic conditions were of any duration, they could quickly affect not merely those who belonged to the reserve of labour but the living standards of the entire community which was associated with economic life of a port. This is what occurred in Liverpool in February 1838 where 'owing to the long continuance of the frost and of easterly winds, which have prevented the arrival of homeward-bound vessels, the sufferings and privations of the numerous and useful classes of porters, carters, and every description of persons who depend for their livelihood upon out-door work are severe in the extreme.' In such circumstances resort could only be made to the resources of private charity, including the ubiquitous soup kitchen, where it was 'painful to see poor children, bare-footed and bare-legged, shivering in the cold, awaiting their turn for soup.'[28] But even without such natural disasters, the true casual was constantly under severe pressure since 'the loss of wages which arises from periodical intervals of short work is not counterbalanced by the addition thereto which occasional overtime enables them to make.'[29]

The initial effect of the introduction of the steam-driven vessel was to multiply his difficulties. For if the advent of steam reduced to some extent the dependence of the carrying trade upon the vagaries of the weather, it at the same time produced a greater emphasis than hitherto upon the importance of speed in the discharging and loading of cargo in order to honour the exacting deadlines of charterers. One immediate social consequence of this trend was to intensify the erratic nature of the demand for casual hands. Stedman Jones has meticulously charted the operation of this process in London.[30] But an identical pattern was to be revealed in every major port. J. Smith Park conceded in 1908 that the Allan Line, whose steamships sailed principally from Glasgow, 'may occasionally have as many as 600 or 700 individual dock labourers at work in a period of twenty-four hours, and again may have as few as 125 in the same line'.[31] Again, the City Line, trading from the same port to India, 'at times, generally lasting only a few days and nights, . . . will employ five hundred hands, at other times we may only have the permanent staff of, say, twenty men employed.'[32] Furthermore, such a trend was not confined to those major shipping companies which, in Glasgow, recruited their own supplies of dock labour. It was also prevalent among the network of tramp steamers whose ships were serviced by teams of dockers in the pay of master stevedores licensed by the Clyde Port Authority. According to W.H. Raeburn, looking at Clydeside's casual problem from the perspective of the tramp steam owner 'you might as well think you could control the action of the planets' as decasualise dock labour, since it possessed its own economic *rationale*. In Raeburn's words:

> the trouble about casual labour is this, someimtes a lot of iron ore steamers may have come in at the same time. For instance, a great deal of iron ore comes from Bilbao in Spain, which has to some extent a bar harbour. If there is a gale of wind in the Bay of Biscay the whole of the tonnage of that port may be prevented from getting out. The first fine day they rush it out and there may arrive at Glasgow, perhaps six or seven steamers on the same tide. Then there is a great rush of labour, stevedores scouring every place to get men. When the six or seven steamers are discharged, then there may be a total blank . . . . No doubt that is one of the greatest difficulties and troubles in this question of unemployment.[33]

In Clydeside, therefore, despite the vigorous denials of shipowners, the dimensions of the labour reserve grew, rather than diminished, over time. As M'Culloch Craig, a master stevedore of considerable experience, observed in 1908, 'unemployment is chronic as regards about one-half' of Glasgow's six or seven thousand harbour labourers.[34] Similar conditions obtained in Liverpool where

> the weekly earnings of the . . . dock labourers [in 1909] are known to be extremely irregular. The best man, in the prime of life, may earn 40s. or even 50s. in one week; 30s., 20s., or 15s. the next. Inferior or old and weakly men vary from 30s. to 4s.6d. or nothing. A very large number are believed to average less than 15s.[35]

But short or longer term increases in the supply of casual labour were not simply a product of the application of steam to shipping. There were at least four other influences which served to promote the same end. In the first place, while the increasing use of machinery for loading and discharging vessels undoubtedly raised productivity, it at the same time reduced the demand for certain kinds of workers. Thus, the transference of grain by suction had, by the early 1900s, halved the number of jobs available for grain porters in London.[36] Secondly, the manner in which employers paid dock workers had a vital bearing upon the spread, or containment, of the casual problem. In London the resolve of employers, in the wake of the 1872 strike, to hire dock labour by the hour rather than by the day was bound to extend the outer limits of the casual market.[37] Again, after the dockers had been defeated in an industrial confrontation, the system of retaining a nucleus of men paid by the week was temporarily abandoned in 1889 by several Glasgow shipping companies, partly on the grounds that reliance upon the labour reserve was a more flexible, and less costly, means of securing their particular labour requirements.[38] Thirdly, the size of the casual labour force was periodically increased as a result of the invasion of the casual market by seasonal hands during the dull months in their own trades and by workers who were drawn from a limited number of unskilled jobs at times of cyclical unemployment.[39] Finally, apart from the element of self perpetuation within the workforce, with the sons of casual dockers frequently entering their fathers' occupation, the docks continued to attract a motley collection of individuals — among them seamen, soldiers, rural migrants and youths who were discarded by employers once they had outlived their usefulness in 'dead end' jobs,   drawn, as at Liverpool, by the lure of 'the nominally high daily pay' rather than 'the actual prospect of [continuous] employment'.[40] But these last two factors, it must be emphasised, operated not merely in the sphere of dock labour but throughout the casual market generally.

Yet while this picture encapsulates the form which the problem assumed in Britain's ports, it should be modified in one respect. For the success of the 1889 strike for 'the docker's tanner' was subsequently to precipitate a determined attack upon the whole problem of casuality in London by the employing class. By 1891-2 dock companies had decided to adopt a system of preference lists for the hiring of hands. At the top of this hierarchy were the permanent staff and Class A dockers who were paid on a regular weekly basis. Below them came Class B men whose ranking within their own grade was systematically revised in the light of their productivity and attendance records. At the bottom was Class C, the casual sector which was primarily used at times of peak demand.[41] This system was later to be revised in certain significant particulars. By the early years of this century the Class C category was abolished and Class B replaced it as the *locus* of the reserve of labour.[42] But such alterations did nothing to mitigate the overall social consequences of these innovations. As Charles Booth showed, by 1894 less work than previously — in that year only 5.6 per cent of the total amount   was being performed by the casual labourer.[43] That pattern, once established, was to hold for the remainder of our period. E.G. Howarth and Mona Wilson, for example, calculated that on average only twenty-five per cent of Class B would be employed on a given day in West Ham's Victoria and Albert Docks in 1905.[44] These findings were confirmed by Steel-Maitland and Squire in 1907 when they concluded that the docker who was neither a permanent hand nor possessed Class A status, could only expect to obtain, on an annual basis, an average of two or three days' work per week. The initial result, therefore, of attempts at decasualisation was to decrease the volume of casual employment without necessarily driving individuals out of the casual market.[45]

Elsewhere few moves were made to emulate this lead. Indeed, only Liverpool of the principal ports produced — in 1912-13 — a comparable registration scheme. But in this specific instance the refusal of all firms to participate and the unwillingness of casual hands to move from their own narrowly defined areas yielded few short-term gains in this direction. As R. Williams indicated in 1914, a massive reserve of casual labour, computed as 'sufficient to supply a surplus of over 8000 on the busiest possible day', continued to exist largely because decasualisation appeared to be a counsel of perfection rather than a readily realisable goal.[46]

While, however, the possibility of decasualisation gave rise to a vigorous debate among contemporaries, there was virtual unanimity about the social hardships which the casual labourer was asked to endure in the age of steam. In West Ham the correlation between endemic poverty and the sharp fluctuations in the demand for dock labour was underlined in unambiguous language by Howarth and Wilson who pointed to the existence of 'a considerable number of men [who] normally earn a weekly wage which is insufficient for the support of their families, and their average wage taken throughout the year is barely sufficient to provide for necessities.'[47] Eleanor Rathbone, at the end of her examination of the casual question in Liverpool in 1909, wrote of,

> the depressing records of poverty and failure, of the decadence of families who have seen better days, of the hopeless struggle of the women with problems in housewifery too hard for them, and for which they have received no adequate training, of the squalid and unabashed poverty of those who have given up or never made the effort.[48]

From Glasgow a similar fate was shared by the housewife of those casuals who were 'only occasionally employed at the docks . . . when the work is in excess of what the First and Second class [of dockers] can overtake, and the formen are consequently obliged to employ them.'[49]

To some authorities chronic impoverishment on this scale was in large measure the product of the unfettered exercise of consumer choice. For it was believed that casual dock work offered a species of social salvation to hordes of individuals who were 'casuals by inclination', repelled by the prospect of the long hours associated with unskilled regular employment. Thus, one employer asserted that Clydeside's casual dockers

> seem only anxious for work when necessity compels, and are, as a result, of little use. A short spell of a few hours satisfies them, and when they receive their wages they disappear for a time. They have no intention of continuing seriously at work or of qualifying themselves for regular and better employment.[50]

Yet, while there is an element of truth in this contention, it must be kept in perspective. Casual dock labour and the poverty which it generated, existed primarily because of the conjunction of specific exogenous forces. The imperfect nature of the unskilled labour market, with its excess supply of hands, and the desire of shipping firms and master stevedores in many cases to maintain their own labour reserves created an economic environment which made it difficult for the casual worker to improve his lot. Indeed, it could be argued that those who were loosely labelled 'casuals by inclination' were drawn from the ranks of those who initial contact with the labour market had been in the role of 'casuals by circumstance' and whose later acceptance of the rhythms of casuality of employment had been shaped by the powerful external restraints operating against regular engagements.

> The question . . . is not whether the conditions of casual employment are the sole cause of the unsatisfactory conditions of life among the labourers, but whether they do not aggravate and perpetuate these conditions, by making the upward path as difficult and the downward as easy as possible. Everything about the system of employment seems to foster the formation of bad habits and nothing to encourage the formation of good ones. The alternations of hard work and idleness disincline the men to regular exertion.[51]

With few alterations this verdict could also be applied to those other groups of casuals — carters, porters and messengers — who had close links with the docks but whose overall contribution to the economy covered a much broader spectrum of activity than quayside employment. At the start of our period casual fringes of porters were to be found in every significant market in Britain. At Liverpool in the mid-1830s this reserve seems largely to have consisted of Irish warehousemen who averaged little more than 7s., or two to three days' work per week over the course of the year.[52] On the other hand, where the problem of underemployment arose elsewhere, it might be more a direct function of the limited nature of the market than the result of employers' decisions to cultivate their own supplies of casual labour. This was the case at Manchester where in 1840 a complaint was levied against

> an assembling of Irish porters who, on market days, are engaged in carrying out goods for the country manufacturers in the neighbourhood, and on the other days, having little or nothing to do, are generally playing at pitch and toss, or some other game, and making a great noise the day through

and at Norwich at a much later point in time where a considerable number of casual hands, subsisting in 'a chronic condition of semi-starvation', was hired on Saturdays to drive bullocks to and from the local cattle market.[53] Furthermore, even in the post-1870 period there was to be little divergence from this basic pattern of irregular employment in those few markets which possessed their own contingents of licensed porters. Charles Booth, while acknowledging the existence of 700 to 800 licensed porters in Covent Garden in the late 1880s, also drew attention to the number of casuals, located in the common lodging houses of the adjacent streets and the district of St. Giles, who lived in grinding poverty outside the short-lived fruit season.[54] Similarly, those 'unbadged' porters who ventured into Manchester's fruit and meat markets in the early 1900s constituted in essence a labour reserve, a misfortune which they shared with that city's casual cloth porters who, despite tentative moves towards decasualisation in 1910, were, on average, engaged for little more than half the year, and with the small volume of casual goods porters who were to be found at major railway freight termini.[55]

Equally erratically employed elements existed among carters in every city and large town. In London such groups had already reached substantial proportions by the 1880s.[56] But the same problem was to emerge at Liverpool, where in 1907 the presence of 'a large number of casual carters who are taken on by the day' from several 'stands' to fill the places of sick colleagues or to meet a sudden upsurge in demand, was recorded,[57] and at Glasgow where Hugh Lyon, Secretary of the Scottish Carters' Association, argued that in the summer of 1909, out of the city's workforce of 10,000 carters, there were 'continually 1000 [horse] men on the streets unemployed.'[58] This last figure must of course be treated with some caution since 1909 was a year of marked industrial depression in the West of Scotland. Lyon's estimate was thus likely to include individuals who in normal conditions were in regular employment but who were the temporary victims of dull trade, as well as a core of permanently casual hands. Nevertheless, when these caveats have been entered, it can still serve as a rough guide to the size of this particular casual reserve, since it almost certainly ignores that 'large number of men [who] flock to drive the horses . . . when other unskilled labour is dull'[59] and those 'tramp' carters who led a peripatetic existence in Scotland, 'moving from place to place, working as carters when there was work, moving on when the wind of trade changed, into the next town.'[60] Yet whether or not the casual carter opted for this migratory form of life – and the overwhelming majority did not – he shared at least one common experience with all who belonged to the ranks of the labour reserve: he was unable unaided to escape for any length of time from the firm grip of primary poverty.

But casualisation reached its peak in the adult male sector of the labour market, not amongst dockers or porters but among those who were labelled general labourers. The sole factor which bound together those who consituted this open-ended group was their inability to offer a would-be employer anything beyond their physical strength. Almost inevitably, therefore, because of the ease of access of this unskilled occupation, there was always a large pool of underemployed men upon whom firms and municipalities could draw. None the less, although such surpluses were a prominent feature of the economy at the start of our period – Anderson has calculated that in 1851 seven per cent of Lancashire's occupied male population consisted of labourers most of whom were casually or irregularly employed – they are much easier to identify in the post-1880 decades when the volume of literature devoted to the casual question had expanded considerably.[61] From such data two basic conclusions can be drawn. Firstly, casually employed general labourers were to be found in every major industry. With some industries – as with sawmills in the Glasgow area and the locomotive works at Aston, Birmingham – casual hands could be hired daily from those who assembled outside the gates at the start of the working day.[62] But in other instances the casual element would be guaranteed a much greater degree of continuity in employment. This was above all true for those who were recruited by municipalities which were firmly committed to 'municipal socialism'. In such localities the casual's employment pattern tended to be task oriented, with a particular job often lasting for a period of some weeks. Sometimes this meant physically exacting work, laying the cables for a burgeoning electricity supply system or extending and improving the permanent way for the trams. In other cases, however, it involved shorter-lived engagements as street lighters 'to allow of holidays being given to the regular staff' or, at periods of intense cold, even more ephemeral employment clearing heavy falls of snow.[63] Finally, in towns without any significant industrial outlets for unskilled labour, the general labourer might — as at Norwich — apply periodically to middle-class householders for casual work as a jobbing gardener at a rate of 2/6d. per day.[64]

The other conclusion which emerged in the post-1880 decades stemmed primarily from the investigative work of those in charge of voluntary unemployment funds, municipal relief schemes and the Distress Committees. For the classification of all applicants for unemployment relief according to the occupation that they had last followed, was usually seen as an integral part of their duties. Almost without exception the category of general labourer loomed largest — and by a sizable margin — in these relief lists. Moreover, it was universally accepted that this grouping consisted of casual hands who resorted to relief works whenever the opportunity arose as a means of easing slightly the pressure of poverty in their lives. But at the same time the limitations of these returns were acknowledged. Above all, it was recognised that such applicants, far from representing the full extent of the casual problem among general labourers in the principal urban areas of Britain, simply comprised the poorest and least capable section of the labour reserve, underfed, frequently unshod, and in some cases suffering from a variety of ailments which limited their prospects of future employment in the unskilled market as a whole.[65]

Usually treated as separate from, but in many respects similar to, the irregularly employed general labourer was the casual labour force within the building industry. Yet although a social phenomenon of long standing, this aspect of the casual problem was only to be thoroughly explored in the post-1900 era, when a growing corpus of information made society aware of the dimensions and causes of casuality in this major sector of the economy. What united the writings of those who had probed this topic was the belief that underemployment pressed more severely upon painters and builders' labourers than other section of the workforce. Thus, the *Glasgow Herald*, emphasising that 'a large number of men . . . are not employed; they are always underemployed, loitering in a stagnant pool about certain large centres of employment, and doing an odd day's work now and again', specifically identified a part of this oversupply of hands with the building industry.[66] And in a West of Scotland context it was clear that the most numerically significant element of that industry's reserve of labour was represented by the unskilled labourer.[67] Again, N.B. Dearle, while aware of the existence of a casual fringe of carpenters and bricklayers in London, concluded that the principal components of the casual problem in the building trades of the capital consisted of labourers and 'still more [of] . . . painters . . . the number of casual painters, especially, being immense.'[68] An identical situation — obtained at York where 'rough painting' was listed as a classic employment outlet for casual hands.[69]

Yet there were powerful reasons why these two occupations were always likely to contribute so heavily to the formation of the labour reserve. In the first place they offered one of the highest hourly rates of pay within the unskilled market — partly, it is true, to compensate for their pronounced seasonal fluctuations — without insisting upon any form of training for new recruits. As Dearle has shown, casual painters alone were drawn from the ranks of soldiers, sailors, coachmen, tram-conductors, butchers, bakers and dockers, as well as 'the drunkard and the lazy'.[70] And it was precisely because the size of this haphazardly recruited reserve grew over time, that casual labourers and painters tended to be firmly rooted to one locality. At the start of this century casuals in London tended to be tied to their own borough or, where it existed, to a large firm, while in Glasgow they were reluctant, if they lived in the north of the city, to cross the Clyde to seek work in the southern suburbs. But the static nature of the workforce was reinforced by the contract system of building which produced 'a continual taking on and discharging of men' in response to sharp shifts in demand.[71] As Dudley Baxter remarked in 1868, 'the smaller masters, especially at the East End of London, engage a large proportion of their [building] hands only for the job, and then at once pay them off.'[72] Inevitably, therefore, the toll which this form of casuality exacted remained, in social terms, high. Part of that burden took the form of a physical deprivation which could be measured. Less tangible but equally real, it also led to the development of a mentality which initially reacted against casual work but which, influenced by the harsh environment of the casual world, was later transmuted into a fatalistic acceptance of its drawbacks. In Dearle's words,

> it is the average man who suffers [from casuality of employment] . . . . Such man are often crowded out of their market by non-*bona-fide* workmen, and their chance of regular or even of a decent proportion of casual labour it taken from them, and they are in danger as their work becomes more casual of sinking to the state of those who are not merely casual workers, but casual in every way.[73]

An identical process was at work in those sectors of the casual market which were linked with the food, drink and clothing trades. In the first of these groups the principal *locus* of adult male casual labour was to be found in those large, integrated bakeries which, in the post-1870 period, started to challenge the position of the small family firm in Britain's cities. To some critics, the formation of this reserve of labour was seen as the logical corollary of the increasing use of machinery to perform tasks which had hitherto been executed by hand. As the National Federal Union of the Operative Bakers of Scotland proclaimed — albeit with some hyperbole — in 1892, 'machinery had to a great extent superseded labour' within the industry.[74] Yet it would be misleading to conclude that casuality of employment could be completely explained within this monocausal framework. For it was also greatly stimulated by the uneven demand for bread. In London, where roughly 1000 bakers were out of work in 1907, the vast majority of casuals could earn 10s. for a fifteen to sixteen hours' shift on

Fridays when in anticipation of week-end sales, many employers virtually doubled the size of their usual labour force. Conversely, during the remainder of the week when consumer demand was relatively static, the casual's climate of expectations was more modest, being compelled to accept an occasional night's employment as and when opportunity arose.[75] In Glasgow, on the other hand, if the creation and perpetuation of the pool of casual workers owed much to the same underlying cause, the hiring policies of certain firms also contributed powerfully to the same end. To quote James MacFarlane,

> the average daily demand on the first five days of the week is doubled, and sometimes more than doubled, on Saturday. Employment is, to a large extent, affected also by the demand for early morning bread, and employers who, for example, require twenty men to turn out their day's work, instead of employing twenty constant men, will work with possibly fifteen constant men, and as against the other five, draw from the un-employed section ten men whom they employ for the first half of the day only, and these are engaged and paid from day to day. Therefore of the 550 to 900 unemployed [trade unionists in the city's baking industry], a considerable proportion obtain half-a-day's work during a part of the week, and they are all probably employed all day on Saturday.[76]

But if this testimony succinctly summarises the desperate plight of the casual baker, he was at least guaranteed, through his union's house of call, a greater amount of employment during the course of the year than those casual hands who sought work in mineral water factories during the summer season. For even during this relatively propitious period their fortunes could fluctuate sharply in the short term. A week of brilliant sunshine might momentarily dislocate the labour supply in the casual's favour. At such times manufacturers, anxious to exploit a buoyant market, could be faced with labour shortages and forced — as in the West of Scotland in the summer of 1912 — 'to send to the model lodging houses and get as many [casuals] workers for night work as we could, and give them fish suppers and 3s. for the night's work.'[77] But such highlights in the casual's experience were usually of limited duration; for if — as at Camberwell — 'the number [of casuals employed during hot weather] varies from week to week', a 'sudden fall in temperature means the dismissal of many . . . and the curtailing of the wages of those who remain on short time.'[78]

Casuality of employment was rarely as erratic as this in the clothing trade. In another sense, however, it was a more broadly based problem, particularly in the opening decades of the nineteenth century when the casual element amongst handloom weavers, engaged in the production of plain fabrics, reached formidable proportions. The initial establishment of this casual labour force owed much more to the vast influx of workers into the occupation during the Napoleonic Wars and the early years of peace than technical change, for the scale of that influx led to a considerable overstocking of the labour market, adverse pressures on piece-rates, and irregular patterns of employment. In the silk town of Macclesfield, that reserve already apparent by 1818 when it was alleged that the weaver 'is very often obliged to stand at play, or in other words, to be without employ for a week together,'[79] had probably expanded by 1830-1 as the result of Irish immigration. At first unable to secure work, these newcomers were later exposed to the intermittent rhythms of the casual market, 'occasionally' obtaining 'a short job as journeymen.'[80] In the silk district of Coventry on the other hand the casual pool in the 1830s largely consisted of female and child labour which was scattered throughout the adjacent villages and which was only effectively used at the peak of seasonal activity.[81] In some respects this pattern was typical of other areas of the country. Casually employed weavers of coarse grade calicoes in Lancashire and the West of Scotland contained within their ranks substantial numbers of women and children anxious to supplement the earnings of unskilled hands of households.[82] Yet this was not a universal role. The 'superabundance' of labour which existed within Leeds' linen weaving community seemed principally to have consisted of adult males, as did the underemployed section of the woollen weavers in the surrounding towns.[83]

But if new technology in the form of the power loom played little part in the formative phase of the development of this labour reserve, during the 1830s 1840s it was to make its own distinctive contribution to the socio-economic difficulties which faced the casual hand. In the first place it affected directly the living standards, and employment prospects, of all grades of plain handloom weavers in the cotton and worsted industries. Progressively undermining the hand worker's trade, it pushed down earnings and enlarged, in the short-term, the casual pool. But its indirect effects were equally important. When underemployed cotton and stuff weavers realised that there was no prospect of any revival in the fortunes of their craft, many of them turned their attention towards those fabrics which had hitherto been hardly touched by mechanisation. Complaints were made in 1835 by Manchester silk weavers that the advent of the power loom in the cotton mill had damaged their prospects 'by causing a great influx of hands into the [silk] trade'.[84] Similarly, the linen weavers of Leeds were

> violently opposed to the introduction of power-looms, which, although hitherto not carried to a sufficient extent in the linen trade directly to injure the hand-loom weavers, still, by throwing many cotton weavers out of employ, these are induced to take up the trade of linen weavers, and thus by increasing their numbers lessen the demand for labour and bring wages down, besides which, owing to the much cheaper price at which cotton goods can be purchased since the introduction of machinery, cotton has been substituted for linen in many articles of clothing.[85]

Initially, therefore, the power loom, by redistributing casual labour within a variegated textile industry, helped to exacerbate the poverty of those who, when in full work, were poorly paid, although ultimately, by transferring manufacturing to the mill system, it was to destroy outwork and, with it, casuality of employment.

But while little remained of a labour reserve in worsted and cotton weaving after 1850, the reverse was true in other important sectors of the clothing industry. Both tailoring and shoemaking were to see their casual supplies of labour expand considerably in the 1850-90 period, although the beginnings of that process in London can be discerned in the early 1830s in the 'honourable' section of the tailoring trade. Indeed, by the late 1840s the casual hand, taken on by employers from the union's house of call 'when there is an extra amount of work to be done', was seen as fulfilling a vital role in enabling tight schedules to be met.[86] Yet whatever the gains which accrued to the employer of such labour, this practice entailed the impoverishment of the casual and his family, since, outside a brief summer season, he was reduced, for ten months of the year, to not 'more than perhaps one day per month's' work in an 'honourable' shop and for the remainder of the time compelled to accept, where available, poorly remunerated employment from sweaters or those who specialised in police and army contracts.[87] Nonetheless, he was more fortunate than those casual tailors who were exclusively used by sweating masters. For the under-employed adult male hand who was solely dependent upon such work for his livelihood, was operating in a more glutted labour market and forced to compete, for a limited amount of wretchedly paid work, against women and — particularly in shoemaking — children.[88]

The casual market, however, did not remain static. As had been shown in the previous chapter, from the 1860s onwards the sewing machine and subsequent technological innovation had a profound impact upon each of these trades. The economic consequences of these changes were the sub-division of work; the increasing use of female labour, particularly in the slop workshops; and, by the 1890s, a definite trend towards concentrating production in shoe and garment factories. Between 1860 and 1890, therefore, the majority of new recruits to an expanding labour reserve in tailoring were drawn from the ranks of women. Yet if the role of adult male casual workers diminished over time, it did not disappear completely. In London male casual hands, their numbers swollen by Jewish 'greeners', were still hired by the week at the 'pig market' in Whitechapel Road during the 1870s and 1880s by sweaters.[89] Again, in Glasgow during the late 1880s casuality of employment continued to flourish in the sweated sector where a sizable number of tailors and machinists were employed, and paid, on a daily basis.[90] Similarly, an irregularly employed element can be discerned in the 1880s among adult male outworkers who were plying their trade as knifers and lasters in the ready-made shoe industry.[91] But by the early 1900s outwork — outside London — was everywhere giving way to the inexorable advance of the factory system. By the end of our period relatively little remained of this particular labour reserve, although in those localities where pools of casual labourers still existed, their poverty deepened since they could only anticipate securing a modicum of regular work during a relatively short-lived busy season.[92]

While the occupations which have thus far been analysed, contributed on a significant scale to the establishment of the casual labour force, the parameters of the male casual market were by no means coterminous with these major areas of the economy. In the pre-1870 era pools of irregularly employed workers could be located among messengers, framework knitters, hawkers and street sellers whose casual section was primarily recruited from the ranks of those labourers whose services were dispensed with during the winter months, and in the Sheffield cutlery trades.[93] Indeed, long after 1870 most of these occupations continued to maintain intact a recognisably casual element.[94] But if there were continuities between the pre- and post-1870 decades, discontinuities in experience were also strong. And the most fundamental of these discontinuities was the shift which occurred in the balance of the casual labour forces during the last forty years of our period. Casual groups, who were of minor importance before that point in time, grew *pari passu* with the development of a mass consumer market. Newspaper sellers; sandwich board men, hired in the 1890s for 1s. to 1/2d. per day; deliverers of handbills; the individual who 'loafs about hotels [and railway stations] touting for travellers' luggage'; cabmen; barbers, taken on for a night and Saturdays from their house of call; and extra hands required for the Christmas mail, were either classically casual workers or in jobs which speedily attracted a casual fringe.[95] Again, in a university town like Cambridge the contours of the casual market were decisively shaped by rises and falls in the residential undergraduate population. To quote Clara Rackham,

> cabmen, newspaper sellers, and many men who are attached to billiard-rooms, shops, or restaurants [in Cambridge] . . . suffer keenly from the drop in the services required of them during the vacations. The result is that there are many men who have no regular employment, but merely lead a hand-to-mouth existence.[96]

Yet these groups were by no means at the bottom of the male casual hierarchy. That place was occupied by those 'otherwise permanent paupers, who leave the workhouse for the fruit, pea, and hop-picking season, or to take advantage of the warmer weather to seek work or pleasure, or, at any rate, variety, outside',[97] and those men with failing physical powers — interviewed by the Salvation Army in 1890 — who slept rough and who were prepared to attempt any task which was offered to them.[98] The poignancy of the lives and the depth of the poverty of this forlorn, but numerically small, element of the reserve of labour can best be illustrated by quoting in its entirety an interview with one of these anonymous figures. 'Number 8,' it was recorded,

> slept here [on the Thames Embankment] four nights running. Is a builder's labourer by trade, that is a handy-man. Had a settled job for a few weeks which expired three weeks since. Has earned nothing for nine days. Then helped wash down a shop front and got 2. 6d. for it. Does anything he can get. Is 46 years old. Earns about 2d. or 3d. a day horse minding. A cut of tea and a bit of bread yesterday, and same to-day, is all he has had.[99]

Casuality of employment, however, was not the exclusive preserve of the unskilled, adult male labour market. Juvenile casual hands were extensively employed in a variety of street trading activities before and after the 1870 English, and the 1872 Scottish, Education Acts; school children were used to assist parents to maximise earnings in certain kinds of home work; and girls were frequently casually hired to work in sweated workshops in the tailoring trade.[100] But of much greater long-term significance than these scattered pockets of youthful casual labour was a burgeoning demand for adult female casual workers, which reached its peak during 1860-90. Much of that expansion was concentrated in the clothing trades where the ubiquitous sewing machine led to increasing specialisation and the vigorous growth of outwork. Shirt-finishing, shirtmaking, basting, vest-making, dressmaking, button-holing, and in the shoe industry, upper-making were all occupations that acquired sizable reserves of female labour which were rarely fully utilised. But in addition to this network of inter-related, irregular patterns of work were also the lot of many female box-makers, paper-bag makers, hook- and eye- carders, artificial flower makers, handloom weavers until their craft was destroyed by the power loom, and, indeed, every other job which was associated with the home work system of production. Yet although these were the main outlets for female casual employment, they do not cover the complete spectrum of the female reserve of labour. Above all they overlook the existence of considerable numbers of underemployed charwomen and washerwomen and the pools of casual labour which factory owners, particularly in the post-1880 era, drew upon to meet their needs for extra hands at the busy season. This was the case in jam and confectionery factories where 'the occasional employment of large numbers [is] absolutely necessary whenever a large quantity of fresh fruit or vegetables has to be prepared for preserving at once.' Now was there ever a shortage of such labour, for, apart from those who were engaged at such times for 'perhaps only two or three days in the week, perhaps regularly for several weeks together,' during high summer 'the [casual] mob . . . stands and fights at the gates in the fruit-picking season, from which hands are chosen, sometimes for a day, sometimes for a few hours only, as occasion requires.'[101] An identical trend, with a sudden upsurge in demand for female casual workers during hot weather, was discernible in lemonade production.[102] Other employers however, were less systematic in their hiring of additional labour. A small number of casually employed women in the leather factories of Bermondsey, 'glad of employment at fourpence an hour which promised to last two or three weeks,' were heavily dependent for work upon the decision of the army authorities to place orders for leather belts.[103] All these factory-based pockets of casual workers were of course largely the creation of the post-1870 decades. But the same was not true of hawking which had its supply of female casual recruits in the 1830s and 1840s and which continued to attract married women, operating on a casual basis, in the early years of this century.[104]

Yet while, for analytical purposes, it is possible to treat the female casual market as a self-contained entity, it is essential, in the context of the poverty question, to explore its relationship with its male equivalent. Contemporaries were convinced that the correlation between the two markets was continuous and close, arguing that while the demand for female casual hands could be attributed to structural changes in the British economy, the necessary supply was only forthcoming because of the prior existence of an adult male casual problem which was bound to lead to widespread poverty unless supplementary contributions were made to family income by other members of the household. In other words, the below subsistence earnings of her husband compelled the wife to seek poorly paid employment in largely unskilled occupations. The inevitable sequel to this search for work was the formation of a female casual reserve. From Glasgow support for this thesis came from Margaret Irwin who asserted in 1907 that it was

> exceedingly difficult to given [sic] even an approximate estimate of the number of women employed in home work, because they are so largely casual workers — women who are driven into it by stress of circumstances. Employers tell me again and again that the supply of workers is very largely regulated by the condition of trade amongst the men. If shipbuilding on the Clyde is in a bad state this sends a number of women into the home work market.[105]

Similarly in the same year it was claimed that casuality of employment loomed so large in West Ham 'because home work is itself to a large extent a form of [female] casual labour, and because male workers are often dependent on the earnings of their wives and daughters at home to eke out their own irregular earnings.'[106]

Nonetheless, despite the general validity of these points, two important qualifications should be entered. In the first place, the female labour reserve did not simply consist of the wives of irregularly employed labourers. It also included in its ranks, especially among outworkers, charwomen and washerwomen, substantial contingents of elderly single women and widows, some of whom received supplementary assistance from the English and Scottish Poor Law authorities, and who, at the lowest level, living in impoverished conditions in common lodging houses, had a 'less eligible' existence than the inmates of the workhouse. It was to this last group that Steel-Maitland and Squire referred when they described those 'poor creatures . . . who use the Salvation Army Shelter in Stepney':

> several of these old women have slept here regularly for years, absent only when they go hopping. Some of them sell flowers and hawk small articles in the streets, others do a little washing for poor families and are fire-lighters and tenders for Jews on Fridays and Saturdays; others work in the seasons at pea-shelling and walnut picking for the Covent Garden market. Many of them live on 4d. a day, paying 2d. for their night's lodging and 1d. morning and evening for a cup of tea and bread-and-butter served out at the Shelter.[107]

Secondly, among the married the relationship between the two casual markets was not as exact as the foregoing analysis implies. Apart from the obvious point that not all wives of casual men entered the labour market, there is evidence from some areas to show that an element of those that did, was able to obtain reasonably continuous work. At Cambridge, for example, where in the early 1900s an 'excess of [male] casual labour' existed, 'many families are kept going more by the earnings of the wife, which are small but comparatively

regular, than by the odd shillings brought in by the husband.'[108] Again, if the
head of the household was in regular but poorly rewarded work, other members of his family might try to augment his income by seeking employment for
themselves in casual jobs. Charles Booth found that this was what occurred
among his Class D of 'small regular' earners:

> in the whole class . . . the women work a good deal to eke out the men's earnings and
> the children begin to make more than they cost when free from school: the sons go
> as van boys, errand boys, etc., and the daughters into daily service, or into factories,
> or help the mother with whatever she has in hand.[109]

In evaluating, however, the living standards of male and female casual hands,
it is wrong to assume that individuals were tied to one specific occupation;
for within the casual market there was a certain amount of internal movement.
An indeterminate number of casually employed women sought to sustain their
earning capacity by switching jobs according to the prevailing state of demand.
In Scotland, for instance, in the early 1900s, 'charwomen do fruit-picking, fur-
pullers go to the "herrings" and the "potatoes", ironers to the seaside, according to the season.'[110] Among male casual workers a parallel trend can be discerned. Handloom weavers in the 1830s and 1840s went harvesting, while
labourers turned to hawking, dockers to general labouring, and casual barbers
to painting. Yet such expedients did little to soften the harsh and unrelenting
poverty to which the casual's family was subjected. The vast majority were
destined to follow the path of the typical Birkenhead docker who 'may have
a few weeks' work, . . . will spend all he earns; when no work is available . . .
will pawn and sell to supply his needs. At the end of his working life he becomes chargeable to the [poor] rates, either indoor or outdoor.'[111] Furthermore, such poverty was on the grand scale. Stedman Jones, reinterpreting
Booth's data, has calculated that around ten per cent of London's population
in the early 1890s consisted of casual workers and their dependants.[112] And
while the casual problem probably reached its peak in the capital, those contemporary comments which have already been quoted, make it clear that few
major centres of trade and industry were without substantial fringes of casual
labour. Given this background, the surprising thing is not that casuality loomed
increasingly large in the literature devoted to the unemployment question in
the last twenty-five years of our period but that it took so long to alert society
to the existence of this waste of human resources in its midst.

Much the same verdict could be delivered upon trades whose seasonal patterns
of employment led to considerable hardship among those elements who were
underemployed or without work during the annually recurring periods of dull
trade. And such hardship, it must be stressed, was not simply a by-product of
the consumer revolution of the post-1870 era. It formed a prominent feature
of the social life of whole groups of workers in communities of markedly different socio-economic structure at the start of our period. Great poverty in Edinburgh in 1840 occurred among 'persons or families generally out of employ-

ment for three or four of the winter months; those are the most utterly destitute class of poor, having no source or fund to apply to for relief.'[113] Included in their ranks were labourers, domestic servants, and 'many cases of single women working in the fields when they can get labour, who during the winter months are in entire destitution.'[114] Similarly in Glasgow, masons and builders' labourers in the mid-1840s, were 'frequently thrown idle in the winter season, [and] are in some instances exposed to great privations, and have no means of obtaining relief except by public begging, to which they seldom or never resort, until every other resourse has failed them,'[115] while a contemporaneous London survey, conducted in St. George's Parish, Hanover Square, made reference to 'a general complaint of the difficulty of obtaining employment during the past season. In winter many families stated that they were in habit of pawning part of their furniture and redeeming it in summer, as they can only obtain employ-ment during the "season".' In particular 'many tailors declare that they seldom get more than three or four months full work in the year,'[116] a conclusion which could be applied with equal force to the capital's shoe-making and cabinet making population. But if seasonality of employment could have a profoundly depressing effect upon working-class living standards, it did not follow that all workers in the seasonal trades shared a common experience. In order, therefore, to probe more deeply the connection between poverty and seasonality, it is necessary to examine the contours, and the nature of the seasonal labour market.

This topic can basically be treated under four main headings. Firstly, there was a seemingly intractable seasonal problem associated with the building industry where 'the key determinant of the amplitude of fluctuations in output and employment was the climate rather than the current state of the housing market.'[117] Evidence from a variety of sources underlines the role of adverse climatic conditions in bringing to a halt all building activity or, more often, leading to a reduction in the length of the working day and the dismissal of the seasonal element of the labour force. The weather, however, did not affect all workers in the same way. Charles Booth noted that on new projects labourers, bricklayers, masons, plasterers and painters were hardest hit by falling tempera-tures. On the other hand the preparatory work of dressing stone which was one part of the mason's craft, was largely uninfluenced by frost.[118] Yet this last case was very much an exception to the general trend, since there was always a sharp rise in unemployment during periods of intense cold. For example, in London and the West of Scotland the 'great frost' of January — March 1895 generated widespread distress among all categories of outdoor workers. But an identical result could also be produced by prolonged periods of rain which hit hard the employment prospects of plasterers, painters and others. Such a situa-tion arose in Glasgow where 'during the month of January [1903] the labouring class suffered considerable hardships owing to the interruption of outdoor work on account of the severe [wet] weather.' In concrete terms this meant that 'amongst the Artisans there are . . . 300 Masons and 500 Painters out of work, also a considerable number of Joiners out of employment.'[119] But quite apart from these occasions when the level of seasonal unemployment reached crisis proportions, there was usually much slackness in the building trades in wintertime. Slaters and, in Scotland during the 1880s and 1890s, paviors encountered formidable difficulties in their search for work in mid-winter.[120] Again, brickmakers were usually discharged after a busy season which ran roughly from April to September, while housepainters might find that two-thirds of their number were either underemployed or unemployed during the opening months of the year.[121] In short, there was a well demarcated seasonal trough, running roughly from November to February, which must have pushed the families of discharged unskilled workers, with no savings to fall back upon, below the primary poverty line. Conversely there was a vigorous upsurge in the demand for labour during the early spring which was well sustained until late autumn. In London part of the initial impetus was provided by the upper classes' need to have their town houses in a good state of repair and decoration for the London season.[122] In most Scottish burghs, on the other hand, 'the Scottish system of yearly house-letting from Whitsunday term causes in busy times a pressure during the Spring months in supplying materials for houses intended for occupation at the term.'[123] Yet however diverse the economic forces which set in motion this annual period of intense activity, it was largely maintained, to the benefit of all sections of the workforce, by repair work undertaken by small jobbing builders and by new house building — increasingly the preserve of larger firms — whose limits were set by the movement of the building cycle.

Work in docks and inland food markets was the second area of the labour market where the well delineated rhythms of casuality of employment were overlaid by a distinctive seasonal pattern. In Britain's ports the most massive and violent seasonal oscillations in the level of work undoubtedly took place during the era of the sailing ship. Reference has already been made to the disastrous combination of frost and 'easterly winds' which brought unemployment to a halt along Liverpool's water front during January and February 1838.[124] But this story was repeated with monotonous frequency in every major dock. In London, where Tom McCarthy recalled in 1892 that 'my father used to be out of work for weeks and weeks together, because owing to the East Wind, the fleet of [sailing] ships could not come up,' a harsh winter had devastating repercussions upon every species of dock labour.[125] In 1854-5 the freezing over of the Thames meant that 'the navigation of ships, steamers and boats is entirely stopped, and the docks are blocked up: the distress amongst the labouring class caused by the suspension of labour is appalling and there are not fewer than 50,000 men out of employ, who have been for several days past subsisting on the scanty relief doled out by the parishes and the unions.' Almost identical crises were to recur in 1860-1, 1866-7 and 1878-9.[126] Even during normal winters, however, the services of certain kinds of workers were invariably dispensed with. Among them were timber 'lumpers' whose busy season began in July and terminated in January but who 'between January and July . . . have little or nothing to do. During that time there are scarcely any timber or deal ships coming in; and the working lumpers then try to fall in with anything they can, either ballasting a ship, or carrying a few deals to load a timber-carriage, or doing a little "tide-work".'[127]

As has been demonstrated, one consequence of the advent of the steam ship was a reduction in the incidence of seasonality.[128] Nevertheless it did not destroy it completely, for seasonal unemployment continued to be an integral part of the economic life of several ports. Moreover, it is possible, from the 1880s onwards, to discern more clearly the unsynchronised nature of the seasonal problem in which the key determinant in producing different monthly peaks and troughs was the type of commodities handled by each group of dockers. For example, the peak period for dock employment in Dundee coincided with the winter arrival of raw jute, so vital for the prosperity of the city's principal industry, while the large-scale import of raw cotton into Liverpool, during a timespan stretching from October to March, led to a seasonal upturn in the demand for hands, with perhaps 2500 extra cotton porters being hired to execute the extra volume of work.[129] Again, those dockers who were engaged by the Manchester Ship Canal Company to unload cotton and fruit were always busiest from September to May.[130] Elsewhere, however, the dull season began towards the end of the year and continued until spring. This was the pattern in the fishing port of Aberdeen where during the mid-winter trough — from December to February — 'this seasonal variation . . . clearly affect [ed] fish porters, women who clean the fish, and others besides fishermen'; in several of the Clyde ports, including Glasgow, where the massive decline in the number of seamen shipped and the movement of labour out of the docks to other unskilled outlets revealed the existence of a seasonal problem of significant dimensions; and the Millwall and Surry Commercial Docks in London where, after an autumn peak, imports of grain and timber fell away sharply in the first three months of the year.[131] Similarly affected by shrinking employment prospects during wintertime were porters in inland fruit markets. Charles Booth highlighted the extreme volatility of the labour market at Covent Garden in the late 1880s where a porter might earn £2 to £3 per week in summer, only to face the doubtful prospects of severe underemployment or unemployment throughout the winter months.[132] Identical situations obtained in the early 1900s amongst 'badged' porters in the Manchester fruit market — its meat market was much more stable — and at Glasgow where the onset of autumn was heralded by the shedding of labour.[133] Overall, therefore, a picture emerges, in the post-1880 world, of a dull season which, despite differences in chronology, occupied three or four months in each year and which could only generate considerable distress among families of the seasonal element of the workforce.

The clothing industry was the third sector of the economy where output and employment conformed in large measure to a seasonal cycle. Seasonality of production was one of the salient characteristics of handloom weaving throughout the 1830s and 1840s. Fancy cotton weavers in Scotland and elsewhere could, for instance, anticipate both a rising demand for their services every spring and autumn and a distinct shortage of work during the summer and winter months, while among weavers of plain cotton goods a busy spring season was usually succeeded by much slackness in summer-time.[134] In fact, looking at the weavers' working year in general terms, a spring peak and summer trough in employment opportunities were an experience which was shared by widely scattered weaving communities engaged upon a variety of fabrics, including outworkers in the Coventry silk trade, linen weavers in the East of Scotland and the majority of woollen and worsted weavers in the West Riding.[135]

In tailoring, dressmaking and shirtmaking, on the other hand, a different cyclical pattern can be traced. 'Honourable' tailors, employed in the bespoke workshops of the West End, spoke, in the late 1840s, about an annually recurring period of brisk business which extended from May to July and a dull season which 'usually begins in August and lasts till the middle of October, or two months and a half,' when an element of bouyancy returned to the trade, inspired by Christmas orders.[136] This short-lived upsurge, however, had spent itself by late November, and from that point in time until March quiet trading conditions led to much short-time work and unemployment among the ranks of this best paid section of the labour force. This pattern was to change remarkably little between 1860 and 1890 despite the introduction of the sewing machine and the rapid growth of the 'slop' sector of the industry. For example, Daniel McLoughlin, a former President of the Scottish Operative Tailors' Society, argued in the late 1880s that customer work in the West of Scotland was still distinguished by a slack season which lasted from January to April, with a further two troughs occurring in September and November in the demand for highly proficient hands.[137] But many small masters, producing ready-made garments for the large wholesale houses in Glasgow, were no better placed, facing six months' slackness in a year and during the bleakest part of that timespan — November to February — being reduced, along with their female machinists, to between a half day's and two and a half days' work per week.[138] Again, in the 1890s 'in the best bespoke shop [of London] the work is fast and furious during the busy season (from March to August and from October to Christmas)' although for the remainder of the year 'the workers are locked out for weeks together.'[139] Finally, in the opening years of this century, Norwich's bespoke tailors fared equally badly during January, February, July and August, while Manchester's tailoring population encountered its period of greatest distress from December to March.[140] In short, whatever other differences existed in the work patterns of the seasonal members of the workforce, they could all expect their prospects of employment to improve in the early summer and to reach the nadir of their fortunes in the opening months of the year.

Scarcely surprisingly, the contours of employment in the dressmaking and shirtmaking trades followed an identical course. Those dressmakers who were hired by large Oxford Street firms in the West End of London during the 1890s had, in effect, two busy seasons, the first lasting from March/April until August and the second — a less spectacular boom — covering at most a few weeks between October and December.[141] For most provincial centres of crafts, however, the summer peak was of briefer duration — Norwich's covered the months of March to June[142] — largely because there was no local equivalent to the London season. Nonetheless, irrespective of locality, the almost exclusively female labour force was badly hit by a falling demand for its services throughout the coldest weeks of the winter. The same was true of London fur-sewers, the bulk of whom, engaged on common work, saw a period of intense activity — May to November — followed by months of either total unemployment or chronic underemployment; and of outwardly disparate groups of workers in the shoe industry in the 1880s — among them outdoor knifers, factory-based lasters and poorly paid female and male employees in the 'sew round' trade — whose seasonal elements during 'the betterest months of the year obtain little or no employment, and frequently suffer great privations.'[143]

The final group of trades to be discussed embraces such a variegated range of activity that it is impossible to classify it under a single heading. Briefly it can be accepted that several of these remaining seasonal occupations were largely the preserve of female labour. They included those domestic servants who during the 1840s in Edinburgh were adversely affected in the spring, early summer and at Christmas by the decision of a section of the *haute bourgeoisie* to travel south for the London season; Glasgow washerwomen who, in the 1900s, could be hit by the decision of their middle-class employers to take up summer residence in one of the Clyde resorts; female college servants at Cambridge, many of whom, at the turn of this century, were still laid off during the summer vacation; and those urban-based female workers in agriculture, gardening and market gardening whose slack period was heralded by the approach of winter.[144] Yet others, in the post-1880 years, were engaged in factory-based seasonal work, for, as we have seen, there was a distinctive seasonal demand for unskilled female labour from jam, confectionery and lemonade firms during summertime. In other factory-based processes, however, the male seasonal element clearly predominated. Labourers employed by dyeing and bleaching establishments in Manchester in the early 1900s were, according to the Secretary of the Operative Bleachers', Dyers' and Finishers' Society, 'out of work six months in the year', although during the dull months for the home trade — from September to March — they were clearly joined by a section of their more skilled colleagues.[145] Similarly those who worked in the india-rubber industry saw a peak period of employment, from July to November, succeeded by a slackness which lasted from November to March and which brought in its wake the dismissal of the seasonal section of the workforce.[146] This pattern of a dull winter season was not, however, exclusively confined to those types of factory work. It was also a prominent feature of cabinet making which, until the end of our period, was still very much a workshop industry in England and Scotland and of those male workers, taken on for the London season — bakers, packers, porters and servants among them — who, in addition to encountering an unemployment problem from July to November when the annual exodus of their employers from the capital took place, had little hope of securing continuous work during the first three months of the year.[147] Yet if winter slackness was the norm, there was a handful of occupations which constituted an exception to this general trend. Gas stokers and labourers, chimney sweeps, coal heavers, carters connected with the delivery of domestic coal and — if the Glasgow experience were typical of the rest of the country — workers who in the early 1900s were employed in the developing electricity supply industry, all experienced their period of brisker business in mid-winter and a decline in the demand for their services during the summer.[148]

To many contemporaries, however, seasonality of employment could not be regarded as a significant source of working-class poverty — and this for four reasons. In the first place, it was frequently only a minority of workers in a given industry who were exposed to the debilitating rhythms of the seasonal market. Furthermore, it was well known that within each seasonal trade there were often considerable differences between the social experience of different groups during the seasonal trough. For example, whereas roundsmen in the 'aerated water' industry were still retained when temperatures started to plunge, there were always widespread redundancies at the same point in time among their fellow workers who were employed as unskilled and semi-skilled factory hands.[149] Similarly in the building industry painters were much more likely to be idle in the winter months than masons, while in tailoring bespoke tailors in London, Glasgow and other centres of the trade faced a more elongated winter trough than their colleagues in 'slop' lines because they were to some extent to the whim of fashion.[150] Secondly, it was believed that the seasonal contingent of the labour market was insulated from the most deleterious effects of dull trade by the abundant opportunities which existed for dovetailing seasonal employment. Thus, handloom weavers in the North of England and Scotland in the 1830s and 1840s turned to agriculture during their slack summer period.[151] Again, from at least the 1880s onwards brickmakers in winter sought labouring work in the gas industry, while a small element of gasworkers — as in Glasgow — might participate, in the summer months, in the Highlands fishing season or go back to Ireland to tend the family plot.[152] Groups of bespoke tailors turned to contract work in the 'slop' sector of the market during their quiet period at the start of the year; chimney sweeps might in summer revert to costermongering; and seamen, when the seasonal downturn occurred, to general labouring.[153] But this interlocking of occupations was by no means confined to the male seasonal market. In the early 1900s Cambridge's female college servants found summer employment fruit-picking, and female hands, dismissed in the autumn by mineral water producers, sought work in pickle factories and as washerwomen and charwomen.[154] This list is by no means exhaustive; but it is sufficient to show that there was some justification for the belief that mobility within the labour market was one means of reducing the impact of the less desirable social consequences of seasonality of employment.

Thirdly, from the 1890s onwards, the number of seasonal dismissals was limited in certain industries by the size, and sometimes the changing organisational structure of the firm. In the building trade it was the practice of large firms in London and the West of Scotland to retain the bulk of their labour force during winter-time by substituting a shorter working week for redundancy.[155] Seasonal unemployment was also a relatively small problem in provincial shoe and garment factories which, in order to keep down their overheads, aimed, as far as possible, at continuous production; and in some food processing factories which overcame seasonality of output, by combining the manufacture of jam and marmalade with its summer peak, with the making of sweets and potted meat in winter-time.[156] Fourthly, amongst those who encountered short-time or unemployment during the inevitable seasonal downturns, there was an artisan element whose wages, when in full work, were thought to be sufficient to tide them over these annually recurring difficult periods.

Yet while these positive influences mitigated, and in some cases removed, the hardships often associated with seasonal dullness, they do not obliterate the reality of the strong relationship between seasonality and poverty. It has already been established that grinding poverty was the fate of disparate groups of seasonally displaced workers in Edinburgh, Glasgow and London in the 1840s.[157] And such a trend was not confined to the early part of our period since the dimensions of this particular aspect of the poverty problem increased rather than diminished between 1850 and 1890 as the seasonal trades themselves grew in size and complexity. Moreover, in most instances such seasonally generated poverty was usually the direct sequel to powerful external constraints upon the seasonal labour force. For one thing the opportunity for dovetailing was usually much more limited than contemporaries were willing to acknowledge. The extent to which this kind of operation could succeed was in a fundamental sense determined by the overall chronology of seasonal peaks and troughs in British industry. In the vast majority of seasonal trades, there was a marked degree of synchronisation between their brisk season — the summer months — and their slack period which ran roughly from December to March. By very definition, therefore, there were relatively few alternative work outlets of a seasonal nature which dismissed employees could seek to enter in mid-winter when there was everywhere a marked surplus of unskilled labour. Indeed, it was only those relatively small numbers of seasonal hands who reversed the normal chronological pattern, such as gas works' labourers, who, during their 'dull' summer, were not consistently haunted by the spectre of a glutted labour market and could attempt, with more hopes of success, to dovetail seasonal jobs.

The adverse pressures which the limited possibility of dovetailing exerted upon the seasonal workforce can be abundantly illustrated from the extant data. Most female home workers, for instance, when seasonally unemployed, had few chances of alternative sources of employment since they suffered from the dual handicap of possessing no skills which would attract the attention of potential employers and of being restricted, either through infirmity, old age or family ties, to the confines of their own house. Yet while occupational immobility existed in its most extreme form among seasonal home workers, there was almost as marked a reluctance among certain other seasonal groups — many of them workshop based — to leave their own trade during the slack season to seek openings elsewhere. In the late 1880s elderly female fur-sewers in London made little attempt, in the dull winter months, to move to any other sector in the labour market.[158] At the same point in time many female machinists and male tailors in Glasgow's ready-made tailoring industry resigned themselves to heavy underemployment and below subsistence earnings rather than venture into other forms of unskilled work, while 'sew round' hands in the London shoe trade faced the prospect, 'through the slack six months of the year', of 'very considerable privations', unless they could obtain employment in another branch of the same industry, which for the majority was a forlorn hope.[159] Partly this pattern of behaviour can be interpreted as a form of social conservatism: workers, at the cost of much social suffering, were prepared to tolerate the seasonal fluctuations within their craft rather than to risk severing the existing connection with their employer by moving temporarily into another sphere of economic activity. But they were principally restrained from making such a transfer by the knowledge, as Stedman Jones put it, that 'dovetailing was always from a more skilled trade into a less skilled one, never the reverse.'[160] Bespoke tailors could thus compete, in mid-winter, for slop work against their colleagues who belonged to the ready-made sector of the industry. On the other hand, if slop tailors sought alternative winter-time outlets, they were pushed into a labour market where the prospect before them was less that of reasonably continuous but unskilled employment and more that of work of a casual nature.

This is little more than arguing that seasonality of employment ultimately led many to experience the more erratic rhythms of casuality of employment. The close nature of this connection has already been amply documented. Some industries, including handloom weaving, tailoring, building, jam and lemonade factories and certain of the home work trades, secured part of their labour requirements at their seasonal peaks from the ranks of the casual reserve. Conversely many classically seasonal elements among paviors, painters and builders' labourers, laid off for three months of the year, availed themselves of such casual employment as was offered to them. But the social sequel to this last interchange is equally important. For the meagre rewards of casual labour gave the families of semi-skilled and unskilled hands who periodically made the transition to the casual market, little hope of eluding, during their slack season, the firm grip of poverty. Yet for the unskilled seasonal workers who could not make that transition, the outlook was even bleaker since they were forced to rely upon a combination of *ad hoc* expedients — private charity, assistance from friends, in England the poor rate, short-term credit and an understanding landlord not to press too hard for accumulating rent arrears — to mitigate some of the economic rigours of the months of dull trade. And for a small element of self-supporting single women, part-time prostitution was seen as the only solution to the pressing threat of lack of food. As Sherwell wrote in 1897, 'it is at present a notorious fact that in the West End of London at least, milliners, and dressmakers, and tailoresses are frequently driven upon the streets in the slack season, returning to their shops with the advent of the new season's trade. In other words, *morals fluctuate with trade*.'[161] It can be safely concluded, therefore, that for all but an artisan elite, seasonality of employment represented yet another route to social deprivation and poverty.

II

The cumulative impact of technological innovation and organisational change upon working-class living standards is in certain areas of the economy more difficult to interpret. Many middle-class contemporaries, firm upholders of the concept of the 'invisible hand,' believed that such change ultimately benefited all sections of the workforce, transferring labour and capital from low wage/low productivity, to high wage/high productivity, occupations and generating only temporary hardship among certain groups of hand workers. In the 1830s this doctrine was enunciated in its most uncompromising form in Andrew Ure's defence of the factory system. But the basic thesis that machinery and factory-based production brought real gains to the working-classes was repeated with monotonous frequency in the closing debates of our period. To Charles Booth mechanisation meant *inter alia* greater regularity of employment.[162] To the Webbs, writing in the late 1890s, it was a sign of the growing maturity of British trade unions that they had abandoned the industrial Luddism of the pre-1850 era for a more flexible attitude towards technical change. The essential feature of this newly found flexibility, which started to manifest itself in the 1860s, was the concern of organised labour to defend the standard rate against a backcloth of technical innovation. In some cases — as with hand paper makers and the bespoke section of the hand-sewn shoe trade — this goal was realised by preserving intact the traditional skills of craftsmen catering for a high-class market, while allowing machinery and the factory to create new openings for semi-skilled hands, concerned with producing an inferior article for a different range of consumers.[163] In other cases the defence of the standard rate was linked with a demand that skilled trade unionists should retain a substantial degree of control over the manning of new machinery as a safeguard against labour dilution. As the Associated Iron-Moulders of Scotland expressed it in 1893, 'machinery is being introduced, such as pipe-moulding machines and plate-moulding machines, but in no case does the Society seek to restrict such beyond preferring moulders at the work.'[164] Similarly the fitters and turners who dominated the Amalgamated Society of Engineers, tried, until their traumatic defeat in the

1897-8 nationwide struggle with their employers, to regulate the recruitment of labour to operate improved machine tools in their own interests.[165] But there were yet other spheres of economic activity where the workmen, with little effective bargaining power, were initially hostile to the factory system but were later to acknowledge the gains in real income which followed in its wake. Among them were file-cutters in the Sheffield region who had opposed the introduction of cutting machinery in the 1860s; those regularly employed bakers in the post-1870 world who secured a rising real income in large, mechanised city bakeries; power loom weavers who fared much better than the bulk of their handworking counterparts; and male hosiery workers in the factories of Nottingham in the post-1870 decades, whose weekly income, from operating the steam-powered rotary frames, raised them well above the poverty line. As George Kendall put it in 1876, when contrasting the former plight of the domestic-based framework knitter with the enhanced economic status of his factory-based counterpart, 'we used to have formerly long periods of depression, but latterly the periods of depression never last so long. People wear better things than they used to generally.'[166] Not all outworkers whose traditional way of life was undermined by new modes of production were, of course, able to secure employment within the mill or factory. But for them it was sometimes possible to seek new work outlets in other areas of the labour market. In Nottinghamshire in the 1860s framework knitters were encouraging their sons to enter the coal industry rather than follow their own lead by taking up a poorly paid, and dying, hand craft.[167] In Preston cotton weavers as early as the mid-1830s sought any form of unskilled work that was available to them 'and when they get it they will not leave it in a hurry,' while worsted handloom weavers in Bradford in 1838 were either 'learning to comb' or 'going to the quarries to work.'[168] Finally, cotton handloom weavers in the West of Scotland turned in the 1840s towards railway navvying and the iron and coal industries, although a minority — as in Airdrie — took up tailoring and hatmaking or set up as small scale grocers and spirit dealers.[169]

Yet this view of a labour market operating in a smooth and automatic fashion to diffuse widely the social benefits of new technology must be qualified. For one thing, there were certain occupations which suffered severely from technological unemployment, with, for the vast majority of those affected, little hope of an immediate improvement in their lot. As we have seen, the final phase of handloom weaving in the cotton and worsted industries, running roughly from 1830 to the mid-1850s, was distinguished by widespread indigence which was a reflection not merely of an overstocked labour market but also of the progressive encroachment of the power loom upon the earning capacity of adult male weavers. Again, the perfection of Lister's combing machine in the mid-1840s increased the social sufferings of Bradford's hand woolcombers — as one observer wrote, 'that their physical well-being was neglected, the emaciated appearance of most plainly betokened'[170] — and within a decade and a half destroyed the economic *rationale* of this branch of outwork.[171] Furthermore, for male domestic workers in the textile industry there were often substantial obstacles to be overcome before they could move into another job. For apart from the fact that power looms were largely operated by women and children, the unskilled labour market which was their most obvious source of alternative employment, was invariably overstocked. In Preston it was freely admitted in 1834 that weavers found 'difficulty in getting into any other employment'; but even among those who were successful in their search, an element would return to weaving in the winter months if they had fared no better in the ranks of inadequately remunerated, and perhaps casually employed, general labourers.[172] One of the principal obstacles to such mobility during these years of searing distress was simply advancing age. The *Morning Chronicle's* correspondent drew attention, in his visit to Ashton-under-Lyne in 1849, to

> a handful of miserable old men, the remnants of the cotton hand-loom weavers. No young persons think of pursuing such an occupation: the few who practise it were too old and confirmed in old habits, when the power-loom was introduced, to be able to learn a new way of making their bread.[173]

In most localities, however, — and almost certainly in Ashton-under-Lyne — elderly weavers remained tied to their craft not because they were reluctant to work elsewhere but largely because they, with their failing powers, had scant chance of attracting the attention of those employers of unskilled labour who placed so much emphasis upon physical strength.

But if the handloom weaving community was the principal victim of technological innovation, it was by no means an isolated case. In the post-1860 era the introduction of the sewing machine led initially in dressmaking, tailoring, shirtmaking and shoemaking to the growth of a poverty-stricken, sweated sector whose numbers only started to diminish with the increasing emphasis which was placed, from the late 1880s onwards, upon factory-based output. Yet even with the arrival of the clothing and shoemaking factory, poverty was not to be entirely abolished. Firstly, although Clapham was correct in his contention 'that the certain and grave evils in the trade were never connected by any responsible person with the coming of the [clothing] factories; rather with its delay,'[174] it by no means followed that sweated female labour was automatically transferred to new jobs with large, provincial firms. For the married home worker the loss of home work, when it occurred, often represented a permanent loss of income which her household could ill afford.[175] Secondly, sweated outwork did not everywhere disappear with the advent of the factory. In London ready-made clothing, produced in the home or the small workshop, continued, until the end of our period, to compete in the home market against the provincial factory.[176] But the result of such competition could only mean additional adverse pressures upon the sweated labour force. A similar pattern emerged in several centres of the shoe industry; for that industry was not, as the Webbs seemed to imply, divided in the late 1890s between a factory-oriented system, using American machinery to manufacture ready-made shoes and a small, hand-sewn bespoke sector.[177] There existed an intermediate layer of hands who in Norwich, London, Bristol and elsewhere worked either in their own homes or under garret masters in the ready-made part of the market and who, by the turn of the century, could be counted amongst the casualties of technical change.[178] The decline in their fortunes was succinctly summarised by a member of the Executive of the National Union of Boot and Shoe Operatives when he argued that many of his members in Bristol in the early years of this century were receiving sick benefit from the union 'merely as an aid in destitution' largely because hand work was being rapidly superseded by machinery. In his words,

> there is absolutely no doubt that machinery has displaced one-third of the men, and the use of machinery is increasing. Machines now turn out twenty-five dozen a day; a man turns out the same number in a week and the demand for boots cannot go far increase as to give employment for displaced men in the trade. A boot hand is no fool and manages to get repairs to do and get odd jobs from various firms, so that he keeps off the [poor] rates; but he earns from 8s. to 12s. a week only, and that casually. There are numbers of such men between 40 and 50 years of age in the boot trade. Their daughters go to the chocolate and tailoring factories and so a wage is made up, none earning a living wage separately.[179]

Needless to say, the families of bootmakers who laced such supplementary income could only have subsisted at a level well below Rowntree's primary poverty line.

Technological and organisational innovation produced similar results in the laundry industry where the integrated steam laundry drew much of its staff from the ranks of single women to the detriment of those married females who had worked as washerwomen either from, or in, their own home; in button-holing where from the early 1870s onwards, outwork, carried out by hand, was being gradually replaced by machinery; in the docks where, in the 1880s, the introduction of grain elevators and 'steam cranes for loading and discharging vessels have materially lessened the number of hands, and work is done in less time'; and in those cities where, as we have seen, large, mechanised bakeries had created among trade unionists a reserve of casually employed jobbing bakers.[180] In this last instance it was precisely because machinery had produced over time a substantial underemployment problem — in the quarter ending 4 January 1909 593 members of the National Federal Union of the Operative Bakers of Scotland were returned as unemployed in Glasgow as against 754 in constant work — that one trade union official was compelled to admit that his own scheme for municipal bakeries encountered strenuous opposition from many of the rank and file who feared that it would lead to more labour-saving devices being used and an increase in the size of the casual workforce.[181] In all these industries, therefore, it is possible to identify an indeterminate number of individuals whose livelihood was either made more precarious or destroyed by the spread of new technology and the trend towards the factory system. This is to do little more than state the obvious: that innovation had, for the hands immediately affected, negative as well as positive results. And yet this point needs to be made because so often the victims of such change, in the worst traditions of Whig historiography, are either ignored by economic historians or the unwarranted assumption is made that they were readily reabsorbed — in full-time employment — elsewhere in the labour market. It was precisely for this reason that home workers were often suspicious of any move, irrespective of the motive which inspired it, designed to undermine their living. To quote Mrs. Brophy, a Glasgow paper bag maker, who gave evidence before the 1907 Select Committee on Home Work, 'I think that it would be awfully cruel to take our home-work away, because it would mean desolation to not a few but a good many. I have a sister who is the upkeep of a house of six children. Her husband is a casual worker in American boots.'[182] And while this plea was inspired by her fear of the economic consequence of government regulations, it can be equally validly accepted as the married female outworker's reaction to the spectre of technical and structural change which could deprive her family of much-needed earnings.

Nevertheless technological advance did not simply threaten the unskilled and the semi-skilled. For if in certain industries it produced new growth points and a demand for new skills, it at the same time dispensed with the traditional role of craftsmen. The rise of an iron ship-building technology was, for instance, an important factor in the gradual demise of the Thames wooden ship-building industry, where by the late 1860s and early 1870s it is easy to discern a drastic decline in the labour force, widespread social suffering, and for those who remained, much underemployment. By the mid-1880s skilled London ship-wrights had been reduced to the status of a casual workforce. But the same process spread to affect riggers who in the late 1880s 'averaged twenty-six weeks work per year', and sailmakers who were employed 'much less'.[183] Yet if the wooden ship-building craftsmen were first, and hardest, hit in the capital, the same process occurred in other areas. From Clydeside the claim was made in the 1890s that although riggers' work — at 5/11d. per day — was more constant than on Merseyside or the Thames, it was still 'very irregular owing to the amount of vessels being built or coming into port . . . . The tendency is also for vessels to carry as little top hamper or spars and rigging as possible, all of which causes lessen work.'[184] Again Scottish shipwrights, no longer required in the era of the iron ship to lay down the hull, were compelled to compete with joiners for the limited amount of wooden work in each iron vessel.[185] Worst hit, however, were the sail-makers, whose impoverished condition was movingly captured by G. Lyon of Glasgow in 1908: 'I am A Sailmaker to Trade but Sailing Ships being A thing of the past also sewing machines taking our place the Trade has left Me and having the misfortune to want the Leg, I go with A Pinleg the trade suited me very well but I cannot get my living at it now upon an average I only work Three Months in A year the little I saved when Trade was good is done now.'[186] In the Steel industry a parallel process was at work, for mechanisation had, by the early 1890s, contributed directly to the impoverishment of an unspecified number of millmen who were concerned with the manufacture of ship-plate and finished rails. To quote John Cronin, General Secretary of the Associated Society of Millmen in Scotland,

in our trade machinery is gradually replacing manual labour. I remember not so very long ago when we used to have 16 men employed on one particular job, to-day a boy and a bit of a machine can do it, and these 16 men are thrown out of employment. There are several cases of that kind, and I find it is becoming more so month by month and year by year. This surplus labour is a menace to us, because they are walking about, and they are always ready to do what we can in our trade black-legging if required by the employers.

And it was made clear that such individuals formed a highly specialised reserve of labour: 'there is a number, owing to the introduction of machinery, who are almost continuously unemployed, and who are unemployed in this sense, that they have no regular work to go to, but look about the works and get an odd day here and there where they can have it.'[187] A similar fate befell adult male ropespinners in the West of Scotland who by the mid-1880s saw their craft challenged by 'the introduction of machinery and the consequent employment of boys and girls,' and male handloom weavers of wirecloth who, in the first decade of this century, complained that their work was being rapidly superseded by the power loom operated by juvenile labour.[188] This catalogue of examples is, of course, far from complete; but it is sufficient to show that innovation could, for certain skilled groups, have the same devastating repercussions upon livelihood and income as it had among the unskilled and semi-skilled.

Two final points need to be stressed about the relationship between structural and technical change on the one hand and poverty on the other. Firstly, from the 1890s onwards trade union leaders and others argued that one adverse consequence of the increasing use of technology was, by speeding up work, to shorten the working life of the artisan and thus to transfer them to the unskilled labour market. As W.F. Anderson remarked in 1907, skilled men at a certain age 'are not so proficient at their trade as younger men. If unable to get employment as labourers on light work, they are compelled to apply for such work as distress committees [set up under the 1905 Unemployed Workmen Act] have at their disposal.'[189] Almost certainly only a small minority resorted to these kinds of expedients. But whenever such downward mobility took place, it took the erstwhile skilled hand — and his family — into an area of social experience which was unmistakably tinged with poverty. Secondly, the factory system, in a few areas of the economy, abetted the growth of the casual labour market by offering 'a large range of occupations in which boys are employed between the ages of fourteen and nineteen, but which offer no permanent position to them at men's wages.' Included in this category were

loom-boys, doffers or shifters in weaving factories, rivet-boys in boilershops, oven-boys in bakeries, 'drawers-off' in saw-mills, packers in soapworks, machine-minders in furniture factories, labelling bottles in mineral water factories, turning the wheel for rope-spinners, and . . . numberless other such positions in which they are performing some simple operation, often as an assistant to a man.[190]

The initial impetus to take up such 'dead-end' appointment was undoubtedly provided by the poverty of unskilled parents. As Tawney argued, 'in the poorest class of all . . . the temptation to the parents of immediately high earnings [from sons entering such outlets on leaving school] is almost overwhelming.[191] Once inside the factory, however, juveniles could expect to be dismissed without any form of craft training from their positions in their eighteenth or nineteenth year, thus to augment the already formidable army of the casually employed. In this way, and in these limited spheres, after the initial short-term gains had been recorded, did poverty and casuality of employment threaten to perpetuate themselves. And, in a wider sense, it is possible to trace the existence of an intimate relationship between technological unemployment and casual and seasonal patterns of work in which 'it was quite possible for an individual to suffer simultaneously from the adverse pressures generated by different forms of unemployment.'[192] Assessed overall, however, it cannot be disputed that mechanisation and the growth of factory-based production, even in the medium-term, led to rising real income and a broadening of occupational outlets for the majority of the working-classes, including elements of the unskilled.

III

While, in any exploration of the connection between unemployment and poverty, it must be accepted that seasonality and casuality of employment and technological and organisational innovation were significant causes of social deprivation, the main generator of widespread indigence in society remained a prolonged period of bad trade. Foster, for example, has argued that forty-one per cent of the families in his Oldham sample were below the primary poverty line in 1847, a year of commercial crisis, compared with fifteen per cent in 1849 which was a much more bouyant phase in the life of the nation.[193] And although the precision of these statistics cannot be endorsed because of the imperfect nature of the data, their broad emphasis is undoubtedly correct. Moreover, if at such times it was those in whose households poverty was a frequent guest, who were the first to be 'thrown out of employment,'[194] social suffering was never as restricted and selective in its visitations as this. Evidence from a variety of sources shows that a cyclical trough of any duration adversely affected a broad cross-section of the labour force, including sections of the artisan elite once they had exhausted, where available, idle benefit from their trade union and private savings.

Just before the start of our period there had been two bouts of intense depression in the economy — in 1826 when the joint endeavours of the London-based Manufacturers' Relief Committee and *ad hoc* bodies elsewhere to soften the blow of mass unemployment were of little more than marginal significance, given the size of the problem, and in 1829 when acute poverty re-emerged to blight the lives of a substantial proportion of the urban working-classes. But in the 1830s the first major check to business confidence did not occur until 1837, in the wake of the frenetic boom which had been a prominent feature of the preceding two years. The bleak fate of the unemployed on this occasion was well documented by comtemporary observers. From Glasgow C.R. Baird wrote about a social crisis of impressive dimensions: 'owing to the depressed state of trade, the consequent want of employment, and the high price of provisions, in the latter part of the spring and the beginning of the summer of 1837, a large number of the working-classes in Glasgow were reduced to very necessitous circumstances.'[195] Similar reports were to be made in other manufacturing centres of the West of Scotland. In the town of Lanark in April 1837 'there were 261 weavers within the burgh, without work, and adding those that are supplied with work in Lanark and reside elsewhere, there are, at least 500 idle in this locality, in that simple employment.' Nevertheless 'the stagnation in trade at present is not confined to one branch of industry. All, or nearly all, are in the same predicament, and many have been so for a much longer time than the weavers.'[196] Again, it was recorded from Paisley in the same month that 'within the last two weeks, the number of the unemployed weavers, dyers, cutters, lashers, etc. has been doubled, and every day is fearfully adding to the amount. Many workmen with families have been out of employment for three, four, five and some even six weeks, and are in consequence on the point of starvation.'[197] What this local manifestation of the phenomenon of cyclical unemployment meant in concrete terms was explained later in 1837 by the Rev. Dr. Burns, a spokesman for the Paisley Relief Committee. 'For the last four months, 14,000 individuals, including men, women and children, had been unemployed who, together with those who from age and infirmity naturally depend on their exertions, leave in round numbers 20,000 in actual distress.'[198] But this was in no way a unique experience. Slackness was equally prominent, and social hardship equally widely diffused among such disparate groups as the cotton workers of Lancashire, lace and hosiery knitters in Nottingham, and largely unskilled workers in Bristol where, out of a survey of 275 households, 96 were described as 'in distress and in great want of food, bedding and furniture.'[199]

In a few areas recovery was under way before the end of the year, although the subsequent upsurge was not to be universally sustained. In particular, reports from some of the principal textile towns were couched in lugubrious language throughout 1840. Adshead showed that 2000 households in the Ancoats, New Town, Deansgate and Portland Street districts of Manchester earned a weekly average of 6/3¼d. per family — or 1/6½d. per head — and that since April 1840 'the subsequently increased pressures of the times will have increased rather than diminished' the already formidable number of goods in pawn.[200] Similarly it was claimed in February 1840 that the cotton industry of Bolton was more depressed than at any period since 1826, with the majority of mill workers unable to obtain more than three to four days' work per week and with little demand for the services of handloom weavers of counterpanes and bed quilts.[201] By 1841 the bleak message contained in these portents of economic deceleration had been amply vindicated when the economy entered a prolonged decline. In October of that year it was possible to speak in Glasgow of a 'commercial depression which has prevailed for some time, [and which] has reduced thousands to the point of starvation, who formerly lived in comparative comfort,' although the same analysis could equally well have been made in other major manufacturing centres.[202] During 1842 the depression deepened to such an extent that some social historians have accorded that year the doubtful privilege of being the worst for unemployment in the whole of the nineteenth century. Not unexpectedly textile workers, both outworkers and mill hands, figured prominently in the lists of those groups who were hardest hit by the crisis. By May 1842 'hundreds of industrious Irish, who have been resident in Manchester for periods varying from ten to forty years, are now wholly without employment, and are daily suffering from hunger and destitution,' having 'pawned and sold almost every article of their . . . furniture' and been compelled to rely, for their sustenance, upon the uncertain bounty of the soup kitchen and private charity.[203] At Bolton 30 mills with 5061 employees were 'standing idle or working only four days a week' at roughly the same point in time, while Provost Henderson proclaimed with some exaggeration that in Paisley in January 1842,

> unemployment was the rule, and employment was the exception. Comparatively few of the workmen of Paisley were employed; they were broken up, and found to be wandering about in every town in the country, begging for bread, independent of those thousands whom they had at home, supported by charity . . . As to the number of mills, there were but few of them at Paisley, some of them were on full, and some of them were on short time. In the neighbouring town of Johnstone, which was exclusively a cotton-spinning place, and which, up to the present time, had never known depression, one-half of the mills had been unemployed for months, and latterly others of them had gone on short time.[204]

But, of course, the social impact of this specific depression was not confined to the cotton towns; it touched the fabric of every aspect of economic activity. In Newcastle-upon-Tyne 'three fourths of the mechanics are out of employment and the demand for labour is less [in 1842] than at any preceding period since the [Poor Law] Union's formation in 1836.'[205] At Bolton approximately one-third fewer iron founders, engineers, millwrights and machine makers were employed in 1842 compared with the boom year of 1836, with the majority on short time, while in Glasgow the unemployed were 'principally composed of labourers; a great many of them belong to the engineering department, and many are hammermen, moulders, and mechanics of all kinds.'[206] Nonetheless the unskilled, at best little removed from a state of poverty during conditions of full employment, fared as badly. This point was well brought out in a survey, conducted in January 1842, of 147 heads of households — 122 of whom were returned as labourers — in the Chisendale Street district of Liverpool. Of this total, 54 were returned as totally unemployed and a further 42 in partial work for three or less days per week as against 33 who worked a full week. Furthermore, 49 of these families were forced to resort to begging and pawning to secure their meagre supplies of food.[207] Viewed against this backcloth the *Liverpool Mercury* scarcely exaggerated when it concluded that 'the distress now existing is unexampled, and this altogether independent of the present severe weather, though, of course, the sufferings of the poor must be greatly aggravated by it.'[208]

Crises of a fundamentally similar nature were to recur, in the mid-Victorian era, in 1847-8 when the collapse of the railway mania had adverse multiplier effects upon employment prospects in an unskilled labour market already overstocked in parts of Lancashire, the West Riding, Lanarkshire and Renfrewshire by the heavy influx of Irish Famine immigrants; in 1857-8; on a more restricted scale in 1862-64 where the American Civil War led to a considerable amount of unemployment and short-time working in the cotton towns of Lancashire and the West of Scotland, with 'the great mass of the cotton workers' in December 1862 struggling to keep their families on 'an average income . . . from all sources' of 'nearly 2s. per head per week';[209] and in 1866-7. At first glance it is less easy to decipher trends in the closing three decades of the nineteenth century. For one thing, despite decelerating production and productivity growth rates, it is impossible, in social terms, to retain the title of the 'Great Depression' for the period 1873-96, since these years coincided with the most spectacular advance in working-class real income in the entire century. Yet the significance of these gains does not obscure the fact that in the cyclical troughs of 1878-9, 1884-87 and 1892-3 considerable increases were recorded in the volume of unemployment and the incidence of working-class poverty in the principal centres of manufacturing industry. Finally, in the last decade of our period, the downturns in the economy which occurred in 1904-5 and 1907-9 led to much social suffering which the efforts of private philanthropy and — in the last instance — of the Unemployed Workmen Act did little to contain.

Valuable insights into the human misery which resulted from these later periods of cyclical dullness can again be gained from the columns of the local press, reports of trade unions and relief committees, statements from Poor Law officials, and, from 1904 onwards, from the campaigning of Unemployed Workers' and Right to Work Committees. Among other things such sources dealt with the length, and nature, of a particular trough, questions of rent arrears and other forms of debt, the role of the pawnshop, and the drastic reshaping of dietary patterns under the grinding pressures of want. This type of evidence which forms the raw materials from which most historical studies of poverty are written, needs, however, to be supplemented, where possible, by the testimony of the poverty-stricken themselves. And this task can be better performed for the cyclically unemployed than for the casualities of any of the other types of unemployment which have been discussed in this chapter, primarily because letters to local relief funds have on occasion survived the ravages of time. In one sense, of course, such correspondence is biased since it tends to be drawn overwhelmingly from the ranks of the unskilled. Nonetheless, after making due allowance for that fact, it is clear that the writers rarely over-stressed the manner in which poverty manifested itself in their lives, not merely because their claims were usually subject to detailed investigation but also because the letters themselves convey a sense of the immediacy and sharpness of a personal crisis.

This point is well brought out in the invaluable collection of letters addressed to the Lord Provost's Funds in Glasgow during the 1907-10 slump which struck Clydeside's heavy engineering and ship-building industries with devastating effect. On that occasion individuals from diverse backgrounds were united in their descriptions of the fearsome social repercussions of cyclical unemploy-ment. Alfred Dailkin, an engineer who, by October 1908, had been out of work for eight months, had 'sold all my furniture except a few things. I had to leave my last house because I was unable to pay my rent. I have 4 Children one is working for 5/6 per week I am in no clubs. I have nothing coming in myself, I am very sorry I have got to ask you [the Relief Committee], for assistance. I must have something at once. I have nothing in the house.' Even more press-ing were the needs of the family of Mrs. Hugh Quinn:

> I am writing to let you know that My husband was payed off last November and we have received since then [relief] tickets at the rate of three shillings a week and that was only five weeks. I have got a paper to be put out of the house and I have a little boy about five years of age and he hasn't got boots to put on. I think it is terrible to be put out and a boy with bare feet. I am as deserving case as any other one. My Husband has tried every way to find out about to get tickets and of no use. I am going to appeal to you. I know you will be able to help us for tickets for if my husband could find work I wouldn't need help. I will be very thankful to you.

With others — as with J. Chalmer — the appeal for assistance was more tersely expressed: 'I have not had any food in the house for 3 day and has pledge all I can pledge and has been out of work for 9 months and cant get any thing to do.[210] Yet however brief or lengthy such personal testimonies were, they underlined the point that in the early years of this century whole sections of the cyclically unemployed were unable to live at the humble level of General William Booth's 'cab horse charter'. For theirs was a poverty which expressed itself not in terms of marginal hardships but of a lack of the basic necessities of life.

Chapter 3
Other Causes
of Poverty
1830-1914

Adverse family circumstances — sickness, widowhood, large families and old age — were always major causes of working-class indigence. Rowntree, for example, discovered that the death of the head of the household accounted for 15.63 per cent, the illness or old age of the chief wage earner for 5.11 per cent, and largeness of family for 22.16 per cent, of the primary poverty which existed in York in 1899.[1] Expressed in another form, almost forty-three per cent of those who were inadequately nourished were in this state because of circumstances over which they had little control. Nor was the experience of York unique in this specific area of suffering. As Table 1 indicates, Bowley and Burnett-Hurst in 1913 found that four areas with very different socio-economic structures — Northampton dominated by the shoe industry, the urban district of Stanley by coal-mining, Warrington where the iron industry was a major employer of male labour and Reading with its biscuit factories — were beset by an identical social problem. But these twentieth-century investigators, while employing a more sophisticated methodology, in one sense simply confirmed the earlier work of Charles Booth who, in the late 1880s had concluded that in the East End of London the prime cause of poverty among twenty-seven per cent of the households in his Classes A and B and nineteen per cent in Classes C and D was what he labelled 'questions of [family] circumstances.'

I

A serious illness contracted by the breadwinner invariably heralded the onset of a period of considerable financial strain in the households of all grades of workers, for as Lady Bell remarked,

we forget how terribly near the margin of disaster the man, even the thrifty man, walks,

Table 1

Principal Causes of Immediate Poverty,
according to Rowntree's Primary Poverty Standard

Immediate Causes of Primary Poverty	Northampton	Warrington	(Percentages) Stanley[1]	Reading
Chief Wage-earner dead	21	6	3	14
Chief Wage-earner ill or old	14	1	6	11
Chief Wage-earner regularly employed:—				
Wages insufficient for 3 children but 4 children or more in the family	9	38	1	15
Wages sufficient for 3 children but more than 3 three in a family	35	27	1	21
All Other Causes	21	28		29
	100	100		100

1. In Stanley's cases, numbers of households quoted.

Source: A.L. Bowley and A.R. Hurst-Burnett, *Livelihood and Poverty* (1915), p.40.

who has, in normal conditions, but just enough to keep himself on. The spectre of illness and disability is always confronting the working-man; the possibility of being from one day to the other plunged into actual want is always confronting his family.[2]

Not unexpectedly, the families of the unskilled were more speedily exposed to the dire consequences which flowed form this kind of involuntary interruption of income than their skilled counterparts. In many urban areas those households of labourers which were solely dependent on the husbands' earnings, lived, during conditions of full employment, 'in a state of actual poverty or so near to that state that they are liable to sink into it at any moment.' Thus, with few resources to fall back upon — many labourers belonged to funeral, rather than sickness, insurance schemes — even a week's illness of the unskilled head of the family led to a sharp decline in an already low standard of living, with 'short rations, or running into debt, or more often both of these.'[3] The availability, however, of this last source of assistance was more limited than Rowntree implied since the shopkeeper's evaluation of the credit rating of customers was largely determined by their economic status within the community. Whenever credit was forthcoming to provide a modicum of food to meet the family's needs during such a crisis, it would usually be restricted in

Table 2

Principal Causes of Poverty in the East End of London

(Percentages)

	Classes A and B		Classes C and D		
Loafers	4		—		
Casual Work	43)		—)		
Irregular Work, Low Pay	9)		—)		Questions of
Small Profits	3)	55	5)	68	Employment
Low Pay, Regular Earnings	—)		20)		
Irregular Earnings	—)		43)		
Drink	9)		7)		Questions
		14		13	of
Drunken or Thriftless Wife	5)		6)		Habit
Illness or Infirmity	10)		5)		Questions
Large Family	8)		9)		of
		27		19	Circumstances
Illness or large family, combined with irregular Earnings	9)		5)		
		100		100	

Source: C. Booth, *Life and Labour of the People in London*, Vol. 1 (1892), pp. 146-7.

amount and relatively short-lived. But, independent of the Poor Law, there were a few other expedients open to the sick person to mitigate the worst effects of primary poverty in the life of his family. Indeed, of the bleak choices open before him, only two had something to commend them. He might, in some of the major cities, seek assistance from one or more of the multifarious charities which were designed to assist the sick. Alternatively he could turn to the pawn-shop. None the less while the sick themselves accepted the pawnshop as a well trusted palliative at times of searing distress, its overall impact in improving their lot was slight. Firstly, resort to the pawnbroker stripped their homes of most of their remaining possessions at a time when they were needed most. Secondly, because of the endemic poverty of the unskilled, the amount which could be realised from this type of transaction was usually small. Finally, when the individual was restored to health, unredeemed pledges represented a burden of debt which had to be cleared if his family and his home were to be restored to their former state. Not surprisingly, when placed against this sombre back-ground, any illness amongst the unskilled which lasted for more than a month could reduce the family to virtual starvation levels. In the moving words of a tubercular slop tailor, interviewed by Mayhew in 1848,

I went on for two years working away, though I was barely able, and, at last, five weeks ago, I was dead beat. I couldn't do a stitch more, and was obliged to take to my bed. Since then we have been living on what we pawned. There was nothing else to be done, and as a last resource we have got up a raffle. We [the slop tailors] generally do assist one another, if we can; but we are all so poor we have scarcely a penny for ourselves, any of us. I have come down to my very last now, and if I don't get better in health what will become of us all I don't know. We can't do without something to eat. My children cry for victuals as it is, and what we shall do in a little while is more than I can say.[4]

A point was thus often reached — and in some unskilled households at an early stage of the illness — when the assistance of the Poor Law had to be invoked. And the extant data clearly highlight the pauperising influence of illness: the sick, where classified, always formed a prominent element in all relief lists. In England and Wales, for instance, from forty per cent to fifty per cent of those who were in receipt of outdoor relief between 1842 and 1866 were sickness or accident cases.[5] Again, looking at those with more deep-seated health problems, 47.2 per cent of the inmates of workhouses in Lancashire and the West Riding in 1854 were non-able-bodied adults, although it is true that this term covered a broader spectrum of individuals than just the pauper sick.[6] Yet, notwithstanding these statistics, what was done to assist the breadwinner and his family was woefully inadequate in every urban area until at least the 1870s. As Flinn has demonstrated, the English Poor Law for more than three decades after the enactment of the 1834 statue failed to guarantee the impoverished victim of sickness competent standards of outdoor treatment. For one thing no attempt was made to establish a uniform code of medical practice, within the framework of the Poor Law, until 1842. But even then the positive gains remained small. Partly this stemmed from the cumbersome nature of the relief mechanism itself: the district Medical Officer had to await instructions to treat a patient from the appropriate relieving officer. But it owed more to the contemporary obsession with economy which resulted in the pauper medical service being starved of funds. As a result many poorly paid doctors were compelled to choose between the needs of the pauper class and their own standard of living since the cost of prescriptions was usually met out of the salaries paid by the Boards of Guardians. The indoor sick fared equally badly, being housed in grossly overcrowded sick wards in the workhouse — sometimes two or three to a bed — and denied the services of properly trained assistants. In Flinn's words, the indoor sick 'were cared for in conditions that were mostly a standing reproach to a nation which thought of itself civilised.'[7] And if from the 1870s onwards there were departures from the harshness of this *modus operandi* — including the use of qualified nurses, improved sick wards, the growth of separate Poor Law infirmaries and after 1885 the enfranchisement of recipients of medical relief — glaring deficiencies still remained in the opening years of this century. In particular those who depended, during illness, upon outdoor relief for the support of themselves and their families were given a level of benefit which left them below that, in Rowntree's basic definition of the term, was a subsistence standard of existence.

A parallel course of development can be discerned in Scotland although improvements in the treatment of the indoor sick were, after 1870, on a much less extended scale than in England. But what was of equal import, until the passing of the Scottish Poor Law Act in 1845 such assistance as was rendered to sickness cases was, from a social point of view, rudimentary in the extreme. Prior to that statute medical treatment was rarely available to the working-classes over vast areas of the Scottish countryside. Yet even in the major towns, where affairs were somewhat better ordered, no humane or consistent policy of treating the sick poor emerged. George Small, Treasurer of the Edinburgh Charity Workhouse, informed the 1844 Inquiry into the Scottish Poor Laws that it was not usual to give any form of medical relief to outdoor paupers in that city.[8] In Glasgow on the other hand defects in the relieving mechanism rather than an objection to outdoor medical relief *per se* often acted against the best interests of the infirm. To quote the evidence of Dr. Fleming,

> in cases of sickness, the district surgeons [attached to the Town's Hospital] do not attend till they receive an order from an elder; and poor people often do not know who their elder is . . . The poor, in moving from place to place, have often a difficulty in knowing the elder of the district. I have seen disease far advanced before medical aid was applied for, and the reason assigned was that they did not know who the elder was.[9]

This, however, was only one of the drawbacks in the pre-1845 Scottish system. An equally popular target of attack for reformers was the parsimony of the financial aid granted to those who were in any way incapacitated. In Edinburgh, for example, it was maintained in 1840 that

> the food of such aged or infirm persons as are dependent on parochial relief, is permanently scanty in the extreme; indeed, those who do not receive additional aid from private benevolence are scarcely one remove from absolute starvation — and there are many such.[10]

The fundamental inequity of such a system of relief was obvious: it pressed most severely upon those whose needs were greatest and whose private resources were least within the pauper class. Above all this meant the permanently disabled who, according to Alison, could anticipate receiving, in Edinburgh and Glasgow, a 'pension' of roughly 1s. per week.[11] And to qualify for this sum, a single person — a married couple could expect from 1/6d. to 2s. weekly in the cities — had to have little prospect of being reabsorbed into the labour market.[12] For the sick paupers themselves, therefore, the social environment created by such close control over expenditure was bleak. For even with supplementation from charity or with some measure of assistance from relatives, such benefits were totally incapable of guaranteeing their recipients a sufficiency of the bare necessities of life.

Yet for all but the chronically sick, illness still represented an admittedly acute, but temporary, crisis in the lives of the working classes. Widowhood or the desertion of his family by a husband on the other hand could result in the permanent impoverishment of the family or, where it occurred in old age, of the surviving partner. Of these two routes to poverty, it is easier to be precise about the economic dislocation produced by the death of the male head of the household since, apart from the information on the plight of widows embodied in some of the social inquiries of the 1840s, it is possible, at certain points in time, to draw the proximate boundaries of this particular problem. Hutchins, for example, calculated that in 1901 6.4 per cent of married women between the ages of 35 and 45 were widowed. Thereafter the statistical chances of experiencing widowhood rose sharply. Between the ages of 45 and 55, 15.8 per cent of married females had lost their partners through death; between 55 and 65, 31.4 per cent; between 65 and 75, 52.1 per cent; and finally over 75, 72.6 per cent.[13] On the other hand it is impossible to quantify, in any meaningful sense, the extent of wife desertion in Britain for any year covered by this study. All that can be confidently asserted is that the problem was sufficiently common to attract the attention of contemporary social commentators — it was pointed out, for instance, that of 2240 females applying for the first time to Glasgow Parish for poor relief in 1905-6, 19.7 per cent had been abondoned by their husbands[14] — and that in some respects their lot was even harder to bear than that of the widow because they were less generously treated by the Poor Laws of England and Scotland. Bearing this last point in mind, I intend, in the ensuing discussion, to concentrate largely upon the socio-economic consequences of widowhood, although in relation to Poor Law policy some attention must be paid to the question of how the treatment of the deserted wife diverged from that of her widowed sister.

In working-class society the economic impact of widowhood was immediately felt. Everywhere the loss of the adult wage-earner's income pushed the widow with young children and her aged counterpart periously close to, or below, the primary poverty line. Inevitably, therefore, many were compelled to seek work in an endeavour to reverse the abrupt fall in their standard of living. In Glasgow in 1911 seven per cent of the gainfully employed female population had been widowed, or, viewed from another perspective, twenty-six per cent of all widows in the city were classified as workers.[15] Again, a sample of home workers, taken in Birmingham in 1906, showed that forty-six per cent of those who answered the questionnaire were either widows or deserted wives.[16] Nevertheless these data probably underestimate the numbers of those in each of these categories who were employed in a given year since much home work, one of the principal outlets for women with dependent children, tended to be organised on a casual or seasonal basis, with the result that a sizable part of its workforce failed to return itself as gainfully employed. Moreover, such statistics make no allowance for widows who were fulfilling a specifically economic function — for instance, child-minding for a married daughter in the textile districts — within the homes of their kin.[17] Finally, they can by very definition take no account of the doctrine of intention — that is, of widows who sought work but who, because of the distinctive socio-economic characteristics of an area, such as coal-mining districts with very low female activity rates, were unable to obtain it.

During the 1830s, 1840s and 1850s this movement of widows from the domestic hearth into the labour market was probably accelerated by the prevailing belief of many Poor Law administrators that outdoor relief to widows — and in 1840-46 widows with dependants accounted for between seventeen per cent and twenty per cent of all adult outdoor cases in England and Wales[18] — should act as a supplement to wages, and then only for a limited period, rather than be sufficient by itself to guarantee an above subsistence diet and adequate supplies of clothing. Thus in Edinburgh in the early 1840s a widow with one child could only initially expect to receive around 1s., or with three children about 1/8d. per week for six weeks.[19] In Glasgow she would be no better placed: a widow with three dependants under the age of ten would be given 10s. per month by the parochial authorities and 'if necessary, she will have 10s at each term to enable her to pay her rent.' But it was argued that — albeit without any attempt being made to test the validity of the argument — this last contingency would rarely arise because 'she is . . . likely to get partial employment in a silk factory, and it is not likely she will require anything in the way of rent.'[20] In Scotland, therefore, the working widow whose earnings were on occasion supplemented by meagre 'doles' of outdoor relief was a reality in most of the principal areas of urban settlement under both the pre- and post-1845 systems of Poor Law management. In England and Wales a similar practice, already firmly established at the time of the 1834 Act,[21] continued to flourish for almost three and a half decades after that. The essence of this system was neatly summarised by the personal testimony of an Irish widow with four children, resident in the town of Bradford, in 1849. In her words,

> The people at the [worsted] mill were very kind . . . They took the little boy [her son], and set him to easy work, and gave him 2s. a week. Then the manager said I might come into the mill and see him, and try if I couldn't learn to do something myself. So I got to know how to pick lumps out of the slubbings, and first I got 5s.6d., and last week I was raised to 6s.; so we have now 8s. a week . . . Well, sir, the parish are very good to me, and give me 3s. a week — 2s. for the rent and 1s. for coals — and we live and clothe ourselves on the other 8s.

But, significantly enough, the family remained tied to the monotonous diet of the poverty stricken: 'we live chiefly on bread. I get a stone and a half of flour every week, and I bake it on Sundays. Then we have a little tea or coffee, and sometimes we have a little offal meat, because it's cheap.'[22]

Yet notwithstanding the modest scale of this Poor Law subsidy, attitudes towards widowhood underwent change over time. Particularly in England and Wales there were strenuous attempts in the 1870s and 1880s to make the condition of widows 'less eligible' by offering specific categories and/or their children the workhouse rather than what was palpably a grant in aid of wages. According to Longley, one of the architects of this deterrent approach to the social difficulties of widowhood, 'the general sympathy for widows had suggested a lax administration of relief to them, and guardians allowed the individual interests of the applicants to outweigh public considerations.' Simply put, outdoor relief had led to the emergence of major abuses. It had multiplied the numbers of widows who availed themselves of this facility — in London alone in 1872-3 one-third of all outdoor cases consisted of 'widows and their dependent children'; — it undermined thrift and the resolve of widows 'to obtain an independent livelihood'; and, lastly, it prevented the wages of those in full employment from rising to their natural level. Hence from the early 1870s strenuous attempts were made to persuade increasing numbers of guardians to revert to the work-house test as a test of indigence. And while this new orthodoxy was never accepted in every area, its success, in the eyes of the Poor Law Inspectorate, was amply demonstrated by the steady fall in the total of widows receiving any form of outdoor assistance from the poor rate. Whereas 53,502 widows were on outdoor relief lists in England and Wales on 1st Janaury 1873, the comparable figure on 1st January 1894 was 38,599.[23] From the mid-1890s, however, there was a further switch of emphasis. Outdoor relief came back into favour in certain areas while in some unions benefits were raised. But assessed overall there was still no sign in England and Wales that widows with dependants, who on 1st Janaury 1907 comprised seventy-seven per cent of the able-bodied females on the outdoor roll,[24] were allotted a sum which would have enabled them, unaided, to raise their families out of a state of poverty. North of the Border the widow was slightly better situated, for by 1908 it was generally accepted that 'the amount of [outdoor] relief given [in Scotland] is uniformly higher' than in England.[25] Even here, however, with the possible exception of the Special Roll, instituted in Glasgow in 1902, to persuade 'deserving' cases to stay at home to look after their children, it is impossible to accept that outdoor relief raised many families above the poverty line, particularly in those localities, Dundee and Edinburgh among them, where the need to correlate the scale of relief to basic needs was 'much neglected.'[26] Finally, deserted wives throughout our entire period, were rarely offered outdoor relief in Scotland, while in England and Wales the Local Government Board Circular of 1871 took a similarly hard line, urging that such females should be denied all forms of outdoor assistance during their first year of separation.[27] Given this sombre backcloth, the decision of many working-class widows and deserted wives to seek paid employment rather than apply for the uncertain bounty of the poor rate becomes easier to understand.

It would be quite wrong, however, to conclude that entry into the labour market solved the underlying economic problems of widowhood or desertion. In the first place their lack of any basic skills pushed the majority of widows into a relatively narrow range of occupations, all of which paid badly. Pre-eminent among them were charing, washing and those workshop or home-based trades which were associated with the sweated system. Of 1398 heads of households who were returned as widows and single women in a survey of

Bristol's working classes in 1838-9, 272 were charwomen; 124, sempstresses and dressmakers; and 104, laundresses.[28] Again, over one-third of 151 widows with dependants who were listed in an investigation into social conditions in St. George's in the East, London, in the late 1840s, were classified as needle-women, 20 as charwomen, 11 as washerwomen, and a further 13 as laundry-women.[29] Mayhew's roughly contemporaneous inquiry into London's poor underlined the accuracy of one aspect of these findings when he showed that widows were strongly represented in the sweated sectors of the tailoring, shoe-making and shirtmaking industries. As one slop-worker, employed in making soldiers' trousers, told him, 'there are many widows with young children, and they give them the seams to do, and so manage to prolong life, because they're afeard to die, and too honest to steal.'[30] This pattern of employment was to undergo no fundamental change for the remainder of our period. Charles Booth's survey of female labour in the East End of London in the late 1880s drew attention to the important role of widows in all kinds of home work, including shirt-finishing where the unskilled 'workwoman . . . is generally elderly if not aged, infirm, penniless, and a widow' who 'never expected to work for a living, and when obliged to do so has recourse to the only work she ever learnt to do.'[31] Similarly widows and deserted wives formed a significant part of Birming-ham's contingents of charwomen and home workers in the early 1800s.[32] Essentially the same picture emerged from a sample of female heads of house-holds with children who were in receipt of outdoor relief in Scotland in 1908 — the overwhelming majority of this group was widowed, — which showed that 'washing and charing' were the occupations followed by twenty-nine per cent of these women in Glasgow Parish and thirty-one per cent in the adjacent Govan Combination.[33]

In most instances the income derived from this type of work, even where augmented by assistance from kin, private charity and/or poor relief, could not remove the shadow of poverty which hung so heavily over the families of widows and deserted wives whose children were too young to enter the labour market on a full-time basis. This outcome was in part the product of those social assumptions which were accepted by middle-class and working-class men as justification for the low levels of earnings accruing to unskilled female labour. The most important of these tenets was the belief that female wages were solely for the upkeep of the single girl, living at home, until her marriage, thereby conveniently overlooking the crises of widowhood, desertion and of the married woman compelled to become the principal breadwinner after her husband had become a chronic invalid. In effect, therefore, as Hutchins pointed out, the widow with dependants was compelled to keep her family upon an income which, at best, was designed for one adult.[34] Nor was this the end of her diffi-culties. For her problems were compounded by the fact that she operated in the worst paid, and most glutted, sectors of the female labour market. Regular employment was thus difficult to obtain while casual and/or seasonal patterns of work could, for many, become the norm, with further deleterious consequences for the level of aggregate family income. Again, because of the precarious nature of their foothold in the unskilled labour market, widows and other females who were engaged in charing or home work were always likely to be amongst the first victims of a rising volume of cyclical unemployment. As Mrs. E. Conway, a widowed washerwoman from the Cowcaddens district of Glasgow, explained during the 1907-9 slump,

> I have not done any work for about 3 months I cannot get anything to do I have two girls one fourteen years the other not sixteen both delicate the youngest was working but lost her place through sickness so I have only one working just now at a very small pay and it takes it to pay the debt I fell into through idleness. I have got notice from the Factor to leave my house and I really dont know what to do I cannot get work having no trade engaged last washing.
> I have a widow householder these last thirteen years. None of my friends can help me they are too poor. As I write this I have neither fire or meat in the house.
> I put in a paper for the unemployed Lord Provost fund a . . . while ago but I have never has any one from the fund to call on me when I put in my paper my girl was giving me 5/- I am now getting six shillings the other one is idle hoping you can help me.[35]

Finally, the socio-economic position of the widow was not helped by the progressive erosion outside London of home work in the post-1890 world.

In the last analysis, therefore, widowhood or desertion usually meant, for those who belonged to the unskilled section of working-class society, material deprivation on the grand scale which would only be alleviated if and when dependants became wage-earners. For the Bradford mill worker whose case has already been cited, it meant a poor diet and furnishings of the most basic kind — a deal table, 'a faded bit of carpeting', and a bed, to serve a family of five, all of which were provided by 'a good gentleman' at a total cost, in the late 1840s, of 15s.[36] The starkness of this inventory of goods was, however, surpassed by that of one of Mayhew's interviewees, a widow striving to support herself making the worst paid kind of convict uniforms:

> there was no table in the room; but on a chair without a back there was an old tin tray, in which stood a cup of hot, milkless tea, and a broken saucer, with some half dozen small potatoes in it. It was the poor old soul's dinner. Some tea leaves had been given to her, and she had boiled them up again to make something like a meal. She had not even a morsel of bread. In one corner of the room was a hay mattress rolled up.[37]

That these microcosmic views of poverty were not unrepresentative of the general plight of unskilled working-class widows in the 1840s was amply demonstrated by the investigation mounted in St. George's in the East, London, where it was revealed that aggregate family earnings of 98 out of 151 households of widows 'with incumbrances', were under 10s. per week; that 86 possessed a solitary bed serving 2.8 persons per household; that 85 families could only afford to rent a single room which accommodated 3.1 individuals; and that the clothing of 81 households was described as 'insufficient but clean' and of a further 15 as 'insufficient and dirty.'[38] Moreover, there is little in the evidence to indicate that in the post-1850 era the lot of this section of society underwent substantial improvement. It is clear, for example, that the 'census' of the unemployed, carried out in the Lisson Grove district of London — admittedly one of the most deprived areas of the capital — during 'the winter . . . of exceptional severity' of 1895, included many widows with dependant children whose material possessions could amount to as little as 'an egg-box, a chair with no back, a kettle and a saucepan in which the woman was cooking some cods' heads for their dinner.'[39] Similarly, Dyos' analysis of the progressive deterioration of Sultan Street, Camberwell, between 1871 and 1891, into an impoverished slum highlights, at the latter date, the disproportionate number of households headed by widows, single women and married females whose husbands were living away from home.[40] But perhaps the most telling demonstration of the relationship between widowhood and primary poverty was afforded by Charles Booth's examination of the socio-economic backgrounds of those who, constituting his Class B, lived in chronic want. In every area of the London that he examined 'widows and their families' loomed large, ranging from a remarkable peak of 45.6 per cent members of that Class in Battersea, to 26.4 per cent in Central London, 18.5 in Shoreditch, 14.3 per cent in Mile End, 13.5 per cent in Hackney, 10.7 per cent in Bethnal Green, 8.8 per cent in Whitechapel, St. George's in the East and Stepney and finally, to 8.1 per cent in Poplar.[41]

Nevertheless poverty in this context involved more than simply material deprivation. For widowhood had other far-reaching social repercussions upon the whole family. In many cases there was a general tendency for the sons of working-class widows to enter a less skilled occupation than that followed by their father. I say 'general tendency' because for sons of labourers this situation obviously did not arise. But children from an artisan background were less likely to take up their deceased parent's trade, and more likely, in response to the immediacy of the pressures of poverty, to seek unskilled, and/or 'dead end', employment outlets where high initial rewards brought much needed additions to the family purse at a social cost of effectively debarring them from subsequent craft training. Unfortunately it is almost impossible to chart this intergenerational process of downward social mobility with any great degree of accuracy. But Tables 3(A) and 3(B), despite their limitations, including a failure to indicate the precise criteria which were used to place individuals into the different categories, show that the sons of those widows whose social background was probed by C.T. Parsons were less well represented in the ranks of the artisan elites of Edinburgh, Govan, Glasgow and Dundee than their fathers had been. On the other hand the evidence relating to daughters is less clear cut, although there are major methodological obstacles to be surmounted — which the data do not permit — before a meaningful comparison between male and female skilled occupations could be made. Lastly, it should be remembered that many widows of craftsmen and commercial clerks had to face the painful trauma of readjusting to a substantial decline in their own social status, which was a direct consequence of their bereavement. As Peter Fyfe noted in his survey of 660 home workers in Glasgow in 1907, while

TABLE 3(A)

The Occupations of the Fathers of those children whose widowed mothers, on outdoor relief, were included in the Sample of C.T. Parsons

(PERCENTAGES)

	Galsgow	Govan	Edinburgh	Dundee
Commercial	4	8	9	5
Skilled	51	60	47	19
Unskilled	41	25	41	67
Other Employment	4	3	3	9

Source:— *Royal Commission on the Poor Laws* Appendix Volume xxiii, 1910, *P.P.*, [Cd. 5075], p. 11.

TABLE 3(B)

Occupation of the children of those widowed mothers who had left school

(PERCENTAGES)

	Glasgow	Govan	Edinburgh	Dundee
MALE:—				
Commercial	9	7	10	–
Skilled	26	37	19	14
Unskilled	55	37	31	79
Other Employments	6	5	35	7
Unemployed	4	14	15	–
FEMALE:—				
Commercial	21	6	9	15
Skilled	33	22	19	28
Unskilled	33	19	48	34
Other Employments	5	11	12	7
Unemployed	8	42	12	16

Source:— *Ibid.*, p.50.

in the majority of instances the husbands [of the 176 widows among them] were low-skilled labourers, . . . it is not uncommon to find widows of highly skilled tradesmen. We found . . . among the outworkers a widow of a photographer, of a jeweller, of a gas manager.[42]

It is, however, less easy to isolate old age as a cause of poverty than certain aspects of widowhood — and this for two reasons. In the first place, as has already been demonstrated, widowhood itself rather than declining physical powers could plunge many women over the age of fifty-five into a state of primary poverty. But poverty in old age was also intimately associated with the problem of sickness, some of Rowntree's Class A fell below his stringent poverty line because of the chronic illness of an elderly member of the household. Typical of those who came into this category was his first case study: 'no occupation. Married. Age 64 . . . The man has not had his boots on for twelve months. He is suffering from dropsy. His wife cleans school'.[43] The same combination of advancing years and physical affliction also played a significant role in the impoverishment of those who slept rough on the Thames Embankment. In the words of one of their number, 'I'm a confectioner by trade; I come from Dartford. I got turned off because I'm getting elderly. They can get younger men cheaper, and I have the rheumatism so bad.'[44] Nevertheless, the most decisive proof of the correlation between old age and sickness was provided not in the pages of Rowntree and General William Booth but in the quantitative returns of the Local Government Board. Thus, a single day count, taken in England and Wales on 1st September 1903, revealed that 60.6 per cent of the total number of indoor paupers who were sixty or more years of age — or 57,942 out of 95,684 cases — 'could not satisfactorily take care of themselves owing to mental or physical infirmity.'[45] In other words, as with low pay and underemployment, old age, sickness and widowhood were mutually reinforcing, rather than completely separate, causes of poverty.

The second difficulty is more formidable since it concerns the definition of old age itself. Most historians of social policy have, not unnaturally, tended to discuss the concept in the context of the vigorous debate which was waged from the 1890s onwards about the desirability or otherwise of non-contributory state pensions for those who were over sixty-five years of age. Yet, despite the enthusiastic backing given to such a proposal by the trade union movement through the National Association of Organised Labour For Promoting Old Age Pensions For All, old age assumed a different meaning in the minds of whole sections of the working classes. Partly this was a reflection of life expectancy. In 1838-54 the average length of a man's life in England and Wales was 39.91 years, that of a woman's 41.85 years; by 1891-1900 the comparable statistics were 44.12 and 47.77 respectively.[46] Given that these figures include members of the upper and middle classes whose life span was greater than that of the working classes, it is clear that for the working man old age began long before sixty-five. This much was acknowledged both by the pension schemes of some of the skilled trade unions — the Amalgamated Society of Brass and other Metal Workers started paying superannuation benefits on member's fifty-fifth birthday[47] — and by the comments of individual union leaders. John Cronin, for instance, speaking in his capacity as General Secretary of the Associated Society of Millmen in Scotland, informed an audience of Coatbridge ironworkers in 1894 that Chamberlain's plan for contributory pensions, to commence at sixty-five, 'was of little use to iron and steel workers, as not five per cent of them lived to be sixty-five years.'[48] But in addition to the problems raised by a low level of life expectancy, the question of defining the term is further complicated by the fact that, in working-class eyes, old age was often taken to refer to that point in time, which varied from trade to trade, when the worker's hold on full-time employment in his chosen occupation started to slacken. Among those who were engaged in jobs requiring considerable muscular strength, this process could begin as early as their fortieth year. Of coal-backers, for instance, who carried coal from the ship to waggons at the quayside, it was written in the late 1840s that 'after a man turns forty he is considered to be past his work, and to be very liable to . . . accidents,' including, under this heading, 'the bursting of blood-vessels.'[49] Similarly in the first half of the nineteenth century a hewer in the Durham and Northumberland coal industry 'is past his prime at forty.'[50] The same pattern can be discerned among skilled hands in the iron industry where many puddlers were compelled to abandon their trade at fifty.[51] In short, whenever employment was equated with physical prowess, there was bound to be a diminution in work outlets for a wide range of skilled workers which could be casually related to their own declining powers. Matters were little better in the 'dangerous trades' where the individual's working life — and indeed, life itself — could be terminated long before he had attained his sixty-fifth year. For example, it was claimed in the early 1900s that 'there are very few old men' in Manchester's bleach and dye works:

> a man has to give up at fifty; he cannot do the work. . . most cannot stand it after about fifty. You hear them say: "I'm done; I'm off to the workhouse." The conditions are extremely bad for health in some departments. Then the sulphur is terribly bad for the men, and lots of cheap dyes are got up by these means.[52]

Again in the india-rubber industry 'the naphtha makes them ill . . . Men suffer from mixing the dough and there is danger of lead poisoning. There are no old men in the trade, they are old at fifty.'[53] Finally, and particularly from the 1890s onwards, the speeding up of work and the increasing use of machinery threatened to shorten the working life of the artisan. As W.J. Davis put it when listing the dissatisfactions of the working classes in 1902,

> the displacement of labour by machinery, and the consequent difficulty of finding regular employment, is one. Another is that men are thought to get old sooner than years ago. A mechanic or a labourer, if on the wrong side of forty-five years of age, when applying for work, is often told that he is too old.[54]

None the less, while old age, assessed from a working-class perspective, was at once a more flexible, and less easily quantifiable, term than it ever was in the hands of middle-class reformers, who tended to regard sixty-five or seventy as the appropriate starting-point for state pensions, most of the date upon which a discussion of the relationship between advancing years and poverty must be based, relates specifically to those who were sixty years of age and above. Pre-eminent among such sources is the considerable volume of information collected by the English and Scottish Poor Law authorities about the incidence of pauper-sim in old age. A series of one day censuses of sixty-five plus pauperism, be-ginning with the Burt return of 1st August 1890, showed that a considerable proportion of the total population of England and Wales who belonged to these age brackets, was in receipt of either indoor or outdoor relief. Looking at the data for 1890-1903 in more detail, it is remarkable how static the percentage of the 'sixty-five plus' population who were on the poor rate, remained, fluctuating from a low point of 18.0 per cent (1st August 1890) to a high of 19.4 per cent, recorded on 1st January 1892.[55] And virtually all of that difference stemmed from the fact that the general trend was for pauperism to increase during winter and to fall in the summer. In Scotland, with its different system of administration, the corresponding figures were markedly lower, one day counts in 1893 and 1894 revealing that 108.67, and 111.09, persons per 1000 people who were sixty-five or more years of age, were paupers.[56]

It was primarily on the basis of the English data for the early 1890s that Charles Booth advanced three general propositions about the poverty-stricken state of the elderly. Firstly, he concluded that eight-ninths of such pauperism must be specifically attributed to the infirmities associated with old age rather than with any moral defects in the pauper class.[57] Secondly, after taking into account the relatively high percentage of the 'sixty-five plus' population who lived in comfortable circumstances, he accepted that between 40 per cent and 45 per cent of those who belonged to the ranks of small traders and working classes had some form of contact with the poor law after they had attained that age. Finally, there was much hidden poverty among the elderly which was quite untouched by this form of institutional relief. As he put it, 'the most acute poverty amongst the old is not coincident with the most widespread pauperism . . . In the towns poverty is most acute; in the country places it is most successfully relieved.'[58] Booth's analysis, however, was not allowed to go unchallenged. Charles Loch, Secretary of the Charity Organisation Society and a sturdy exponent of self help, argued that these statistics exaggerated the amount of indigence amongst the elderly and effectively concealed the long-term trend which was towards less dependence upon the poor rate in old age. According to Loch's own calculations, whereas the 'percentage of paupers 60 and upwards to population 60 and upwards' stood at a figure of 21.7 per cent — on a single day count basis — in 1871, by 1891 it had fallen to 14.0 per cent and was to decline still further to 13.8 per cent at the end of the next decade, before rising slightly to 14.7 per cent in 1905.[59] That these were at best only proximate estimates Loch himself acknowledged, since his pre-1891 calculations were based upon certain assumptions about the age composition of 'not able-bodied' paupers, and not upon actual day counts.[60] But to Loch this did not invalidate the overall pattern and the underlying powerful social forces which shaped its contours. In particular, the enforcement of the workhouse test as a test of need had done much to reduce, where applied, old age pauperism to a residual problem. If only, therefore, it were adopted in every Poor Law Union,

> it is not too much to say that in a comparatively short time instead of one in seven or 14 per cent of the population over sixty being paupers, old age pauperism might be reduced in the country to a minimum, and in the metropolis and other towns by more than half.[61]

The fact that such fundamentally divergent conclusions could be extracted from the extant statistics means that the evidence must be handled with care. But a full review of these and other data indicates that more reliance can be placed upon Booth's lugubrious assessment of old age than the roseate optimism of Loch. Thus, while Loch was undoubtedly correct in ascribing the 1871-91 decline in the proportion of the population who resorted to poor relief to the crusading zeal of the English Local Government Board, with its fierce denunciation of outdoor 'doles', he made a fundamental error in assuming that the incidence of poverty amongst the elderly could be equated with their willingness to enter the workhouse. In reality, before and after those two decades, the workhouse was an institution which the poor would go to considerable lengths to avoid, including living at well below the poverty line. Charles Booth was not giving vent to his own prejudices but summing up the findings of widely scattered correspondents when he wrote that 'as regards entering the workhouse, it is the one point on which no difference of opinion exists among the [aged] poor. The aversion to the 'House' is absolutely universal, and privation will be endured by the people rather than go into it.'[62] Now was this an exclusively English phenomenon? Captain Miller argued in 1844 that aged persons in Glasgow much preferred to be relieved at home 'if their wants could be properly supplied', while Sir John McNeill reported from the Highlands in 1869 that,

> we find the greatest difficulty in inducing elderly women, especially those who have cots of their own, to go into the poor house, even when they are in a most miserable condition. . . They have a most catlike tenacity to the cottage they have lived in.[63]

Rather, therefore, than concluding that indigence could only be accurately measured where the workhouse test was rigorously applied, Loch ought to have accepted that the size of the problem was much broader than his own interpretation of the statistics suggested.

The validity of this last point can best be illustrated not so much from the writings of Booth who continued to base much of his analysis upon Poor Law returns, as from subsequent revelations about the incidence of poverty — as distinct from pauperism — among the elderly. Rowntree, for example, calculated that 21.39 per cent of York's 'sixty-five plus' population was directly affected, in 1899, by either primary or secondary poverty.[64] But equally significant was the light which was shed upon the question when a state non-contributory pension of 5s. per week was introduced in 1908 for those over seventy who could survive rigid character and means tests. For quite apart from the vast numbers who were rendered ineligible for the benefit as a result of being paupers — on 1st September 1903 19.7 per cent of the population of England and Wales aged between seventy and seventy-five, 26.1 per cent of these between seventy-five and eighty, and 30.2 per cent of those who were above eighty, were in receipt of poor relief,[65] — the fact that roughly 27 per cent of the 'seventy plus' age group in the United Kingdom, in all slightly less than half a million people, were the beneficiaries of this new departure in social policy was a conclusive demonstration 'of the need for state relief and of the depths of severe, hidden, respectable poverty among the aged.'[66] In other words, a sizable proportion of the elderly, before the advent of state pensions, had viewed the Poor Law with the same antipathy as the Lancastrian working man of an earlier generation who had 'as soon ha' gone to prison as do it . . . just to go up there before the [Poor Law] Board [of Guardians] , – see what they thinks of poverty there, – then, maybe, you'll know why we working men had rather clem (starve) than trouble them.'[67]

The poverty of the elderly was, of course, in large measure the product of the distinctive character of the 'sixty plus' population. For the greater longevity of females meant that they were not merely in numerical terms the predominant sex but that if they were living alone – whether widows, deserted wives or single persons, they were more likely, with advancing years, to be undernourished as their work patterns became more irregular. Among those worst affected, 'a class in the lowest depth of poverty which stops just short of destitution,' were the elderly inmates of the Salvation Army Shelter at Stepney who, in the early 1900s, 'by living on the minimum of food and being content with the barest form of shelter and the meanest of clothing' – in themselves a reflection of the meagre rewards of charing, washing, hawking, flower selling and 'work in the seasons at pea-shelling and walnut picking' – 'manage to escape pauperism.'[68] But as we have seen, only marginally better situated were ageing widows and spinsters who eked out a miserable existence in the sweated trades, haunted by the fear, as one of their number expressed it in the late 1840s, that they would ultimately be compelled to acknowledge that 'for . . . old age there is nothing but the workhouse.'[69]

Elderly men, if living alone or with their wives, were equally hard pressed if they came from the ranks of the unskilled. For in the unskilled labour market old age was unmistakably associated with casuality of employment. In the docks, for example, the point was reached, sometimes before and sometimes around the age of sixty, when the individual found himself in the position of the Liverpool docker who 'gets practically no work . . . His age . . . is against him, but besides this he has the look of a permanent "out-of-work", and no foreman would be likely to pick him unless very short of men.'[70] This experience was repeated in the lives of other unskilled groups for whom advancing years meant employment as hawkers, billposters, night-watchmen and in Coventry and elsewhere 'calling artisans in early morning', although by the 1890s it was claimed that 'steam whistles have superseded' that particular outlet for casual earnings.[71] This brief summary of unskilled casual openings, with their below subsistence incomes, which were available to the aged, relates specifically to the 1890s. But fifty years earlier the same basic trend obtained. For instance, many farm labourers came to Edinburgh from the surrounding countryside in the 1840s in search of less arduous, but more casual, work. And, as John MacKay indicated, they were on the whole successful, 'for there are many light sources of work in Edinburgh, such as acting as porters, running messages. There are a great number of employments about little jobs in Edinburgh for such people.[72] Exceptions to this general picture of casualisation were relatively few, although elements of paternalism were sometimes discernible in the iron and steel ship-building yards of Clydeside and Birkenhead and in some of the coalfields where light, unskilled, but regular employment was offered to small numbers of elderly men 'who have grown grey in the[ir] service.'[73]

Nor was the lot of the majority eased to any marked extent by financial assistance from the Poor Law. Where such aid was given to the aged in Scotland, it was often, in the years before the 1845 Scottish Poor Law Act, derisory in amount. This was particularly true of the Highlands where the annual contri-bution to their well-being could be as little as the 20s. allocated to bed-ridden old men in the parish of Alness (Easter Ross) or the 10s. to 11s. to elderly parishioners in Sandwick (Shetland), although in this last instance some supple-mentation could be secured from licensed begging.[74] These token payments were, of course, the inevitable sequel to the great emphasis which was placed in a rural context upon meeting the requirements of the poor from voluntary contributions. But in Scottish urban society, where the levying of an assess-ment was usually an integral part of poor law practice in the pre-1845 era, benefits still fell far short of subsistence, as in the case of Glasgow where it was admitted that the sums, ranging 'from 4s. to 6s. a month,' which were distri-buted to elderly outdoor paupers, 'cannot support such persons.'[75] In England and Wales, however, the scale of payments to the same grade of pauper was certainly more generous in the early part of our period when figures of 1/6d. to 2/6d. per week were sometimes mentioned. On the other hand, many of those who were over the age of sixty suffered severely in several, but not all, areas — among them Birmingham and some of the Poor Law Unions in the East End of London[76] — when during the 1870s, 1880s and early 1890s the 'undeserving' aged poor were cut off from outdoor relief, and compelled to enter the workhouse if they required assistance. Only in the late 1890s and early 1900s, when more humane attitudes informed the treatment of the aged, was there some indication that these attitudes were being relaxed. And even then the considerable degree of autonomy exercised by each Board of Guardians meant that the system of workhouse deterrence was not everywhere abandoned. Yet where more flexible attitudes operated, it is a mistake to believe that outdoor relief was adequate; for in England and Scotland — the two systems had grown closer together over time — the levels of outdoor assistance — usually between 2/6d. and 3s. per week — still did not suffice to raise its largely unskilled recip-ients, without outside earnings or supplementary aid, above the primary poverty line.

Outside the labour market the only source of supplementary aid which was of general application — private charity including almshouses, coal and bread charities had at best a marginal impact upon the overall problem of poverty amongst the aged — was that which was provided by the elderly person's own family. In some instances such aid assumed the form of a periodic money allowance to meet a specific contingency, such as part of the rent, although the limited means of working-class sons and daughters, often with children of their own to rear, effectively excluded any widespread adoption of this expedient.[77] When, therefore, attempts were made to alleviate the wants of the aged they were usually confined to an offer of food and shelter in their offspring's own home, with the unwritten assumption that any income accruing to elderly parents, whether in the shape of outdoor relief or, after 1908, an old age pension, would largely or wholly be devoted towards the budget of the enlarged household.[78] This practice seems to have been well developed in Lancashire where thirty-two per cent of Preston's 'sixty-five plus' population who were examined in Anderson's sample of the 1851 Census, resided with a married or widowed child and a further thirty-six per cent with unmarried children.[79] This was not in itself a surprising development since, in an area with a high female involvement in the labour market, aged parents – and particularly a widowed mother – could undertake household and child-minding duties while daughter or daughter-in-law worked in a mill. None the less this kind of arrangement in other areas – and almost certainly in Lancashire itself – owed more to the sense of social obligation to one's kin than to specifically economic forces. For example, it was asserted in the late 1840s that 'old pitmen' in Durham and Northumberland, living in communities with low female activity rates, 'are very generally supported in whole or in part by their grown-up families – a filial duty, the performance of which is far more common in the mining than in the manufacturing districts.'[80] Again, it was not unknown for the discharge of these filial obligations to result in the impoverishment – at least in the short-term – of the whole family.[81] To argue thus, however, is not to discount the strong influence of economic forces upon the strength of kinship links. For where grinding poverty already obtained in the homes of unskilled sons and daughters, it could either rule out any form of assistance to parents, or, if given, generate considerable social and psychological tensions among the elderly who would classify themselves as a burden upon their children.[82] It was probably for that reason that old age pensions were, in 1908-9, so rapturously greeted by sections of the aged, since in their eyes, it restored to them some of their lost independence. In the words of John MacLeod, a Gaelic-speaking bard from Shawbost, Isle of Lewis,

Like the warm wind of May serenity and hospitality are now reflected in all faces; men's spirits will no longer be affected by fear for their livelihoods, so they can now rest and sleep peacefully. The younger generation will no longer instruct the aged irately to move away from the fire and those of the latter who may even reach a hundred years need not die of starvation as food now awaits them . . . .

It is now more or less promised that poverty will disappear; the elderly man's feet will be protected from the cold and, provided the merchants of the north do not run out of butter supplies, he need no longer eat dry bread. Despite the fact that time is running out for them the condition of the aged has been considerably improved as a result of this Bill – so much so that the coming generation need no longer sing in praise of Mac Cholum Ruadh [traditionally famed for his generosity].

He who existed in a hovel, living in destitution, lacking self respect and with his home in chaos, without frown or moan, will be uplifted and his affairs will be set in order. Instead of washing in cold, or even dirty, water he will use 'Sunlight' [soap] ; he will have decent socks to clad his heels; he will have meat for his food and a tea-pot to place on his fire.[83]

The historian could not endorse in its entirety this enthusiastic verdict upon a measure which at most guaranteed a weekly pension of 10s. to an elderly couple, retained its pauper disqualification clause until January 1911 and left untouched 'old age' poverty among those who were below the age of seventy. But, stripped of its hyperbole, its emphasis is surely correct. For not merely did state pensions enable those who were living with kin, to contribute in a meaningful fashion to aggregate family income; it also permitted all its recipients to meet the hardships associated with old age with a greater degree of optimism than had occurred among any earlier generation. Yet having said that, the fact remains that the climate of expectations of the elderly was still modest, for the level of benefit was never enough by itself to remove want from their lives. As one working-class critic of Joseph Chamberlain's proposal for a contributory pension of 5s. per week commented in 1894,

a pension of less than 15s. a week was of no use. The option of that ought to be given after a man had enriched the community by his labour for say 30 years. They did not want pensions to save them from becoming paupers. They wanted pensions so that they could reasonably enjoy the closing years of their existence after a life of toil.[84]

II

Not all poverty was the product of exogenous forces which the individual was powerless to influence. It could also stem from personal failings. Indeed, until the appearance of Charles Booth's first volumes in the late 1880s and early 1890s, the self-inflicted wound was the central feature of most middle-class attempts at delineating the salient characteristics of poverty. Such a stark framework of reference had, of course, long antecedents. In the late eighteenth century it was accepted as axiomatic that most urban poverty reflected a wasteful pattern of expenditure rather than inadequate income.[85] Subsequently the complexity of some of the issues involved in this discussion of self-induced poverty were to be explored in greater detail by Colquhoun who in 1806 tried to distinguish between 'culpable' and 'innocent' indigence;[86] by Malthus who castigated the working man for his indifference to the wise counsels of prudential restraint; by the 1832-4 Royal Commission on the Poor Laws whose vigorous advocacy of 'less eligibility' and the workhouse test as the best means of containing able-bodied pauperism was based upon the belief that the Old Poor Law perpetuated the impoverishment of the working classes by destroying their moral fibre and sense of social responsibility; and, from the late 1860s onwards, by the more unbending spokesmen of the Charity Organisation Society.

Almost inevitably the plethora of literature devoted to this theme contained many generalisations which were never tested and even more solutions, often underpinned by moral judgments, which had little relevance to the condition of the working classes. But not all writers operated at the level of the sepulchral or pious platitude. A serious attempt was made to define the principal causes of self-inflicted, or what Rowntree later called secondary, poverty. In broad terms the problem was treated under two principal headings. Firstly, attention was drawn to the sizable amount of money that was squandered upon drink and gambling. Secondly, the existence of a residuum within working-class society was postulated which, for part of the period under review, was denounced for its reluctance to maximise its earnings by not seeking, or not holding on to, full-time employment.

Of those two theses the last is perhaps the easier to deal with. The concept of the residuum formed one of the main themes of the 1832-4 Poor Law Inquiry where the allowance system to the able-bodied was blamed for inhibiting labour mobility, creating an environment in which the hardworking individual was penalised for his thrift, and encouraging a long-term dependence upon the poor rate for subsistence. As Stedman Jones has shown in a London context, these fears continued to dominate middle-class thinking until at least the 1880s. During the intervening decades the residuum came to be identified with an underserving element whose main contact with the labour market was confined to those areas of economic activity where casuality of employment prevailed, although some writers sought to narrow this concept by restricting it to 'wastrels' and the criminal classes. Thus in Manchester in 1866 it was argued that 'the lowest depth' of working-class society was 'composed of the beggar or criminal class, whose offspring are brought up to beg or to steal, and to lead an utterly immoral life.'[87] On the whole, however, this circumscribed perspective was rejected in favour of the more comprehensive assessment of the residuum which has been outlined above. Partly this was because, for some, the existence of the 'criminal class' posed quite different social problems, but it owed even more to the fact that the majority of writers, including Charles Booth, treated the petty criminal and the vagrant as integral elements of an imprecisely defined residuum. What united those who subscribed to this enlarged view was the belief that its peripheral contact with the unskilled labour market was not an indication of imperfections in the market itself. Rather it was a product of deliberate consumer choice, encouraged by either assistance from the poor rate or the indiscriminate bounty of private charity. In the eyes of the Rev. J.R. Green of Stepney,

> it is not so much poverty that is increasing in the East, as pauperism, the want of industry, of thrift or self reliance — qualities which the legislation of 30 years' ago has ever since been with difficulty producing among the poor, but which melt and vanish in a couple of minutes before the certainty of money from the west . . . Some half a million people in the East End of London have been flung into the crucible of public benevolence and have come out of it simple paupers.[88]

Even more scathing was the criticism made by another opponent of the largesse which had been distributed to the unemployed by the 1866-69 Mansion House Relief Fund: 'with every gift of a shilling ticket, he had done 4d. worth of good and 8d. worth of harm. The 4d. represented the food that went into the stomach of a wretched population; the 8d., the premium given to their wasteful and improvident habits.'[89] The offensive against outdoor relief which was mounted in the 1870s and 1880s owed much of this type of analysis, in which the residuum was at once the creation of, and demoralised by, the mistakenly humane treatment of Poor Law officials. Again, the plea of the Charity Organisation Society for a scientific approach towards charitable assistance was specifically aimed at reducing the dependence of the underserving upon all forms of voluntary aid. Such a stringent policy of deterrence would, it was hoped, remove the enervating influences which had hitherto enabled the residuum to remain satisfied with a low threshold of expectations and to compel it, through self help and regular work, to improve its economic status. What had to be changed, therefore, was less the economic system and more the social values of the residuum, for in the last analysis its social problems were the creation of 'incorrect' moral attitudes rather than economic forces.

These views were to persist in certain circles until long after the 1880s. When in 1893-4 the Board of Supervision tried to break down the unemployment problem in Scotland into its component parts, it explicitly referred,

> to that large section of the fourth class, which consists of dissolute, vicious, worthless loafers, who have no wish or intention at any time to do an honest day's work for an honest day's wage, and whose highest ambitions is to procure by fair means, or otherwise, a few pence for a lodging-house bed, breakfast and supper, when these necessaries are not provided for them out of the public rates in the poorhouse or the prison,

although it was made clear that the membership of this class was much more restricted than that of the entire casual labour force.[90] Drage was equally convinced in the 1890s that irregular employment was linked with faults of character, including 'habits of intemperance, idleness, or dishonesty.'[91] Again, many witnesses before the 1905-9 Royal Commission on the Poor Laws continued to refer to the 'unsettled habits' of the residuum as a basic cause of their casual patterns of work.[92] Yet by the latter date, while *critiques* were made of 'the unemployable', a term which by the late 1890s was widely used as a synonym for the residuum, the idea of the self-inflicted wound was being slowly modified.

This shift in social thought owed everything to a fresh approach to the poverty problem. By the mid-1880s the first glimmerings of this new approach were dimly discernible when a few isolated individuals started to argue that the poverty of the residuum was not exclusively the product of personal failings which had been assiduously cultivated by ill-conceived acts of public or private benevolence. Instead more stress was placed than hitherto upon environmental influences, including bad housing, inadequate feeding and the role of heredity, in producing a residuum which was essentially an inefficient pool of labour, only likely to be fully used at times of peak demand, and which was quite incapable by its own efforts of raising itself above the poverty line. According to Arnold White, writing in 1885, forty per cent of the poor were 'physically, mentally and morally unfit, and there is nothing that the nation can do for these men except to let them die out by leaving them alone.'[93] Similarly, while Booth was to describe his Class B of irregularly employed men in bitingly moralistic language — they were a 'leisure class', 'many of' whom 'from shiftlessness, helplessness, idleness, or drink, are inevitably poor', — environmental factors also guaranteed that their low productivity — their work as 'inefficiently done, both badly and slowly' — would always confine them to the ranks of casual labour.[94] In this analysis, therefore, the deeply ingrained poverty of the majority of members of the residuum became in most circumstances less the outward sign of moral turpitude, although heavy drinking continued to be stressed, and more the penalty imposed upon them by the impersonal workings of a form of Social Darwinism. Compounding their difficulties was the chaotic nature of the casual labour market, which, with its uncertain rewards, undermined the strength, and limited the horizons, of its adherents. In a word, rather than classifying them along with other groups who were firmly placed in the category of those suffering from secondary poverty, most who belonged to the residuum had more in common with those working men who belonged to Rowntree's 'race of the unfit' and who, in normal times, lived below the level of subsistence. As Rowntree wrote,

> such men have at all times to be content with the lowest paid work, and they are the first to lose their situations as soon as there is any slackness of trade. At the time when this inquiry was being made trade was good, and probably the proportion of 'unfit' workmen who were in work was above the average. The position of these workmen is one of peculiar hopelessness. Their unfitness means low wages, low wages means insufficient food, insufficient food means unfitness for labour, so that the vicious circle is complete. The children of such parents have to share their privations, and even if healthy when born, the lack of sufficient food soon tells upon them. Thus they often grow up weak and diseased, and so tend to perpetuate the race of the 'unfit'.[95]

On the other hand the evidence which relates to drink is outwardly quite unambiguous. All the quantitative indicators point to the fact that working-class society was a society heavily addicted to drinking throughout our period. G.B. Wilson's data for liquor consumption in the United Kingdom highlight, in relation to beer alone, two distinct trends. In the first place, beer consumption rose only slowly and by no means uninterruptedly from an average of 21.6 gallons *per capita* per annum during the 1840-4 quinquennium to 22.0 gallons for 1850-4. Thereafter, however, the rate of increase was both sharper and more sustained until the record level of 33.2 gallons per head per year was reached in 1875-9. The second trend, which emerged in the 1880s, suggests that society was becoming marginally more temperate; for from the late 1870s to the mid-1890s, when the data are evaluated on a quinquennial basis, a slow decline in *per capita* intake can be observed, with the annual average for 1890-4 standing at 29.8 gallons. In the late 1890s and early 1900s there was a temporary, but scarcely spectacular, reversal of this movement, the comparable statistic for

1895-99 being 31.2 gallons, until the downward march was resumed in the last decade before the outbreak of the First World War, when a post-1870 low point was reached in 1910-14, with an average annual *per capita* consumption of 27.0 gallons. The pattern of spirits consumption followed a much less systematic course although as Table 4 indicates, the 1830s, 1850-54, 1865-79, 1890-1904 were all quinquennia when the average annual intake of spirits per head of the United Kingdom's population exceeded one proof gallon, while the post-1904 era was, as with beer, a period of increasing abstemiousness, with the lowest quinquennial average in the entire post-1830 era − 0.67 gallons *per capita* per annum − being recorded in 1910-14.

These data are of course not completely satisfactory since they do not bring out fully the r ional differences in working-class drinking habits, with the Englishman and Welshman firmly committed to beer and the Scotsman and the Irishman to whisky. Furthermore, they take no account of differences between towns of different socio-economic structure − Wilson has argued that ports and mining communities were the centres of heaviest drinking − or of any divergence in experience between rural and urban society. Moreover, they make no allowance for the home-brewing of beer which was well established in the English countryside in the pre-1850 era, or for the production of illicit spirits which, unlike the late eighteenth and early nineteenth centuries when the industry was heavily concentrated in certain towns and the Scottish Highlands and under the control of the indigenous population, had, by 1830,[96] come under the sway of Irish immigrants in their areas of heaviest settlement. Thus, in Manchester it was claimed that throughout the 1830s and 1840s the Irish monopolised the distillation and retailing of illicit spirits, frequently using as whisky hawkers 'their females' who, carrying their supplies 'in bladders with tin necks and a cork . . . retail it to the servants at back doors, in exchange for food, clothes, etc.' and to the clientele of lodging-houses and beershops where it 'fetches about half price.'[97] In Liverpool on the other hand there is fragmentary evidence to show that attempts were sometimes made to supplement home distilled supplies with poteen, smuggled through the customs in the guise of firkins of Irish butter.[98] How widespread or significant these developments were, it is impossible to calculate. But their very existence indicates that the difference between the pre- and post-1850 consumption levels of beer were narrower than the official statistics suggest, while, in the sphere of spirits consumption, a case can be made out for regarding the 1830s as the second most drunken decade of our entire period. Finally, the official data afforded no indication of how much alcohol was drunk by the separate social strata of the working classes and no insight into the dominant drinking role of the adult male.

Yet, as the whole weight of contemporary comment confirmed, heavy drinking was largely the preserve of the male head of the household.[99] Now was this surprising since the public house played a large part in shaping his social life and cultural *mores*? In the first place it was extensively used by trade

TABLE 4

Liquor Consumption in the United Kingdom 1830-1914
(Quinquennial Periods)

Years	Average yearly consumption of Spirits Proof Gallons *per capita*	Average yearly consumption of Beer Standard Gallons *per capita*
1830- 4	1.11	21.6
1835- 9	1.17	22.9
1840- 4	0.87	19.5
1845- 9	0.86	19.4
1850- 4	1.08	21.1
1855- 9	0.99	22.0
1860- 4	0.07	24.6
1865- 9	0.31	28.8
1870- 4	1.14	31.1
1875- 9	1.21	33.2
1880- 4	1.05	29.2
1885- 9	0.94	28.4
1890- 4	1.00	29.8
1895- 9	1.03	31.2
1900- 4	1.04	30.2
1905- 9	0.86	27.3
1910-14	0.67	27.0

Source: G.B. Wilson, *Alcohol and the Nation* (1940), p. 335.

unions as a 'house of call' for time-served artisans and by employers as a hiring place for certain grades of unskilled labour. But in either case — whether it was Mayhew's tailor waiting for an outlet in the 'honourable' sector of his trade or the London coalwhipper who, until he was protected by legislation in 1843, was virtually dependent upon the good-will of the publican for employment,[100] — the waiting hours were usually spent drinking, often on credit extended by the landlord. Heavy drinking, however, was not confined to those who were temporarily unemployed. For, before the beginning of effective restrictions upon licensing hours, many men fortified themselves with beer or whisky before they started their day's work. For example, the Select Committee on Railway Labourers (1946) found that there was some correlation between injuries incurred by navvies during the construction of the Sheffield and Manchester Railway tunnel and early morning visits to the beer house, while in Glasgow, before the Forbes Mackenzie Act of 1854, it was asserted, albeit with much hyperbole, that 'the morning dram was an institution with all the ordinary workmen.'[101] Again, copious supplies of beer were drunk in many parts of England during the course of the working day — among London hatters in the early 1830s 'two pots or even ten pints, a day being a frequent consumption by a man not accounted a "fuddler",' although by the late 1840s 'few' drank 'more than a pot a day whilst at work',[102] — until the more rigorous demands of factory discipline made themselves felt. Finally, the ties between drink and the work context were in some towns even more firmly cemented by the practice of paying wages in the public house.[103] But, as Brian Harrison has argued, the pub discharged, or fulfilled, equally important social functions. It served as a recreational centre at a time when alternative forms of leisure, in the pre-1870 years, were few in number; it was an avenue of temporary escape from intolerable social conditions at home — in this respect, as in so many others, the wife was less fortunate; and, until the late 1860s when there were signs of perceptible improvement, it often guaranteed to the working man a purer, and more regular supply, of refreshment than existing supplies of water.[104]

In assessing the incidence of secondary poverty in society, however, it is more difficult to decide how far this pattern changed over time. At first glance the available statistics do not lend much support to the view that the Temperance Movement in its various guises had had, as late at 1914, a significant impact upon working-class drinking customs. Nevertheless those historians who have explored the problem in depth, have argued that by the 1870s ameliorative forces were at work in British society which acted as countervailing influences to drink. Harrison has listed changing consumer spending habits; the restrictions which, from the mid-1860s onwards, were placed in England and Wales upon week-day opening hours — the check in Scotland had come a decade earlier; the development of rail travel and, after 1870, the increased range of sporting activities open to the working classes as forces which made for greater sobriety, while Dingle has emphasised that the rise of the mass-market, trends in real earnings and by the early 1900s a more rational appraisal by the working man of the relationships between drink and living standards had a similar effect for much of the 1876-1914 period.[105] Wilson, on the other hand, while laying stress upon the influence of positive forces operating in favour of a reduced consumption of alcohol, has also argued that, in this country, less socially beneficial habits, among them gambling and smoking, worked to promote the same end.[106] Indeed, gambling itself was denounced as an undesirable social development among Middlesborough's iron workers by Lady Bell; as a contributing factor in the impoverishment of many girls in London's mineral water factories who, according to O.C. Malvery, were known in the early 1900s to squander their earnings at the week-end upon horse racing; and by Rowntree as one of the principal routes to secondary poverty in York.[107] Nor was the rise of professional football from the 1890s onwards seen in a more favourable light by some critics since it could again lead to advances in real income being frittered away. In the words of W.F. Anderson, Deputy Chairman of Glasgow's Distress Committee,

> I think there is a very big proportion of these people who spend their money foolishly on Saturday, not only in drink but on sport. They do not care how much they spend in going to a football match, and in taking a cab there, and in paying for a grand stand seat, and having a fish tea after it is all over. We could do better if we could inculcate a little thrift in them.[108]

Although this last verdict was wildly exaggerated even in a Glasgow context — at the time it was delivered, 1908-9, my own team, Partick Thistle, was facing problems posed by a dwindling support, little money in the bank and lack of a ground, having to play many of its home fixtures at Ibrox Stadium, the home of Glasgow Rangers![109] — it at least demonstrated that secondary poverty was a more variegated social phenomenon than the contemporary obsession with alcohol tended to imply.

Nevertheless, despite these new forms of working-class entertainment, it is unrealistic, in the post-1870 period, to dispute the central role of drink in producing self-induced poverty. And its massive contribution can be illustrated not merely from *per capita* consumption figures but also from two other sources. Firstly, there are estimates of the amounts of money spent by the working classes upon alcohol. For example, while it was thought that the average working-class household in the late 1870s expended between £15 and £20 per annum on drink, it was apparent that many families disbursed between one-third to one-half of their earnings upon this single item.[110] Almost twenty years later Rowntree painted an equally black picture when he accepted that in England and Wales roughly 6s. per week per household were channelled in this same direction which 'would absorb more than one-sixth of the average total income of the working classes of York.'[111] Secondly, the consensus of opinion among social investigators was that over-indulgence in alcohol was the principal cause of self-inflicted poverty. William Hoyle, writing in 1871, estimated that one-sixth of the population of England and Wales fell below the poverty line because of this habit, although this figure, it must be stressed, was not based upon any detailed analysis of working-class earnings.[112] Charles Booth's more scientific approach to the question did not disagree with this emphasis; for, treating drink in a narrowly defined fashion — as the prime generator of poverty — he discovered that in the East End of London in the late 1880s nine per cent of his Classes A and B and seven per cent of his Classes C and D owed their impoverished state to alcohol.[113] (In this instance, however, it is not strictly accurate to place any of these households into the category of secondary poverty since, whether or not they drank, they would still have fallen below the poverty line because of inadequate family income. This point is discussed below.). Lastly, Rowntree underlined the paramount contribution of alcohol when he argued that it was the overriding factor in reducing 18.51 per cent of York's population to a state of secondary poverty.[114]

But having argued thus, certain qualifications must be entered. In the first place, as Booth's data show, the heaviest drinking frequently occurred among those who already lived in conditions of chronic deprivation. Drink, in other words, was used as an antidote by sizable elements of the working classes who were exposed to the devastating rhythms of casual employment and whose scanty earnings were incapable, no matter how scientifically they were spent, of removing the blight of primary poverty from their lives. Murray has already drawn attention, in a Scottish context, to the paradoxical situation which arose among handloom weavers in the 1830s and 1840s when their consumption of spirits rose at the same time as aggregate family income was falling.[115] The same situation, covering a broad spectrum of the unskilled labour market, still obtained in Glasgow in the late 1860s when it was observed that,

> the very class of people that cannot afford to drink whisky at all, drink most. People that have no shoes upon their feet, no stockings upon their legs, and very few clothes upon their backs, are much more frequently in the dram shops than those that are well-clothed and comfortably provided for.[116]

Yet this was not an exclusively Scottish phenomenon. In London casually employed coalwhippers in the 1840s and casually employed dockers in the 1880s were united both by their meagre incomes and by their addiction to beer.[117] As Dr. Niven observed in 1904, when discussing the question of casual labour in Manchester, 'it is right to say that not only is intemperance a cause of poverty, but poverty is a cause of intemperance. People who have not enough food turn to satisfy their cravings to drink and also to support their enfeebled hearts by alcohol.'[118] Secondly, many of those who penalised their families through drinking were often victims of their drab domestic environment rather than masters of their own fate. In the words of General William Booth, drink was

> a natural outgrowth of our social conditions. The tap-room in many cases is the poor man's only parlour. Many a man takes to beer, not from love of beer, but from a natural craving for light, warmth, company and comfort which is thrown in along with beer, and which he cannot get excepting by buying beer.[119]

In more prosaic terms this assessment was to be endorsed by Rowntree a decade later.[120] Thirdly, particularly in the pre-1870 decades, employers in certain localities helped to impoverish their work forces not simply by using pubs for the payment of wages, but, as P. McGowan, a 'dock excavator' working at Liverpool docks, put it, compelling them to spend 'a portion of their earnings every Saturday night at the public-house at which they are paid.'[121] Lastly, in some cases a household could find itself struggling to attain a subsistence diet not so much because its male head consumed vast quantities of alcohol but becasue aggregate family income was so low that even a modest amount of social drinking was sufficient to turn the scales of poverty against it.

This final point is, of course, central to any analysis of what secondary poverty actually meant. For those who castigated the working classes for their wasteful use of resources very often failed to relate income to total family needs. This was particularly true of the majority of attacks which were mounted against 'unscientific' household management throughout our period. In the litany of incompetence which was recited against the 'feckless' wife, child neglect always figured prominently. Margaret Loane and Mrs. B. Bosanquet were both certain that, in the closing decades of our period, the health problems of working-class infants were more often a tangible sign of 'improper feeding' rather than of underfeeding.[122] But child neglect could assume another form, when a housewife sought paid employment in the labour market, to the detriment of her social obligations to her family. Again, housewives were denounced for their profligate patterns of expenditure, buying commodities 'dear' in small quantities, and for preparing monotonous and ill-balanced meals. There was, of course, some truth in this *voyeur's* approach to poverty. Infants were frequently unscientifically fed and quietened with alcohol in the form of 'Godfrey's Cordial' and other sleep-inducing concoctions. Furthermore, the culinary skills of the majority of working-class women did not extend far, while money was often not spent to the family's best advantage.

Yet having made these points, that does not by itself advance our understanding of the reasons behind this form of behaviour or enable us to decide whether or not this way of life was an outward sign of secondary poverty. Such evidence as we do possess in this field, however, goes some way towards at least softening the acerbity of this catalogue of denunciation. For instance, as surveys of mid-nineteenth-century Preston and early twentieth-century Birmingham revealed, while many wives were forced into the labour market by the poverty of the family unit,[123] it by no means followed that neglect of the household inevitably followed in the wake of this decision. Similarly, the practice of acquiring food in small amounts was often, but not always, a sign that a family subsisted in a state of primary poverty. This habit was most deeply ingrained among casual workers whose wildly fluctuating earnings compelled the housewife to meet her needs on this daily basis, although an additional factor in promoting this trend was the shortage of storage space in working-class homes.[124] None the less it was also true, as Rowntree showed for York, that high but irregular earnings which ought to have kept the family free from want, could defeat the budgeting skills of the wife and this lead to secondary poverty.[125] In a word, few households, when confronted by the problem, made the necessary social readjustments to cope successfully with the difficulty of 'equalising an irregular income with regular recurrent needs.'[126] Furthermore, if reformers were correct to stress 'that the diet of the poorer . . . children is insufficient, unscientific, and utterly unsatisfactory,'[127] it was increasingly recognised, in the early 1900s, that many of these wounds were not deliberately self-inflicted and that, although owing something to ignorance of nutritional values, bad cooking and inadequate feeding were often a manifestation of primary rather than secondary poverty, which would not be removed simply by teaching future generations of school children the rudiments of domestic science.[128] As Mrs. Pember Reeves asked in 1913,

> What person or body of persons, however educated and expert, could maintain a working man in physical efficiency and rear healthy children on the amount of money [roughly £1 per week] which is all these same [Lambeth] mothers have to deal with? It would be an impossible problem if set to trained and expert people. How much more an impossible problem when set to the saddened, weakened, overburdened wives of London labourers?[129]

Finally, it is often impossible to explain secondary poverty within the mono-casual framework of bad housekeeping. For in many households imprudent budgeting and heavy drinking were the twin foundations upon which working-class poverty was built.

Chapter 4

The Alleviation of Poverty among the Able-Bodied 1830-1914: A Study of Palliatives and Expedients

Any account of primary and secondary poverty during these years must give due weighting to the dynamic nature of the poverty problem itself. At the most basic level the stresses and strains generated by social and economic deprivation were causally related to the movement of the trade cycle, with cyclical troughs invariably leading to a sharp increase in the incidence of primary poverty in British society. Nevertheless, at the micro-economic level of the individual household, the family's ability to ease or to remove the harsh burdens imposed by poverty depended upon many more factors than the seemingly inexorable seven to ten years' swings of the conventional Juglar cycle. As we have seen, the head of the household's physique, age, and possession or lack of specific skills were important determinants of his status, ability to command regular employment and earning capacity in the labour market. But a family's relationship to the poverty line was also in some measure influenced by the extent to which it could successfully exploit an assorted range of expedients to mitigate some of the worst effects of poverty. In broad terms these expedients can be classified under three headings. Firstly, there were those palliatives which were designed by outside agencies — town councils, Distress Committees, Poor Law authorities, and private philanthropy — to deal with the plight of the able-bodied, above all but not exclusively at times of cyclical unemployment. Secondly, a more ambiguous role was played by debt and debt agencies in alleviating, in the short-term, some of the more pressing needs of working-class society. Thirdly, a very limited range of options were open to the working classes which, if properly used, could either produce real improvement in their standard of living or do something to soften the debilitating pressure of indigence during a crisis.

I

Under this last heading the most obvious, as well as the most efficacious, solution to those socio-economic difficulties which confronted the households of the unskilled was to seek to maximise, at the earliest opportunity, family aggregate income. That, of course, did not mean that supplementation of the earnings of the male head of the household by other members of the family was *per se* a sign of primary or secondary poverty. In certain parts of the country high juvenile and female activity rates were, throughout our period, an integral part of the traditional pattern of local employment. This was true of certain of the cotton towns in Lancashire where the wife worked to maintain a standard of living which was already above subsistence level. Such a situation clearly obtained at Blackburn in the early years of this century where a substantial proportion of married women sought employment in the local mills in order to support 'a high standard of life . . . comfortable houses and money to spend on excursions, holidays and amusements are considered essentials.'[1] Again, a small number of wives actively engaged in home work not because their income was essential to preserve their families from want but because they were attracted by the prospect of earning 'pin money'. As James Pitkeithley, a partner in the Glasgow wholesale clothier firm of R.S. Muir and Company, observed in 1889, albeit with much exaggeration, 'the outside workers that do our shirts are generally the wives of artizans and various other workmen, who have nothing to do at home in the absence of their husbands, and it is so much money earned, when otherwise they could have gone idle.'[2] Similarly some of the part-time work outlets still available to children in the post-1870 era when factory and educational legislation had severely curtailed the opportunities for factory employment at an early age, were often occupied by the offspring of members of the artisan class. Thus a survey of sixty-nine Board schools, undertaken by Glasgow School Board in 1901, revealed that eighty-four per cent of the fathers of 4628 schoolchildren who worked for wages — almost half of this total delivered milk — belonged to skilled or semi-skilled occupations. As *Forward* argued, fathers from this kind of background 'might be presumed to earn enough to support', by their own labour, their families, although it conceded that the small contribution of the child to the household budget — perhaps 2s. per week — 'represents a very helpful addition to the purchasing power of a working-class family.'[3] Yet when these qualifications have been entered, they cannot obliterate the continuing strength of the relationship between the threat or reality of poverty on the one hand and the speed with which, and the rate at which, dependants procured gainful employment on the other.

There can be little doubt that the decision of many wives to take up unskilled work was prompted by the inadequacy and/or irregularity of the incomes of their husbands. Attention has already been drawn to the strong economic ties which bound together the casual markets for male and female labour, and in particular to the fact that the married component of the workforce in the sweated trades consisted 'chiefly of the wives of labourers whose pay is small and whose employment is casual '[4] It was essentially this type of economic motivation — the desire to 'cover minimum consumption needs' — which pushed the wives of London-based Irish labourers into the unskilled labour market in the 1850s and which, four decades later, persuaded the women, married to the impoverished and casually employed men who constituted Charles Booth's Class B, to accept work 'of a rough kind' in order to supplement the meagre earnings of their husbands.[5] A similar picture emerged in Birmingham when Cadbury, Matheson and Shann discovered that in the majority of cases the decision of a wife to seek employment was stimulated either by an adult male wage which was 'insufficient for comfort' or by the heavy drinking and idleness of her spouse which threatened to keep the family permanently in a state of secondary poverty; in Liverpool where the uncertainties which surrounded quayside employment made the wives of casual dock labourers anxious to avail themselves of any opportunity of making a modest addition to aggregate family income; and in Glasgow where the wives of labourers were often compelled to turn to ill-paid home work and charing if they and their children were to have any hope of eluding the grip of primary poverty.[6]

But if the struggle for subsistence was the principal driving force behind this kind of involvement in the casual labour market, an identical motive informed the decision of many married women to turn, for employment, to mills and factories in those spheres of economic activity which made extensive use of female labour. Anderson, for example, has shown, in his sample drawn from the 1851 Census of Preston, that sixty per cent of the wives who worked in the local mills, did so because their earning capacity had to be exploited if their families were to have a chance of rising above the primary poverty line.[7] Moreover, more than half a century later there had been no basic shift in this situation for a section of the female workforce. For the detailed inquiry, conducted by Rose E. Squire in 1904, into the motives which persuaded female mill hands in Preston to return to work as soon as possible after the birth of a child — often before the expiry of the statutory waiting period of four weeks — underlined the paramount influence of poverty. In the words of the official report,

> in one-third of the cases of early return to the mill investigated by Miss Squire . . . the reason was poverty due to insufficiency of the father's wage, and in two-fifths of the cases it was due to that and lack of employment [for the male head of the household] combined.[8]

Nor were these results unique, for contemporaneous surveys stressed the correlation which existed between the presence of substantial numbers of wives in the jute mills of Dundee and the pottery works of Stock-upon-Trent and 'serious struggling poverty.'[9] In other words, as at Preston, the force which pushed these women, married to labourers 'whose earnings [in Dundee in 1904] do not exceed £1 a week', from their homes into the labour market was again economic in origin.[10]

Much the same conclusion emerges when the employment patterns of the offspring of poor and unskilled parents are examined. Particularly in the pre-1850 decades the temptations to transfer such children from the school or the street to wage earning employment was overwhelming. In parts of the North of England and the West and East of Scotland this might involve a child giving some form of assistance to sorely pressed fathers during the final and painful phase of the handloom weaving industry.[11] It was more usual, however, for those who were, in the 1830s and 1840s, at the bottom of the labour hierarchy in the textile districts to seek a menial form of factory employment for their sons and daughters, sometimes at the risk of violating the law itself. What this last ploy usually involved was the falsification of a child's age in order to circumvent the Factory Acts, although when it was resorted to, it was more the product of poverty than of parental cupidity. Probably typical of such cases was that of Mary O'Brien who was found guilty at Bolton in 1843 of forging a baptismal certificate; 'but as she was in wretched circumstances and had a large family, including an infant in arms, she was not sent to prison, but punished by being made to bear the costs of the prosecution'.[12] But it was not, of course, simply the cotton mill in the pre-1850 era which attracted, and made extensive use of, juvenile labour. The same held true of the flax and worsted mills of the West Riding where the 'pull' of supplementary earnings far outweighed the benefits of free education in the eyes of the poorest category of parents. Several children, for instance, who had been allocated free places at St. Marie's Roman Catholic Day School, Bradford, were returned, in September 1854, as 'often absent, but I understand at work,' 'gone to work in a mill,' or more simply, 'not regular.'[13]

This Bradford experience encapsulates one of the social responses to the presence of want in the lives of an Irish immigrant community. Yet it was not unique either to Bradford or, in a broader sense, to the textile towns of Britain. For it was to be repeated in other areas of heavy Irish settlement which possessed a fundamentally different economic structure. In London, for instance, the young offspring of Irish families were to be found in a whole range of casual jobs — hawking, street singing, rag and bone collecting — which enabled them to contribute something towards the family purse, while in Newcastle-upon-Tyne the 'constant migration of the parents, who are nearly all Irish labourers' and the counter-attraction of casual jobs for schoolchildren meant that 'the attendance [at St. Andrew's Roman Catholic Day School] is . . . irregular and composition of the school so fluctuating.'[14] Again, in some of the major cities, Liverpool and Manchester among them, contemporaries pointed to the presence of a small group of professional beggars of Irish extraction who sent out their children to beg on the streets and with instructions not to return home until they had acquired a fixed sum of money.[15] In short, the pressure of poverty led to a brief period of schooling and an early start to their working lives for the majority of the children of Irish immigrants. As T.M. Marshall observed in 1850-1,

> although it [the short-lived school career] is an evil apparent, more or less prominently, in all the classes and communities into which our community is divided, it assumes very exaggerated dimensions amongst the Roman Catholic population, in which the proportion of the poor to the rich is probably very much greater than in any other religious body. Teachers in certain districts are constantly complaining to me, not merely of the early age at which their scholars finally quit them, but that all their efforts are frustrated by the fluctuating attendance of the majority, whose intense poverty leaves them without defence when tempted by the prospect of the small conceivable gain. The inducement of 6d. per week to be earned by the sale of chips, periwinkles, or matches, will entirely quench the faint desire for instruction which is its only counterpoise, and reduce a promising class to a skeleton, whilst its members are scattered over the country, often for several weeks together, in pursuance of their vagabond craft; and everybody must feel the unreasonableness of condemning such lucrative vagrancy, if it does but add a few loaves to the attenuated store of the starving family at home.[16]

Yet this pre-1850 pattern was not an exclusively Irish phenomenon. For it was reproduced, on a larger scale, in the homes of those Scottish, Welsh and English parents who, like their Irish counterparts, were unable to attain a subsistence standard of existence by the exertions of the head of the household alone. But, equally important, some of these trends in juvenile employment were not confined to the opening twenty years of our period but persisted in some form throughout the whole of these eight and a half decades. This kind of continuity was particularly strong in relation to certain categories of 'street children' whose activities attracted the attention of social reformers in the late 1860s and who formed the subject of at least one of the lesser known Victorian social novels — *Our Benny* — with its preoccupation with the changing fortunes of an orphaned match seller in late nineteenth-century Liverpool.[17] And they were still a sufficiently numerous group in the early 1900s, notwithstanding attempts to curb their activities through a system of licencing and regulation, to be presented as a major social problem in Glasgow, created by the poverty of their parents and in their turn living and working in an environment likely to perpetuate that impoverishment in their own adult lives.[18]

Outwardly, however, there were also marked differences in the nature of juvenile employment between the pre- and post-1870 worlds. In the first place, as has already been noted, legislative intervention by Parliament progressively closed several of those outlets which had formerly been open to young children. Educational reforms in particular were explicitly designed to lengthen the school-life of the working-class child. One of the prime purposes of the 1872 Scottish Education Act, for example, — to introduce a system of universal and compulsory schooling — was accepted as a realistic social goal at which to aim by England and Wales in 1880, while subsequently measures were adopted in all three countries to raise the minimum school leaving age. Apart from this legislative programme, the 'half-timers' became an element of diminishing significance in the labour force of the textile mills of England and Scotland. Indeed, it was openly acknowledged in Dundee in 1904 that it was only the indigence of 'the very lowest class' which was responsible for the continuation of this system, albeit on a much reduced scale.[19] Finally, the changing structure of British industry led, in the post-1870 decades, to a broadening of the spectrum of unskilled jobs which were the preserve of youthful labour, in the manufacturing and tertiary sectors of the economy.

Yet although these discontinuities were real enough, the impact of some of them upon working-class life can easily be exaggerated. For instance, it was clear that the early educational acts permitted a good deal of flexibility to those families where supplemention of the father's income by his children was still important. Thus an 1878 Scottish statute incorporated in its clauses a provision which permitted a parent to remove a child from school at ten years of age, once he or she had shown a degree of proficiency in reading, writing and arithmetic. And while the 1901 Scottish Education Act closed this loophole and raised the leaving age to fourteen, it was still possible, 'in cases of real necessity and on very strict conditions', to obtain merit and labour certificates which exempted children from further attendance at day schools after their thirteenth birthday.[20] Similarly, compulsory attendance regulations were very laxly applied until at least the late 1880s in England and Wales. As Rowntree observed in 1899,

> many of the parents in this class [Class D where aggregate family income exceeded 30s. per week] left school very early, for until 1888 the compulsory education clauses were very imperfectly enforced in the city [of York], and it was comparatively easy to obtain special orders from the magistrates exempting children from compulsory education at an early age.[21]

But while it was possible to frustrate the intentions of the creators of the new educational structures of England, Wales and Scotland by operating in this fashion — that is, strictly within the framework of the law, — the evidence also suggests that certain sections of the poor were prepared to ignore those statutory obligations which they incurred as parents for the education of their offspring, if they conflicted with the economic needs of their families. The incentive to pursue this course of action was clearly much stronger in England and Wales during the laxer climate of the early and mid-1880s. Nevertheless the socio-economic status of the father and/or mother was another significant variable in determining the levels of absenteeism, with those in sweated or casual employment being more likely to seek to realise the earning potential of their children while they were of school age. To quote a London matchbox worker in 1883, 'of course, we cheat the School Board. It's hard on the little ones, but their fingers is so quick — they that has most of 'em is the best off.'[22] And in the post-1890 era when the School Board Inspectorates of England, Wales and Scotland were quick to highlight such infractions of the law, it was still the pressures of want which often led to truancy and irregularity of attendance. This type of correlation clearly existed in the area of Lanarkshire covered by the Rutherglen School Board in 1909-10 where it was noted that 'nearly every case [of absenteeism] is directly traceable to poverty in some form; casual labour and unemployment being the contributory causes in the bulk of the cases', although the complexity of the motives which underlaid this pattern was also acknowledged. In particular it was pointed out that it was often the practice amongst the unskilled to keep the eldest child away from school during a period of parental illness. Even so, if the victim of sickness was the male head of the household, then the social role of housekeeper which was fulfilled by such children had also positive economic effects, since it allowed the wife and mother to re-enter the casual labour market and to 'try to earn something at washing or cleaning work of any kind' at a time when the living standards of the entire family had fallen below the primary poverty line.[23]

Yet, with the fragmentary material at our disposal, it is impossible to decide, with any great degree of accuracy, the overall efficacy of this strategy in easing or removing the pressures of poverty amongst the households of the unskilled. In certain areas of economic activity it was obvious enough that the contributions of supplementary wage-earners made a meaningful difference to the family's standard of living. Thus the average aggregate incomes of the households of 363 labourers which were investigated in St. George's in the East in the late 1840s amounted to 19/1d. per week, although the average earnings of the adult male head of the household were only 15/7d. Similarly, while 34 porters in the same survey averaged 17s. per week, the average weekly income of their families was 20/8d.[24] But by very definition such data which encapsulate the 'average' experience, obscure the economic position of the individual family unit. Bearing in mind, however, the distinctive socio-economic feature in the life cycle of each household — the changing ratio of dependants to wage-earners — it is logical to conclude that supplementation in some instances was on a sufficient scale to guarantee, with prudent management, an above subsistence level of existence. Moreover, in the pre-1870 world an identical pattern was to be reproduced among working-class communities of widely divergent economic backgrounds. Anderson, for example, has shown that the vast majority of wives in his sample who, in response to the pinching effects of want, obtained work in Preston's mills in 1850, were able, by dint of their own supplementary earnings, to keep their families marginally above the poverty line.[25] Again, H. S. Chapman in 1840 commented upon the positive role played by children in boosting the aggregate earnings of the households of worsted weavers in the West Riding and in enabling a proportion of them to experience a modest, but ephemeral, measure of comfort in their lives, while Lynn Lees, in her study of the largely unskilled Irish immigrants in London in 1851, emphasised the crucial contribution made by co-residing sons and daughters in the struggle to attain 'minimum consumption needs.'[26]

Even after 1870, despite a secular rise in working-class income which was only checked in the early 1900s, supplementation remained the essential precondition in many households if they were ever to break free from the inadequate diet associated with primary poverty. As we have seen, it was for this reason that groups of parents saw a conflict between the economic needs of the family on the one hand and the educational obligations which were placed upon them by the state on the other. In a word, the insistence upon compulsory education and a marked reduction in the employment of children under the age of fourteen imposed considerable hardships upon the households of the unskilled, which juvenile part-time or casual work could only partially alleviate. As in the pre-1870 era, it was only when youthful dependants started to become full-time employees, that it becomes possible to trace a slow but sustained improvement in the economic prospects of every working-class household. And in the case of the unskilled it was the working out of this process that largely represented for them the difference between poverty and prosperity. The validity of this analysis was amply illustrated by Rowntree who showed that a basic cause of primary poverty among his Class B was the non-productive role of children. Of the average weekly income of 19/9d. which accrued to families who were placed in this class, only 3.5 per cent (8¼d.) was contributed by male supplementary earners and a further 3.8 per cent (9d.) by their female equivalents. On the other hand, in Class D, where aggregate family earnings in excess of 30s. kept households in a tolerable degree of comfort, 17.4 per cent — or 7/3¼d. — of the average family income of 41/9¼d. was earned by sons and 5.2 per cent — or 2/1½d. — by daughters. Equally significant, one of the two major components of this class consisted of 'families in which the fathers are unskilled workers earning less than 30s., but where the total family income is raised above that figure on account of the sums contributed by children who are working.[27] But while the economic function discharged by offspring formed the central feature in Rowntree's discussion of supplementation, it is impossible to overlook in certain areas the vital contribution of working wives. To quote from Dr. Robertson's exhaustive inquiry into infant mortality rate among the poorer sections of the working classes in St. Stephen's and St. George's Wards, Birmingham, in 1908-9,

> in many cases the additional income brought in by the mother had an important influence in the prevention of poverty, which is the one great cause of infant mortality . . . many women who go to work being thrifty and energetic and determined not to get below the poverty line, nor yet to neglect their home duties.[28]

To obtain, however, a balanced view of the economic role of supplementation, this picture must in certain respects be modified. In the first place, as Charles Booth showed in relation to the casually employed elements of his Class B, supplementary income did not *per se* produce a subsistence standard of living. But, of much wider application, supplementation has to be placed against the sombre backcloth of the poverty — prosperity — poverty cycle of the unskilled which was formulated by Chapman in 1840 and refined by Rowntree some sixty years later.[29] According to this theses, a labourer could look forward to two periods of relative affluence, the first occurring before marriage when he was 'earning money and living under his parents' roof', and the second when his own children became in their turn wage-earners. Conversely he would be 'in poverty, and therefore underfed', in childhood,'when his constitution is being built up'; 'in early middle life — when he should be in his prime'; and, finally and irretrievably, in his old age.[30] And even this assessment, it can be argued, is too optimistic in tone since it fails to take account of those adverse factors which could drastically shorten at least one of the periods of prosperity. In particular it does not explore the nature of the relationship between the movement of the trade cycle and the work cycle of the individual family, for it was perfectly possible for the unskilled hand's offspring to try to enter the labour market during a prolonged depression, such as 1839-42, 1904-5 and 1907-9, when job prospects were discouraging and the opportunities for maximising aggregate family income correspondingly reduced. Reinforcing the braking influence of this exogenous variable was the social fact that once erstwhile dependants were gainfully employed, they were less likely to stay within the household of unskilled parents than their equivalents from an artisan background. Partly this was simply a reflection of the earlier age of marriage amongst the unskilled, particularly among those who were engaged in physically exacting tasks where the full adult wage-rate could be achieved in the opening years of a man's working life. But this is very far from providing a total explanation since many sons and daughters left the family home long before they were married.

This last development cannot be satisfactorily treated within a monocausal framework of economic determinatism, primarily because social influences, such as parental cruelty, could often be the key expulsive cause.[31] At the same time, however, it is clear that poverty itself could also shape the individual's decision to depart. In some cases the demands which were made by parents, acting in response to the pressures of poverty upon the earnings of adolescent workers, were sufficient to persuade their children to move into lodgings where they could enjoy the individual fruits of their labours.[32] But what was outwardly the same result could also be achieved under a very different set of social conditions. Where, for example, the income of the child did not cover the cost of his own upkeep, he might in his turn be 'turned adrift'. How often this kind of parental sanction was invoked, must remain the subject of speculation, although probably only a tiny minority viewed their offspring in such a coldly economic light. Yet that it was used by a section of the poor was conclusively established by Charles Booth, who concluded that among a section of the casual labour force in the East End of London, 'boys who do not bring in enough . . . are likely [in the late 1880s and early 1890s] to be turned adrift, being in that case apt to sink into Class A [of loafers and semi-criminals].'[33] Again, there must have been many instances of children breaking away from their family at that point in their lives when their wages were sufficient for their own needs without yielding any surplus for the support of other members of the household. It was this kind of situation that a Bradford woolcomber described in 1849 after his daughter, then earning 6s. per week, 'went plump over the door and left us.' As he noted, 'perhaps it's as well. When children grows up, their keep and their clothes takes their wages fully.'[34] In the last analysis, therefore, the threat of reality of poverty, for a sizable element of the unskilled, neither strengthened the ties of kinship nor taught their families to act as a single economic unit. Indeed, it can be said of those who reacted in the manner that we have just been describing, that 'the assertion of independence [by offspring leaving home], linked no doubt to their ability to support themselves in a city which employed much child labour, shows the family economy at the point of disintegration.'[35] Finally, if the majority of the unskilled probably exploited to the full the economic possibilities of supplementation, the substantial short-term gains which accrued to their households were to some extent counterbalanced by the fact that sons and daughters were pushed into 'dead end' jobs, offering high initial returns but bleak employment prospects in adulthood.

None the less, compared to any other step which the poor could take on their own behalf to raise their living standards, supplementation was the only really effective answer to the socio-economic problems posed by indigence. Mutual assistance, for example, although an integral part of working-class social life, above all at times of sickness, was usually on too small a scale to raise its recipients above the primary poverty line. Similarly economic crime, whether it assumed the form of bread riot or the drift of the able-bodied during a period of cyclical unemployment into petty theft, only appealed to an insignificant element who were either totally destitute or who failed to appreciate that the risks involved were not commensurate with the small and uncertain rewards it yielded. But the majority of those unmarried and unskilled women who turned to part-time prostitution, because they were badly paid and/or because they were unable to obtain regular employment, fared scarcely any better. In short, whole sections of the working classes, outside those often brief periods when most members of the household were wage-earners, could do little, without external assistance, to mitigate the crushing social burdens which were imposed by limited financial resources.

II

Outside assistance was not, however, universally accepted as a salve for some of the more distressing aspects of poverty. Indeed, it was widely accepted by those elements of the middle class who were keen to persuade the working classes to seek social salvation through the practice of the virtues of thrift and self-help, that external aid, unless scientifically and sparingly disbursed, could perpetuate the depressed state of the poor. Given this social philosophy, it was scarcely surprising that they were scathingly critical of the role which the licenced pawnbroker fulfilled in the lives of the working men and women. To David Macrae, writing in 1862, the morally corrupting influence of such short-term credit was everywhere apparent, for 'like a upas-tree, it [the pawn office] so taints the moral atmosphere around it that religious and other bene-volent agencies can scarcely live in it.'[36] Almost forty years later Mrs. B. Bosanquet endorsed this verdict when she represented the pawnshop as the antithesis of those concepts which formed the cornerstone of the Smilesian creed:

> thrift is the characteristic of the steadfast mind, reflecting the unity and necessity of life and the universe, and exercising self-control in the present for the sake of ensuring that the future shall at any rate approximate to it in value. The mind which yields easily to the temptation of pawning, on the contrary, is one to which the future is merely an uncertain chance, good only to be robbed for the sake of the present.[37]

Again, Beatrice Potter, accepting that the casual pattern of employment which operated among dockers in the East End of London in the 1880s 'encouraged . . . wasteful patterns of expenditure,' concluded that the inevitable sequel to such a system was to breed reliance upon the pawnbroker for funds which could be used to buy drink. In her words, 'the most they can do in their forlorn help-lessness is to make the pawnbroker their banker, and the publican their friend.'[38] Nevertheless the intimate relationship between the pawnshop and the pub was not simply a distinctive feature of the social life of the East End dock labourer. An identical pattern was reproduced in every major city throughout our period. In Glasgow, for instance, it was acknowledged that parents in the 1840s fre-quently pledged furniture or dress 'for the purpose of raising a few pence to satisfy their insatiable craving for whisky', with the result that they were 'in misery from one end of the year to the next.'[39] Little had changed in this respect by 1870 when Alexander M'Call, the city's Chief Constable, informed the Select Committee on Pawnbrokers that the monies raised upon goods pledged for sums of less than 10s. were, in the majority of cases, spent upon alcohol.[40] But the spread of secondary poverty and the intensification of the pressures of want which were linked with primary poverty were not the exclu-sive product of this one form of credit. They owed as much in the pre-1869 era in England and Wales to the limited amounts of credit which were made available to the customers of the ubiquitous beershop and, until a much later date, to the existence of a similar arrangement in public houses in certain parts of the country.[41]

While, however, a clear correlation can be established between credit on the one hand and drink and gambling on the other, it is a mistake to treat the topic within such a narrowly defined framework of reference. For credit was sought, and obtained, by working-class consumers for quite different purposes. More-over, in these other areas of consumer activity it was widely acknowledged by the working classes themselves that this kind of advance acted as a palliative which could guarantee a measure of immediate relief when they were beset with a pressing economic difficulty. This was particularly true of the advances made by the pawnshop which, quite apart from providing funds for drink, served four distinct, but inter-related ends. In the first place there was the provision of short-term credit 'in what are called the weekly trades, where the goods [usually clothing] are pledged on the Monday and redeemed on the Saturday.'[42] The advantage of such an arrangement, with its modest rate of interest, was that it enabled a family to anticipate its income to purchase food without becoming tied to a single, and perhaps high-cost, retail outlet. Secondly, some groups of workers pawned their goods on a longer term, seasonal basis in an attempt to mitigate the harsh impact of the seasonal trough upon their living standards. Among others who operated in this manner were seasonally hired hands, resident in St. George's Parish, Hanover Square, in the early 1840s, who 'were in the habit of pawning part of their furniture [in winter] and . . . [redeeming] it in summer' and those seasonally employed building workers whose socio-economic background was investigated by N.B. Dearle in 1908.[43] In this case, however, unless the slack period was of relatively short duration, this form of expedient could have had only the most marginal effect in softening the rigours of under-employment and unemployment. Thirdly, as has already been noted, pawning was often resorted to at times of sickness. When illness confined the head of the household to his home, the proceeds from this type of transaction were rarely sufficient to meet the specific needs of the sick person and the general needs of his family for more than a brief period of time. On the other hand when 'a little extra ready-money' was required for the sick child of an unskilled labourer, such a policy could be attended with more success. As Lady Bell observed, 'if any extra nourishment . . . is ordered for the sick child [in Middlesborough in the early 1900s] whose father is living, or trying to live, on 20s. a week or a little over, the only way to get that nourishment is to pawn something.'[44] Finally, insistent demands were made upon the services of the pawnbroker at times of cyclical unemployment, although it was precisely during these periods of economic dislocation that brokers as a group were likely to be more cautious and discriminating in their dealings with customers.[45]

But the exercise of sound judgment was a counsel of managerial prudence which had to be constantly observed, since it was in the individual broker's interest not merely to turn over his stock as rapidly as possible, but also to avoid accumulating in his own hands too many forfeited pledges which, when offered for sale in the open market, would not necessarily realise the amount of the initial advance. In the words of J.F. May, a Salford pawnbroker,

> we want people who pay us regularly from week to week; and, in fact, our trade is a regular one, and our profit is got where the money is lent and lent again, and not from persons who want to get the money and leave the goods.[46]

Expressed in another form, most pawnshops were happy to deal with persons who were in receipt of a regular wage and who, by very definition, 'are not the very poorest people. They are sometimes getting good wages, but they manage to run a little beyond them, and they have to speculate upon the receipt of their wages next week.'[47] Conversely there were certain sections of the working classes who were treated as unacceptable risks. To quote J.F. May again, 'we do not care about destitute customers, those people who are coming down, and gradually descending, who begin with pledging their plate, and end, perhaps, with pledging their shoes.'[48] Where, of course, this line was drawn in practice varied enormously from town to town. In York, for instance, some pawnshops conducted a vigorous weekly business with members of Rowntree's Class B, most of whom lived in a state of primary poverty.[49] Yet however far down the social scale the individual broker's business descended, a point was ultimately reached when pleas for accommodation were rejected because of the poor quality of goods which were proffered as security.

Individuals who were confronted by this situation, were compelled to turn to other, more expensive forms of credit which were open to the working classes. In the pre-1870 era this above all meant, in Scotland, the 'wee pawn', and, in England, the 'dolly shop' where the rate of interest was rarely less than one penny per week for each shilling which was advanced.[50] Nevertheless, despite the prominent position which these institutions assumed in working-class localities, their great period of growth was already over by the mid-1850s. For example, whereas 200 'wee pawns' flourished in Glasgow in the mid-1840s, the majority of them heavily concentrated in the impoverished weaving strong-holds of the East End, that total had fallen to around 100 by 1870.[51] This trend, which was faithfully reproduced in other areas, was largely the product of their uncertain status, for in the post-1856 world the activities of the unlicensed pawnshop were subject to powerful legal constraints. Those unlicensed dealers, therefore, who continued to operate after that date, either took grave risks or sought to circumvent the letter of the law by claiming that they were acting as purchasers and sellers of second-hand goods rather than as brokers who were exacting a return from their clientele roughly twenty times greater than the legal limit of twenty per cent per annum.[52] Given this background, it was perhaps inevitable that the unlicenced broker should become a figure of rapidly diminishing significance in the post-1870 decades, to be replaced in part by the small money-lender.

In one crucial respect the money-lender emulated the practice of the un-licensed broker by charging his or her customers a cripplingly high rate of interest which in Liverpool in 1909 stood at '2d. per shilling for the first week, sometimes rising to 3d. in subsequent weeks.'[53] Yet the full extent of working-class indebtedness was very often concealed by these exorbitant interest rates, since the money-lender, 'having in most cases no security whatever for her [or his] loans,' might also insist upon additional payments being made, as in Lambeth in 1913 where a 'tip' of 2/6d. was extracted from the borrower after the capital and interest had been repaid.[54] In Liverpool, on the other hand, where the functions of money-lender and retailer were sometimes combined, this kind of exaction could assume a more subtle form. In the words of Eleanor Rathbone, 'some money-lenders keep small shops and others hawk fish or more rarely meat, and part of the loan has to be taken in kind. Thus, in order to obtain 2s. in cash a woman has often to take 1s. worth of fish as well . . . Her debt is then entered as 3s. 4d.'[55] Faced with demands of this nature, it was clear that not merely was the journey 'from the pawnshop to the money-lender . . . a distinct step downwards,'[56] but also that those who undertook that journey were reluctant travellers, propelled in that direction by the sparseness of their material possessions and the chronic inadequacy of their earnings to support a bare subsistence level of existence.

But in most circumstances the funds which were realised from this source and from the pawnshop could be spent according to the dictates of the individual's own conscience and the needs of his family. Such flexibility in the application of a loan was, however, largely absent in the case of most of the remaining avenues of credit which loomed large in working-class experience. Of these alternative outlets, the limited amount of short-term credit which was extended to select groups of customers by the local shopkeeper in order to purchase essential household commodities was at once the most widespread, as well as the most eagerly sought after, form of advance. As Olive Malvery observed, when writing about South London in the early years of this century, food shops

> generally run on a weekly credit system, the customers having a book in which the goods they take away are entered. They settle their account on Saturday night . . . as I found, this system often helps a poor woman to tide over a serious moment and to provide a meal for many a little mouth that would otherwise be empty.[57]

Supplementing this kind of activity was the provision of credit for the acquisition of clothing. In the pre-1850 period, and probably later, such an arrangement might be concluded on an informal, *ad hoc,* basis between a craftsman-retailer and a customer whose income fluctuated markedly during the course of a year. For instance, James Brennan, a Manchester-based master weaver of Marseilles toilet covers, who gave evidence before the 1834 Select Committee on Handloom Weavers' Petitions, obtained his supply of shoes from a local shoemaker who respected his integrity, trusting him to pay something towards their cost 'whenever he can.'[58] At a much later point in time traces of this type of transaction lingered on in the second-hand clothing trade conducted by licensed pawnbrokers with their regular clients. As at Liverpool in 1909, such items were usually acquired by

> 'leaving on' a few pence weekly when pledging their own bundle. These pence are apt to be forgotten or rather deducted from the amount received for the pledge. The clothes bought in this way are often astonishingly cheap. One woman when given 5/6 to buy boots for her husband, explained apologetically that she had supplied herself and two schoolboys of 10 and 13 as well, and the footgear displayed certainly looked worth the money.[59]

It was more usual, however, for advances for this specific purpose to take place within a relatively formal framework of reference. In its most widespread form this would bring the working class into contact with the peripatetic tally-man, with is antecedents stretching back into the late eighteenth century, who provided cheap fabrics and clothing on the weekly instalment principle.[60]

None the less, from the consumer's viewpoint, this system possessed two substantial drawbacks. In the first place it was a dear way of acquiring clothes since it left the housewife 'at the mercy of the tallyman, who may palm off on her at a given price something which is usually sold far below it.' Secondly, the quality of the goods could sometimes lead to considerable dissatisfaction, primarily because 'she has . . . to buy the thing unseen from a sample shown to her.'[61] It was for this reason that Lady Bell extolled the superior merits of the clothing ticket which circularised in Middlesborough in the opening decade of the twentieth century. In her words,

> these £1 tickets are sold by men who buy them for cash down at certain shops in the town, getting the tickets for 18s. or even less; and the women, who buy these in their turn, pay 21s., payable in instalments of not less than 1s. per week, and usually 2s.6d. for the first week. These tickets are available either for one shop or two, sometimes 10s. goes to a bootshop and 10s. to a draper. The advantage of this system over that of buying from the 'tallymen' or hawkers, is that, although in each case the woman has to make a weekly payment, in the case of the £1 tickets she goes to the shop in the town, and can get the goods that she sees at the prices marked in the windows.[62]

But from the 1850s onwards loanable funds from this kind of purchase were increasingly generated within working-class society itself through the formation of its own boot and clothing clubs. As early as 1860 it was noted that in Glasgow a number of 'large and seemingly respectable' warehouses and shops vigorously touted for the custom of possessors of 'club tickets', so styled 'because a certain number of workers club together to guarantee each other's debts.'[63]

Nevertheless such schemes multiplied much more rapidly after 1880 in response to rising real wages when their scope was extended to cover working women. Charles Booth, for example, drew attention to the adoption of this system by London factory girls in the late 1880s, while single women, engaged on unskilled work in Birmingham's metal trades in 1906, also adapted this practical application of the precept of self help to meet their own clothing requirements.[64] Furthermore, by the latter date this form of organisational structure embraced married women who banded together to establish money clubs, designed, like some male-dominated and pub-based investment societies, to meet 'any special expenses, boots or furniture, or the payment of a debt.' In this last instance, however, this type of institution might, as at Liverpool among the wives of dock labourers, merely serve to strengthen the hold of the local money-lender over her clientele, particularly when she undertook the task of organisation by 'getting, say, 16 of her clients to pay her a threepenny entrance fee, and a shilling a week for 16 weeks'. Subsequently, at the conclusion of each week 'lots are drawn and the woman to whom it falls draws the 16 shillings',[65] to be spent, if the money-lender were a retailer, at her own store or shop.

The only other significant aspect of credit which must be discussed — the accumulation of rent arrears — was in one sense unique, since it neither entailed the transfer of money from creditor to debtor nor the levying of even a purely nominal rate of interest. But, equally important, it is notoriously difficult to generalise about this facet of working-class life simply because the level of arrears was powerfully influenced by a whole host of mutually interacting social and economic variables, among them the movement of the trade cycle, the competence and attitudes of housing agents and landlords, the number of empty houses in a borough at a particular moment in time and the social class of the tenants, with 'the movement of arrears', as at West Ham between 1888 and 1905, tending to be 'both irregular and at a high level' in areas dominated by casual labour.[66] Yet, notwithstanding the complexity of the factors which shaped the contours of this problem in areas of widely divergent socio-economic structure, it is still possible to highlight two distinct approaches to the question. Firstly, there was the arrangement arrived at between landlord and seasonally employed worker which permitted the tenant to incur debts during the slack season on the understanding that they would be promptly cleared during the months of brisk trade. In a relatively small number of cases such an agreement denoted the existence of 'tied' housing in which the landlord, acting also as his tenant's employer, insisted that the paying off of arrears was the first charge upon income. In a microcosmic form this situation obtained at Bramley in 1839 where one handloom weaver of woollen cloth bitterly complained that 'I owed him (the manufacturer for whom he was working) some rent, owing to the distress of last year; when I commenced work, I owed him £11, and he would not agree to give me work, unless I paid half what I earned. If I earn 15/- a week, I receive 7/6; the other goes against the debt.'[67] The overwhelming bulk of seasonal workers, freed from the restraints associated with this king of relationship, would, however, only be allowed to run into arrears if they had attained the status of trusted tenants. This was true of two adult needle-women, interviewed by Mayhew in 1849, who had shared accommodation and worked together during the preceding four years. As Mayhew expressed it,

> they were obliged to allow their rent to go to 12. 6d. in arrears the first winter of all [1846]. But they paid it directly they had work, and since then the landlady never troubles them during the winter for the rent — never, indeed, asks for it. She is satisfied that they will pay it directly they can. They are convinced that no one else would do the same thing, for their landlady is very kind to them, and allows them the occasional use of her fire.[68]

Secondly, and of more general application, the amount of unpaid rent rose rapidly during periods of economic dislocation, simply because whole sections of the working classes lacked the means to meet this weekly contractual obligation. At such times the landlord might decide to leave his tenants undisturbed on the grounds that to evict them was a counsel of despair, involving the abandonment of all hope of recovering any part of the accumulated debt and affording no guarantee that the same problem would not recur in the immediate future. On the other hand he might decide to take active measures to protect his financial interests by seeking to distrain his tenant's possessions in lieu of payment of rent. This approach was vigorously pursued by some agents at West

Ham in the early 1900s who 'will put in brokers if the rent be owing for a week or two, even where the tenant is of long standing.'[69] But the success of this expedient, measured in purely monetary terms, was not always guaranteed since it depended upon the socio-economic position of the householder — were his goods worth acquiring? — and the speed with which this manoeuvre was executed. For any delay, at a time of deepening cyclical depression, would mean that the most valuable items had already been pawned. Thus, although it was claimed in January 1842 that 'of the rents of tradesmen's houses and loom-stands [in the burgh of Pollokshaws, situated on the outskirts of Glasgow] due at Martinmas last, not one in 10 has yet been fully paid', the severity of the economic crisis effectively ruled out sequestration as a practical solution to the landlords' difficulties. As John Ralston, one of the principal house factors in the burgh, put it, 'the tenant's effects would not in one case in ten pay the expenses of sequestration . . . in numerous instances . . . families have no bed-clothes, and . . . in almost every case ornamental or valuable furniture had disappeared from the houses.'[70] Finally, there remained the ultimate sanction of eviction which seems to have been employed with much greater frequency in the post-1870 world, a product in part of the more professional management of house property. As has been already noted, when it was invoked, it often entailed short-term financial losses to the landlord. But its impact upon the impoverished and dispossessed householder could be more devastating if he were required to produce a line of 'good conduct' and to pay rent in advance when seeking comparable accommodation elsewhere. For, as in Glasgow, particularly in the post-1890 period, failure to comply with these criteria could compel him and his family to turn to high cost, and weekly leased, furnished housing — the so-called 'farmed-out' house — which was the special preserve of the poorest elements of working-class society.[71]

Assessed overall, it must be concluded that credit, in its various shapes, played an important role in the economic life of working-class society. Yet, however crucial it was in meeting a specific contingency, it bestowed a far from unmixed blessing upon its recipients. This was, of course, obviously true when it assumed a socially harmful form, as in the case of the truck shop and of the insidious links which were forged between certain species of retailers and workers in the sweated trades. The *raison d'etre* of this last kind of relationship was the poverty of the 'slop' worker who, unable to provide a prospective employer with adequate financial security, turned to 'bakers, publicans, chandlershop keepers, and coal-shed keepers' to act on his behalf. But, as Mayhew pointed out in 1849, there was nothing of an altruistic nature which motivated retailers who acted in this fashion:

> they [the retailers] consent to be responsible for the workpeople upon the condition of the men dealing at their shops . . . The parties becoming securities thus not only greatly increase their trade, bur furnish a second-rate article at a first-rate price. It is useless to complain of the but quality or high price of the articles supplied by the securities, for the shop-keepers know, as well as the workpeople, that it is impossible for the hands to leave them without losing their work.[72]

None the less, equally formidable drawbacks, all of which had a significant bearing upon the poverty question, attended the credit structure which has just been analysed. Firstly, the cost of borrowing inevitably depressed the family's real income, although this fact has scarcely been acknowledged, never mind explored, in any of the recent studies of working-class living standards. What mattered in this context was not simply the interest rates charged by money-lenders and licensed and unlicensed pawnbrokers, but also, at the most basic level, the high cost of provisions which were acquired from credit-granting shopkeepers, since it was alleged that 'shopkeepers charge more for such credit than the pawnbroker does for the loan of his money.'[73] That verdict was applicable to every area where this practice obtained, including South London, where Olive Malvery regarded it as axiomatic, in the early 1900s, that 'the person receiving [shop] credit has to pay a much higher price for his goods than one who pays cash.'[74] Secondly, once those who were living at, or below, the poverty line became enmeshed in the web of credit, difficulties could frequently be encountered in repaying the 'dead interest' and the capital sum borrowed, again to the detriment of the family's standard of life. Sherwell highlighted the presence of such a pattern in the lives of tailors working in the ready-made sector in the West End of London during the 1890s, who operated 'for a large part of the year in a chronic state of bankruptcy, pledging one week's earnings (in the slack season, several weeks' earnings) to eke out another.'[75] Precisely what this entailed in terms of material deprivation was captured in one of Rowntree's case studies, made during his 1899 survey of York. Mr. and Mrs. T., with two dependent children, were unmistakably afflicted by primary poverty during the three weeks for which they kept their record of income and expenditure. But, as Rowntree pointed out, their current difficulties were compounded by the burden of debt, inherited from an earlier period. In his words,

> the father has been out of work for several months before he obtained his present situation [as a labourer], and the family are still suffering from the privations they then endured. They are also labouring under a debt contracted during this period, and are paying off 'back rent'. In addition to this, Mrs. T. is paying for a wringing-machine in weekly instalments, thus the margin of income available for ordinary expenditure is seriously reduced.[76]

Thirdly, credit generally — and not merely that which was provided by the licensed pawnshop — tended to be less freely available when it was most needed. During 1842, for instance, a year of high unemployment and widespread bankruptcies among small shopkeepers, many retailers, in the interests of solvency, were compelled to refuse all requests for further credit. As shopkeepers in the Gorbals and Anderston districts of Glasgow put it, 'respectable people they had formerly trusted were so reduced, that they were not able to pay their old scores; and that now they could not trust, without certain loss, or at least very great risk.'[77] In a word, for the working man 'employment is, in the matter of food, almost, and in the matter of clothing, entirely, a *sine qua non*'[78] when his credit rating was evaluated. At times of economic crisis, therefore, he might be compelled to join the chronically impoverished sections of the working classes — the elderly, the sick and those whose lowly earnings made them unacceptable risks for shopkeepers — in availing himself of the expensive services of the ubiquitous money-lender, the 'dolly shop' and the 'wee pawn'. In short, if reliance upon credit were usually a symptom rather than a cause of poverty, it still imposed the heaviest burden upon those least capable of bearing them and mortgaged future earnings for the satisfaction of immediate needs. But for their survival it was none the less a necessity.

III

The last type of palliative with which we are concerned, can best be defined within a broad framework which does full justice to the complex nature of its component parts. In the first place there was the role assumed by private charity in meeting, in a partial fashion, some of the requirements of the working classes at times of acute or chronic personal difficulty. Secondly, municipal authorities became increasingly involved in mounting 'make work' projects to mitigate some of the devastating social consequences of cyclical unemployment. Thirdly, there were those acts of intervention in the sphere of social policy which were approved by the state. And if before 1905 the horizons of Parliament in this particular legislative area were largely confined to the provision and modification of systems of poor relief for England, Wales and Scotland, it is equally valid, after that date, to speak of the beginnings of a revolution in welfare as the Liberals turned to deal with the plight of specific groups outside the constricting scope of the Poor Laws.

An attempt has already been made to evaluate the practical achievements of certain of these initiatives, particularly those which affected the economic status of the elderly, the sick and the widowed.[79] Rather than duplicate that earlier work here, it is my intention, in the remainder of this chapter, to adopt a narrower perspective by concentrating upon those strategies which were specifically designed to grapple with the poverty question amongst the able-bodied unemployed.

In this more restricted context it might, at first glance, appear that the unemployed were most harshly treated at the hands of those who carried out the exacting clauses of the New English and Scottish Poor Laws, since the enactment of both of these measures represented a triumph for the rigidly individualist school of social philosophy. Thus, in the case of the 1845 Scottish act, the able-bodied were to be totally excluded from what were regarded as the enervating effects of institutional relief, a policy which was less a solution to the poverty-inducing pressures of unemployment than a reaffirmation of traditional views by all those who subscribed to the teaching of the Rev. Thomas Chalmers. And while the New Poor Law Act of 1834 shrank from invoking this ultimate sanction in England and Wales, it still derived its inspiration from a Royal Commission which firmly believed that the doctrine of deterrence was the only effective way of containing the problem of able-bodied pauperism. As the Poor Law Commissioners expressed it in a circular, issued in 1835, the Poor Law was to be 'the harshest taskmaster and the worst paymaster.'[80]

Yet despite the uncompromising tone of this language and the initial intentions of those who had shaped this legislative structure, a crucial gap quickly emerged between what the law intended and the manner in which parish authorities reacted to the social strains and stresses generated by unemployment. In Scotland, for instance, the able-bodied unemployed who, in the pre-1845 era, had sometimes been relieved as 'occasional poor', continued to be so treated in a few urban areas for most of the 1850s until the practice was declared illegal in 1859.[81] But, even then, uniformity of administration proved a difficult goal to attain, for outdoor relief subject to a work test was periodically awarded in some of the major centres of population, among them Paisley and Glasgow, up to 1866 when the House of Lords ruled that it was 'ultra vires to expend the poor rate' for such purposes.[82]

As in Scotland, so in England and Wales the day-to-day administration of the New Poor Law speedily diverged from the general strategy which had been outlined in the Final Report of the 1832-4 Commission. Such a development owed much to three factors. In the first place a considerable amount of ambiguity surrounded the concept of the able-boded, for the term was sometimes applied to adult males alone and sometimes to members of both sexes.[83] Again, it was difficult in reality to classify those whose fading physical powers made it unlikely that they would ever be reabsorbed into the labour market on a full-time basis. Thus, while T.C. Parsons showed that there were virtually 10,000 inmates of workhouses who, in March 1906, were returned as able-bodied, almost twenty-five per cent of this total 'were over 55 years old, an age when employment was hard to find.'[84] Furthermore, minor physical deficiencies fuled out the possibility of a sizable, but imprecise, percentage of those who remained, performing heavy labouring work. Secondly, from the outset Boards of Guardians adapted the Poor Law to meet specific local needs, although it was sometimes impossible to reconcile the conflicting claims of the able-bodied and the ratepayers. Finally, there was the acceptance by the Poor Law Commissioners (1834-47) and their successor, the Poor Law Board (1847-71) of the view that it was, in some areas, quite impracticable to treat poverty which stemmed from unemployment and underemployment within the walls of the general mixed workhouse.

The upshot was that by the 1840s the doctrine of the workhouse test had been openly abandoned in many of the principal towns and cities of England and Wales. Such an outcome owed much to the directives which were issued from London and the repercussions of the 1839-42 economic crisis upon the able-bodied in urban society. From the start the Poor Law Commissioners had permitted large urban unions to give outdoor relief, on a temporary basis, to the unemployed until their workhouse building programmes had been completed. This concession was placed on a firmer basis in 1842 when, confronted by the daunting size of the unemployment problem, the Commissioners issued the Outdoor Labour Test Order which, in the Webbs' words, represented during the ensuing decade, 'the temporary embodiment of an alternative policy [to the workhouse] of the Central Authority.'[85] In 1852 matters were taken further when the Out-Relief Regulation Order formalised the system of outdoor relief to able-bodied men subject to a work test and, unlike its 1842 predecessor, to able-bodied females without conditions, in those parts of the country where its writ ran.[86] This trend, once sanctioned, was, in geographical terms, to spread during the 1850s and 1860s until the stone-yard and/or oakum picking became in many areas the normal way of testing destitution at times of cyclical unemployment. Scarcely surprisingly, therefore, able-bodied paupers between 1859 and 1874 comprised less than twenty per cent of the cases which were treated within the workhouse.[87] But this was by no means the only significant departure from the spirit of 1834. For wages subsidies continued to be paid out of the poor rate in such widely scattered communities as Durham, the East End of London and Lancashire throughout these decades,[88] notwithstanding the scathing attack on this 'abuse' which had been delivered by the 1832-4 Royal Commission. And if with the decline of some of the lowly paid outwork trades, including handloom weaving, this practice did not feature as prominently in the post-1870 world in the lives of unskilled male workers, it tenaciously survived into the twentieth century in the form of 'doles' which were sometimes given to irregularly employed women who were located in the sweated sector of the labour market.

During the early 1870s, however, a further switch of policy occurred when, inspired by the Goschen Minute of 1869 and its own Circular of 1871, the newly constituted Local Government Board launched a crusade against outdoor relief in all its forms. Working through its inspectorate, it sought to persuade guardians, wherever possible, to revert to the workhouse test, while in the cities it encouraged the establishment of test workhouses where the able-bodied could be effectively isolated and exposed to the practical application of deterrent principles. Moreover, in those urban unions where outdoor assistance had already been approved under the terms of either the Labour Test Order or the Out-Relief Regulation Order, it was stipulated that work tasks should in no circumstances be waived; that investigation into the background of each applicant should be undertaken; and that 'orders to able-bodied men for relief in the labour yard should only be given from week to week.'[89] The impact of such a campaign was, in the medium-term, quite dramatic. In London — first at Poplar and later at Kensington, — Manchester and Birmingham test workhouses were set up which, during their life-span, succeeded in reducing the amount of indoor able-bodied pauperism in very much the way that their supporters had predicted.[90]

Judged by statistics alone, this pattern was reproduced in workhouses through-out England and Wales where from the 1870s onwards the able-bodied pauper population remained at a relatively low level, only once exceeding, between 1886 and 1912, a figure of 12,000.[91] But, from the perspective of the inspec-torate, what was a cause of even greater satisfaction was the sharp fall which took place between the 1870s and the early 1890s, in the number of individuals who were in receipt of outdoor relief. Nor was this to prove to be a short-lived development, for, despite the evolution of a more humane and flexible climate of opinion in the 1890s, the Poor Law was never again destined to become a major source of outdoor assistance for the unemployed in the pre-1914 era.[92]

Yet if the Poor Law loomed larger in the lives of the unemployed in the pre-1870 decades, the fear, expressed by the advocates of deterrence, that departures from the tenets of 1834 would lead to a rapid growth of able-bodied pauperism, proved groundless. For it was only during a protracted slump, such as occurred nationally in 1842 and regionally in the Lancashire Cotton Famine of the 1860s, that its services were used by a significant minority of the working-classes. Nor was this surprising since the Poor Law, before and after 1870, possessed substantial drawbacks which drastically reduced its appeal to the workless. For one thing the stigma which was attached to poor relief, was sufficiently real for it to be regarded by many as a last resort, to be invoked only after every other expedient had been tried and exhausted. That stigma was most overtly expressed in the workhouse test. But the work test itself, most popularly embodied in those tasks — stone breaking, oakum picking and chopping wood — which were carried out in the labour yard, was viewed in a similar light by whole sections of those whom the Victorian middle class desig-nated the deserving poor. Little changed in this respect when, from the mid-1880s onwards, many urban unions either stripped the labour test of its more exacting requirements or put the able-bodied pauper to more constructive work than hitherto.[93]

Reinforcing the repellent nature of this system were the meagre benefits which were usually distributed in the form of outdoor relief. Such a policy was clearly pursued at Manchester in the spring of 1848 where a deputation from the local labour yard pressed the guardians to show a greater measure of generosity. In support of this claim, they had little difficulty in demon-strating that it was impossible to maintain a family on a scale of payments which amounted to less than 1s. *per capita* per week.[94] Manchester's contin-uing adherence, however, to the doctrines of parsimony and deterrence was in no sense untypical. For despite the existence of areas such as Poplar where the unemployed pauper was temporarily freed, during 1904-5, from some of the less pleasant features of less eligibility, below subsistence levels of assistance represented the general trend in Poor Law administration in the majority of urban unions until the outbreak of the First World War.[95] Given, therefore, the expulsive effect of these adverse influences, it was perhaps inevitable that after 1870 the poor rate was increasingly called upon to support the chronically underemployed casual worker rather than the regular workman at times of mass unemployment, thereby ironically strengthening the structure of the casual labour market.[96] Finally, and what in the context of this discussion is equally important, it must be accepted that the admittedly imperfect data which relate to able-bodied pauperism are as inaccurate a guide to the dimensions of the unemployment problem and the wants of the unemployed as the aggregate pauper statistics are of the incidence of poverty in British society.

Nevertheless, it is a mistake to argue that the number of able-bodied who sought assistance from the Poor Law was usually kept within manageable limits through the exercise of consumer choice. In at least two distinct areas of policy attempts were consciously made to exclude specific categories of the able-bodied from all, or certain, kinds of rate aid. In the first place single unemployed men were often excluded from the stone yard and thus compelled to choose between entering the workhouse and trying to maintain themselves independently of the Poor Law.[97] Secondly, the laws of settlement, more especially in the 1830s and 1840s, could effectively deprive those who had failed to obtain a settlement in the town to which they had moved in search of work, of all right to institutional relief. These laws pressed most harshly upon the Irish immigrant communities who, in England, were heavily concentrated – outside London – in the industrial towns of Lancashire and the West Riding. Largely unskilled and placed firmly at the foot of the socio-economic hierarchy, such groups possessed few material resources to shelter them from the deleterious consequences of unemployment. At such times, therefore, they tried to avoid the often inevitable sequel to approaching the Poor Law authorities – the granting of temporary relief on condition that they would agree to be passed back to Ireland – by begging, pawning, mutual assistance and utilising, where possible, the resources of local charity. But, as was amply illustrated in Adshead's 1840-2 survey of Manchester, these ploys still left the individual family in deep poverty. Typical of such households was that of 'Sarah Cunningham, Pot-street, Ancoats. An Irish family, nine in number; one of the children earns 4s. 6d. They pay in rent 1s. 6d. The husband cannot obtain work; and is disqualified to receive relief, having only resided four years in Manchester.'[98] At the extended level of the town, the invocation of the same spectre of removal could speedily reduce, at times of heavy unemployment, the local Irish community to a similar state of want. As the *Leeds Times* recorded in February 1841, 'hundreds of families at Leeds are, at the present moment, in a state almost of absolute want. This is particularly the case of the poor Irish who are peremptorily refused relief, unless they consent to sign a pass to have themselves and their families carried back to Ireland.'[99]

In mitigation it can be argued that before and after the 1834 Poor Law Act, Manchester and Liverpool, the two cities with the largest Irish contingents in the North of England, operated an informal arrangement which allowed immigrants of good character and a specified period of residence – a minimum of from ten to fifteen years – to obtain relief in an emergency without being subjected to the harrassing process of removal.[100] Moreover, in Liverpool and a handful of other northern areas,

> the law [of removal] has always been carried out . . . with humanity and discretion. No pauper is removed who up to the last moment expresses his desire to make a renewed effort at self-support; facility is even afforded him to accomplish that object, by granting occasional relief in seasons of temporary distress.[101]

In addition, as the relief lists of some urban unions demonstrate, able-bodied Irishmen were relieved at times of cyclical unemployment, without any close observance of the law of settlement, since their services would be needed in the ensuing upswing phase of the trade cycle. Finally, starting with *9 & 10 Vict. cap. 66* (1946) which bestowed irremovable status on those applicants for relief who, without possessing a settlement, had been resident in a parish for five consecutive years and ending with the Union Chargeability Act of 1865 which reduced the qualifying period to one year and extended the area of residence of the irremovable poor from a parochial to a union basis,[102] Parliament itself undertook to alter an aspect of the Poor Law which had been the subject of frequent complaints among Irish immigrants generally. For until the emergence of these more positive steps, there was justification both for the claim of Leeds' Irish community that 'we . . . are made to feel more acutely our distressed condition from the circumstances of our being compelled to leave this country on receipt of relief, though that relief be only temporarily required in consequence of sickness or loss of employment', and the demand of their counterparts in Manchester, made in 1842, for the acceptance of the principle that 'they have a just and equitable claim to relief *in that place where they have worked longest and have most contributed to increase the general wealth.*'[103]

The task remains of evaluating the contributions of charity and municipal 'make work' projects in alleviating poverty amongst the unemployed. At one level these two approaches were, of course, quite distinct from one another, for while most philanthropic bodies possessed relatively limited financial resources, they were, paradoxically enough, usually concerned with a broader range of social problems than those posed by unemployment alone. At another level, however, it is misleading to regard them as mutually exclusive initiatives since the closest co-operation commonly prevailed between the Town Hall and those acts of private philanthropy which were made by prominent citizens in an attempt to reduce the intensity and incidence of social suffering in their own locality during periods of bad trade. In such cases the mayor or provost might play the key role in launching an appeal for funds which could in part be used to finance a programme of municipal works. Similarly, a local authority might secure the services of the casework specialists of local charities — particularly, in the post-1870 era, those of the Charity Organisation Society — to undertake the investigative work which was necessary to establish the *bona fides* of all applicants. And if in many instances this kind of formal arrangement was lacking, the degree of overlap which usually existed between the personnel of the council chamber and the administrators of unemployment relief funds ensured that each would, as far as possible, concentrate upon different facets of the unemployment question, hopefully for the benefit of the unemployed themselves.

On the credit side this form of initiative undoubtedly helped to soften the devastating effect of cyclical unemployment upon the standard of living of a section of the unskilled. This was above all true of the multitude of *ad hoc* expeidents which were extensively adopted in areas of widespread material deprivation, although the manner in which such benevolence was exercised depended upon how the exigencies of the poor were viewed by middle-class subscribers. In the vast majority of localities the soup kitchen — the cost of its operation having been underwritten by donations — was usually allocated a prominent role in sustaining the needy. Yet while it loomed large in virtually every private relief programme, it was rarely expected to discharge the function of feeding the unemployed unaided. Thus, it was by no means uncommon to find an assorted range of voluntary organisations, including the churches, supplementing, on a temporary basis, the ubiquitous efforts of the soup kitchen by either providing free meals for the children and wives of out of work men or giving cash and in kind assistance to families pressurised by poverty. On the other hand these short-term manifestations of charity might concentrate part or all of their energies upon other aspects of the social problem. This was what occurred in Manchester in 1840 when almost £3800 was raised to procure supplies of bedding and clothing for destitute members of the working classes and in Glasgow in 1895 when gifts of coal and garments were distributed, through the medium of the local Lord Provost's Fund, to carefully selected households.[104] Furthermore, as has already been noted, the administrators of such funds were not simply preoccupied with the task of dispensing relief; they were frequently concerned with testing hardship by financing or mounting unskilled 'make work' schemes for the unemployed. In some instances, especially in the pre-1850 period, a part of the task which was exacted — for example, the giving out of webs to unemployed weavers[105] — would be completely independent of any outside agency. Increasingly, however, private philanthropy looked to local government to discharge this duty, although it was sometimes able to offer financial guarantees, designed to cover the cost of a specific project, to the individual municipality. Nevertheless, the involvement of municipal authorities in the 'make work' field cannot be adequately explained by concentrating upon its contractual relationship with charitable endeavour. For from the mid-1880s onwards other forces pushed municipalities to act in this way. In England and Wales the Local Government Board Circular, issued by Joseph Chamberlain in 1886, encouraged Town Halls to embark upon a programme of rate-financed public works at times of cyclical unemployment in order to keep the deserving artisan free from all contact with the Poor Law. Again, the Unemployed Workmen Act of 1905 meant that in practice local Distress Committees, including those which had established their own Farm

Colonies, turned instinctively towards local government to set in motion un-skilled projects of general utility which would be open to those of their appli-cants whom they deemed to be deserving.

In the last analysis, however, this kind of interventionism left untouched the vast majority of the unemployed, while in hardly any case did it raise the recipients of its bounty above the poverty line. But in part its failure to do more was inherent in its *modus operandi*. In the first place, while some of these initiatives — and above all the soup kitchens — adopted the limited brief of trying to prevent the occurrence of mass starvation, other relief organisations and committees confused supporters and the unemployed alike by failing to define, in a clearcut fashion, the social objectives they were trying to attain. Secondly, the raising of relief funds was in any case dependent for its success both upon the degree to which the social consciences of the middle class were attuned, at the local level, to the problem of unemployment and upon the social structure of different urban communities. For example, amidst the con-siderable amount of distress which was generated in 1879 by mass unemploy-ment, the Charity Organisation Society successfully stifled the charitable im-pulses of London's wealthy citizens by preventing the launching of an appeal on behalf of the impoverished population of the East End.[106] Conversely, many districts where the need was greatest, were often unable to do much — either through private philanthropy or municipal works — to alleviate social suffering because they lacked a numerically significant middle class.[107] In the third place none of the expedients which have been described, rested upon very firm financial foundations. Appeals for donations at times of depressed trade often evoked a very poor response because the middle class itself was also adversely affected by the general commercial crisis. This facet of the question was succinctly summarised by C.R. Baird when he described the uncertain progress of Glasgow's unemployment fund in 1842. As he put it, subscriptions

> came in very slowly, and we experienced some difficulty from the fact that the mer-cantile class was much depressed. I went through the street in which I have my own chambers [Baird was a lawyer], and a number of parties whom I might reasonably have expected to get subscriptions, declined to give any from the circumstances of the times. Had it not been for large subscriptions from the banks in Glasgow, I do not conceive we could have carried on as we did.[108]

In a Glasgow context this was to be a recurrent complaint, for the efforts of private philanthropy to assist the city's workless population were halted in 1878-9 and 1907-8 not because it had successfully discharged its brief but because its resources were exhausted.[109] But this was by no means an exclu-sively West of Scotland phenomenon. As contemporary comments illustrated, this pattern was to be reproduced in most of the principal centres of industry in England during a protracted slump. From Manchester came the claim in May 1842 that the funds of the Manchester and Salford Soup Charity had virtually dried up 'at a time when it appears as much needed as ever, and when the poor are greatly alarmed at such a prospect'; in Leeds in the same year the

ad hoc unemployment relief fund had disbursed its income long before the
return of good trading conditions; and in Bradford those who had mounted
a similar effort on behalf of the unemployed, were compelled temporarily to
suspend operations in February 1843.[110] In other words, as these parochial
examples, taken from the 1842 crisis, make plain, the resources of *ad hoc* and
permanent charities became so stretched during a slump that they were rarely
able to deal, for more than a brief period of time, with a small percentage of
those who were thrown out of work. But the problem of limited means also
affected those initiatives taken by local authorities which, with no powers to
levy rates for unemployment relief *per se*, were largely content with a restricted
programme of unskilled labouring work. Nor was this picture changed with the
passing of the Unemployed Workmen Act since the financial restraints which
were imposed upon Distress Committees guaranteed that they would be unable
to cope with the kind of cyclical crisis which occurred in 1907-9.

But such initiatives often failed in a more profound sense, since they rarely
reached that section of society — the deserving poor — whose needs they had
been designed to alleviate. To some extent this was because the nature of the
tasks associated with most 'make work' schemes — digging, trenching, levelling
waste ground, laying out park land, banking and paving — made them fundamentally unattractive to the artisan class.[111] None the less such objection was
neither the prerogative of the tradesman nor applied exclusively to public
work projects. It could extend to other forms of relief which were seen as
stigmatising their recipients. Thus, it was argued in Paisley in 1829 that only the
'low Irish and other dregs of society' would avail themselves of the services of
the local soup kitchen since the unemployed indigenous weaver, 'if he once
stooped to such degradation . . . would never be able to hold up his head among
his fellows.'[112] Similarly, during the severe frost of January-February 1895
which brought Glasgow's building trades to a virtual halt, relatively few building workers, skilled and unskilled, turned to the Lord Provost's Fund for support.
As A.J. Hunter, Secretary of the local Trades Council expressed it,

> perhaps a few of these men applied for relief; but very few, I think; they are not men
> who do that sort of thing. What I want to show is that, although not many of those
> men applied for relief, there was an immense number of them that might have applied
> [because of their poverty] , and not be blamed very much if they had done so.[113]

But the stigma which such expedients possessed in the eyes of a substantial
proportion of the working class was reinforced by two other considerations.
Firstly, where investigations into the background of applicants was carried
out — and this was increasingly the trend from the 1880s onwards, — the
'deserving' often refused to apply, despite pressing personal needs, because they
interpreted such a mode of inquiry as an extension of the methods of the Poor
Law and the profoundly distrusted Charity Organisation Society. In the Scottish
situation, to quote Hunter again, 'in connection with relief funds, many of the
workmen have at all times had very strong objections to being subject to the

investigations of the Charity Organisation Society.'[114] The same kind of hostility was also periodically manifested in an English context, as in Liverpool in 1893 when a deputation of the unemployed resolved to have nothing to do with the Central Relief Committee because of its work test.[115] Secondly, the 'less eligible' structure of wages, whether paid in kind or in money, which was invariably linked with the 'make work' proposals of philanthropy, municipality and Distress Committee, and the relatively limited period for which an individual was hired, further reduced the appeal of such initiatives.

Despite, therefore, the persistent attempts at introducing character, and other, tests of suitability — a minimum period of residence in a town was usually insisted upon and single men, along with male residents from model lodging houses, single women and able-bodied widows were rarely catered for — the 'task work' aspect of this programme tended over time to become the special preserve of largely casual hands. And this applied equally to measures which owed their origins to the Chamberlain Circular and the Unemployed Workmen Act as well as to those which owed nothing to such acts of state intervention. For those thus situated such employment might provide an important, albeit short-lived, supplement to what, on a yearly basis, were below subsistence earnings, without raising them above the poverty line. For the majority of the cyclically unemployed, however, such palliatives had little relevance to their own social problems. Outside the realm of public works they might accept the utility of alternative sources of charitable assistence — clothing and coal charities, aid from the churches, and Poor Children's Dinner Funds among them — as partial salves for some of the needs of their families and concede that the beginnings of a state-run scheme of sickness and unemployment insurance was an augury of a better future. But, in concrete terms, none of these steps had, before 1914, more than a marginal impact on the dimensions of that part of the poverty problem which could be directly attributed to unemployment.

Chapter 5
The Socio-Economic Characteristics of Poverty 1830-1914: Food and Housing

Any discussion of the socio-economic characteristics of poverty must begin with an evaluation of the food consumption patterns of the poor, primarily because the cost of foodstuffs absorbed the major part of family income. Nevertheless the proportion of earnings which was channelled in this direction could vary enormously over time and between different unskilled occupations. At one end of the spectrum weaving households in Dundee were devoting eighty per cent of their meagre incomes during 1934 to acquire the limited range of foodstuffs which comprised their inadequate diet.[1] At the other extreme, expenditure upon food accounted for only fifty-one per cent of the average total outlay of those members of Rowntree's Class I — weekly family earnings under 26s. — whose budgets were subject to detailed scrutiny in York during the years 1898-1901.[2] In the vast majority of cases, however, it was rare for the food purchases to amount to less than fifty-five to sixty-five per cent of an unskilled household's aggregate income.[3]

Yet while a study of working-class eating habits can shed light upon the nature of the poverty question, it is necessary to be aware of the limitations and deficiencies of much of the surviving evidence. In this context it is important at the start to stress that there were considerable differences between regions which can be effectively disguised by concentrating upon the experience of London. In their most obvious form there were differences, more marked before 1860 but not completely obliterated by 1914, in the type of food consumed. Thus, while the unskilled urban worker in Scotland still retained a firm commitment to oatmeal in the first half of the nineteenth century, his counterpart in the South of England was equally attached to the wheaten loaf. Again, if in England whole sections of the unskilled working class, from the late 1880s onwards, bought imported frozen meat on account of its cheapness, their Scottish equivalents tended to shun it in favour of home-produced boiling beef, 'mince and sausages sold as low as 4d. per pound.'[4] There were also sizable regional differences, in the middle years of the nineteenth century, in the working classes' consumption of fish. Whereas Mayhew proclaimed in the 1850s that 'the rooms of the very neediest of a needy metropolitan population always smell of fish, most frequently of herrings', fish only appeared in a minority of those households in the provinces whose living standards formed the basis of Dr. Edward Smith's 1863 *Report on the Food of the Poorer Labouring Classes in England*.[5] Similarly, while the poor in York displayed in the early 1900s an antipathy to vegetables, the families of labourers in Barrow and Lancaster held them in high esteem.[6]

But in addition to such dissimilarities it is also possible to discern a distinctively regional experience, in the pre-railway era, in the realm of retail and wholesale prices. For although much of the historical research in this particular sphere has still to be undertaken, Gourvish's study of the real incomes of the working classes in Glasgow in the opening three decades of the nineteenth century, with its emphasis upon the size of the differentials between West of Scotland and London prices, is by itself sufficient to demonstrate the reality of this phenomenon.[7] Yet if such differences were in part a product of poor transport communications, they were not to be completely removed when the railway network started to expand. Thus, while Perren, in his examination of wholesale meat prices in Britain between 1846 and 1862, has concluded that 'there were no consistently wide differentials in regional prices,' his data still enable a hierarchy of price levels to be clearly defined, with London being the most expensive city for mutton and Glasgow occupying a comparable position for beef.[8] It must, of course, be accepted that for those at or below the poverty line these differentials were of little more than academic interest since few of them at that point in time were consumers of flesh meat on a significant scale. That, however, was less true of the retail index of commodity prices, constructed by the Board of Trade in 1905, which, in addition to fuel, included many items, among them bread, tea, bacon, sugar, butter, potatoes, and flour, that figured in the budgets of the urban poor. In this case the cost of the 'basket' of goods upon which the index was based, again high-lighted the existence of local and regional price variations. At the level of the individual English town the index moved between a 'high' of 106, recorded at Dover in October 1905 (London prices equalled 100) and a low point of 88 which was reached in Wigan and Stockport. In regional terms the Southern Counties (102) were the dearest, and Lancashire and Cheshire (92) the cheapest, areas in which to live.[9] Nevertheless, valuable as such inter-regional studies are, they do not, by their very nature, take into account the last form of price difference whose existence must be acknowledged in any discussion of urban poverty. Throughout our period there were often differences in the cost of what were outwardly the same kind of foodstuffs within the individual town. Where such fluctuations can be identified — and much of the evidence here is of a qualitative nature, — they were usually tangible signs of a community pressurised by poverty. In short, dearer food denoted either the reliance of the poor upon the credit facilities of local shopkeepers and their practice of acquiring their supplies in small quantities, or the pernicious influence of the truck system.

Quite distinct from the regional factor, the impact of unemployment in all its guises upon working-class feeding patterns must be acknowledged, although several contemporary surveys of the budgets of the unskilled effectively ignored this dynamic dimension of the poverty question. As has already been argued, the downswing of the trade cycle not merely exacerbated the material impoverishment of the casual and largely unskilled sectors of the labour force; it also reduced a proportion of those from an artisan background to a state of want.[10] In concrete terms, cyclically generated unemployment led to monotonous and below subsistence diets for many, and among whole elements of the unskilled to either dependence upon institutional and voluntary assistance for most of the food they consumed or days when nothing was eaten by the whole family. As Thomas Wright pointed out in 1973,

> the industrious poor are, for the most part, unskilled and only casually employed labourers, members of trades that have been superseded, or of branches of existing trades that have fallen under the sway of sweaters — needlewomen, charwomen, and washerwomen . . . They have to live hardly and from hand to mouth even at the best of times, and when evils come — when employment cannot be found, or through sickness, cannot be followed — they suffer terribly in the struggle to keep body and soul together. The hungry stomach, the scantily-clad back, the fireless grate, the foodless cupboard, and worse than all, in many instances, the cry of their children for bread they cannot give, becomes familiar to them. To keep themselves at all, at such times, they have to part with their little belongings, and get into debt with petty tradesmen, and then they are encumbered when what is to them prosperity returns again, and their whole life becomes a heartbreaking struggle with the bitterest poverty.[11]

But other forms of unemployment pressed equally hard upon those who lived below, or perilously close to, the poverty line. Rathbone's inquiry into Liverpool's dock labourers and Charles Booth's description of his Class B underlined the fact that casually employed hands were likely to experience considerable fluctuations in their intake of food over a relative short time-span since their living standards were primarily influenced by the rhythms of the casual market. In Rathbone's words,

> it is . . . difficult to convey by means of any general statement a correct picture of a diet of which the most marked feature was its fluctuations of plenty and scarcity, according to the quantity of the family income. In the matter of food even less than the other necessaries of life, an irregular supply is not the equivalent of its average since neither physiologically nor in any other way can privation at one time be compensated by a surfeit at another.[12]

Much the same held true of unskilled workers whose earnings were adversely affected by seasonal slackness. This trend was succinctly captured in Mayhew's description of a London brickmaker in the 1850s, although, judged from the nature of his meat diet, he fared a good deal better than the vast majority of seasonally employed labourers in the building industry.

> In the long fine days of summer the little daughter of a working brickmaker used to order chops and other choice dainties of a butcher, saying, "Please, sir, father don't care for the price just a-now; but he must have his chops good; line-chops, sir, and tender, please — 'cause he's a brickmaker." In winter it was, "O please, sir, here's a fourpenny bit, and you must send father something cheap. He don't care what it is, so long as it's cheap. It's winter and he hasn't no work, sir — 'cause he's a brickmaker."[13]

Similarly, any evaluation of feeding patterns must take note of questions of family circumstance. For apart from the immediacy of the crisis which followed in the wake of widowhood and sickness of the head of the household among the unskilled, the life cycle of the individual family could produce, even if no measure of social mobility took place, substantial changes in the eating patterns of its members. Where, for example, the husband, working in an unskilled or sweated occupation, was the sole breadwinner, undernourishment was invariably a feature of the family's diet. As one observer of Huddersfield's woollen handloom weavers proclaimed in 1849, 'if they have young families . . ., that is, families over young to help them by working in the mills, they don't get half enough to eat.'[14] That verdict was of much wider application than this relatively restricted group of outworkers, was endorsed fifty years later when Rowntree in York and Cadury, Matheson and Shann in Birmingham examined the socio-economic position of labourers' households in which there were no supplementary wage-earners. Labourers' children, it was concluded, 'fare worse during infancy than at any other time, unless indeed they grow up to marry labourers and try to bring up families on an irregular 18/- to 20/- a week [in 1906]. These children often live for weeks or even months at a time chiefly on bread and tea, and it is no uncommon occurrence for the supply to run out.'[15]

Finally, old age and declining physical powers meant for the unskilled individual whose limited income during his working life had been barely sufficient 'to provide the absolute requirements of food, clothing and shelter',[16] a desperately inadequate diet to which, in the absence of external aid, he was tied until death. Among those who were severely hit by the social crisis associated with old age were the relatively small bands of labourers who, having attained their sixtieth birthday, saw their hold on the labour market slacken but who, having married late in life, still had a substantial number of dependants to support. The paucity of the dietaries of those who were thus situated can be starkly illustrated by quoting in full the plight of 'Mr. P', a Liverpool docket 'over 60' who, in 1909, was rarely hired but who, with only two children gainfully employed, had to try to feed a wife and five other dependants.[17] As Table 5 illustrates, such attempts were doomed to failure, with chronic malnutrition the invariable outcome. But all was not loss. In this case as in other households of the unskilled, there was some hope of a modicum of social betterment in the medium term. To reiterate the point made in Chapter 4, when children started to contribute on a significant scale to aggregate income, labourers' families could expect, until their offspring left home, to rise above the primary poverty line. In short, any assessment of food consumption patterns is misleading if it focuses its attention upon occupation *per se* and ignores the economic life cycle of the family and the changing nature of the demand for unskilled labour.

These *caveats* by no means exhaust the list of shortcomings in the surviving evidence. In the first place major gaps remain in our knowledge of trends in the *per capita* consumption of certain kinds of foodstuffs. In the pre-1850 period, as the standard of living debate illustrates, we cannot be certain about whether or

Table 5

Menu of Meals during Week 2 of Mr. P's Budget

	Breakfast	Dinner	Tea	Supper
Sunday	Bread Margarine Tea Fish 9	Meat Potatoes 8	Bread Margarine Tea 9	—
Monday	Bread Margarine Tea 8	Cold Meat Potatoes 9	Bread Margarine Tea 8	—
Tuesday	Bread Margarine 5	Soup 5	Bread Margarine 6	—
Wednesday	Bread Margarine 5	—	Bread Margarine 8	—
Thursday	—	Bread Margarine 8	Bread Margarine 7	—
Friday	—	Bread Margarine 6	Bread Margarine 8	—
Saturday	—	Bread Margarine 8	Bread Margarine 8	—

The figures indicate the numbers present at each meal.

Source:- *How the casual Labourer Lives: Report of the Liverpool Joint Committee* (1909) quoted in W.H.B. Court, *op. cit.*, p. 312.

not wheat production outstripped the inexorable growth of Britain's population, although the answer to that problem would in its turn give a more accurate insight into the nature of the role of the potato in working-class households. Furthermore, while several pre-1850 investigations raised the question of the part played by meat in working-class diets, they are usually impressionistic in tone, giving no indication as to the quantity consumed and often failing to distinguish between bacon, mutton and beef. Outwardly some of these difficulties appear to be reduced in the post-1870 decades. For one thing national data relating to food consumption patterns become more profuse. But what is of greater importance, the post-1870 era was distinguished by a more systematic approach to the study of the relationship between food and social class. In some respects the results of this comparative approach have to be handled with care. Some of its findings can scarcely claim to be representative because of the narrowness of the sample upon which its conclusions rest.[18] Yet, whatever its weaknesses in terms of statistical precision, this kind of survey fulfils a positive purpose, since it enables the historian of poverty to highlight those points at which the diets of the unskilled diverged from those of other social groupings. In particular it underlines the extent to which national averages often obscure, rather than illuminate, the socio-economic position of the poor. Two examples to illustrate this point suffice. Long after the advent of milk cooling techniques and improved transport facilities had overcome the problem of supplying the major towns and cities, fresh milk − as opposed to buttermilk and skimmed milk − was still relatively little used by those at or below the poverty line. According to R.H. Rew, for instance, whereas in 1891 the daily consumption of milk in Britain amounted to 0.33 pints per head, the comparable figure for the impoverished East End of London was a mere 0.086 pints.[19] Again, while a Committee of the Royal Statistical Society computed that in 1904 members of the households of artisans and mechanics within the United Kingdom consumed twelve gallons of milk per annum, those from a labouring background used a mere five gallons annually.[20] Similarly, in the early years of this century the consumption of butter by labourers, urban and rural, lagged behind that of the artisan elite.[21] In both cases, however, if the size of these differences can be attributed to corresponding differentials in earnings, they were also in some measure a reflection of the way in which low pay compelled the unskilled to resort to cheaper substitutes in the form of already sweetened condensed milk, skimmed milk and buttermilk and, from the late 1880s onwards, margarine.

But while, in the closing years of our period, increasing attention was paid to charting the nature of the relationship between diet and poverty, a less systematic approach was made in two other significant areas of the subject. Firstly, we still know too little about the role of outside bodies in meeting part of the food requirements of the poverty stricken. In one form, as Rathbone demonstrated in Liverpool in 1909, such supplementation could involve mutual assistance, operated on an informal basis, among the poor themselves. Thus, 'No. 19' of her budget keepers, a family of eight supporting itself on an average income of 19/4d. 'and where poverty is acutely felt from its contrast with former days of prosperity', invited 'a poor old woman', without any relatives, 'to come for all her meals.'[22] At another level, however, it could take the form of payment in kind, provided by a vast range of institutional outlets. Outside those *ad hoc* expedients adopted by private benevolence for dealing with mass unemployment, external assistance could mean soup kitchens, ostensibly designed to cater for the deserving poor during the winter months; bread charities; free breakfasts which were organised in some cities by religious bodies for the children of the poor; and, starting in the 1870s, the provision, initially by private philanthropy and after 1906, by local authorities, of school meals for necessitous school children. Finally, as with a section of the needlewomen examined by Dr. Edward Smith in 1863 who 'received aid from the parish, which comprised a loaf of bread, and this was made the basis of the weekly dietary, other elements of food being added as the variable income might permit,'[23] The Poor Laws in both England and Scotland provided a modicum of 'in kind' assistance to sweated, and frequently elderly, female outworkers. Viewed overall, it can be accepted that the combined efforts of these multifarious agencies helped to contain, to a limited degree, the amount of social suffering which marked the lives of the impoverished elements of society. But it remains doubtful if, with the possible exception of free school meals which, as at Bradford in the early 1900s, led to weight gains being recorded among their recipients,[24] these forms of aid did much to lift the veil of primary poverty in urban Britain.

The last methodological point which must be raised concerns the deficiencies of many extant working-class budgets and the difficulty, because of the unsatisfactory nature of the evidence, of deciding whether or not whole groups of people were the victims of primary or secondary poverty. The principal defect in several of the budgetary exercises that were carried out by contemporary investigators was that the prominent position played by drink in working-class society tended to be played down. This omission could assume one of two forms. In the first place it could be the direct consequence of the type of individuals or families whose expenditure patterns were selected for scrutiny. Thus, few of the witnesses who appeared before the Select Committees on Handloom Weavers' Petitions in the mid-1830s drank on any scale. Representing the best paid sections of Manchester's cotton weaving community was James Brennan, a master weaver in the fancy branch of the trade, who, out of an aggregate family income of 19s. per week, devoted a mere 4d. to 'malt liquor' on a Saturday night.[25] Again, with one exception, the York budgets compiled by members of Rowntree's Class I between 1898 and 1901 were selected from 'the steady, respectable sections of the labouring classes, who spend practically nothing upon drink.'[26] Secondly, the budget keepers themselves might try to project a misleading image of sobriety by seeking to minimise the significance of alchol in their returns. For example, it was accepted that it was impossible to assess the proportion of income diverted to drink by those labourers whose living standards were examined in Liverpool in 1909,

> such expenditure being usually covered by the noncommittal heading "kept by the husband," and sometimes no doubt concealed under an apparent excess of income over expenditure. But in our forty families, ten husbands are noted to drink more or less immoderately, and of several wives the same thing is suspected.[27]

With the first of the groups, therefore, the question arises as to how far, at a time when roughly one-sixth of working-class income was channelled towards the publican and the off-licence, the diets of Rowntree's budget keepers, even if they all fell below the poverty line, mirrored those of the bulk of their unskilled contemporaries. With regard to the second kind of omission — the attempt to conceal expenditure upon beer and spirits — it is simply an additional complication when an attempt is made to draw the dividing line between primary and secondary poverty.

Many of the problems of definition in that sphere have already been touched upon. Here, in the light of that earlier discussion, it is enough to repeat that some of the attacks of the middle class upon feckless housekeeping were misconceived, mistaking what, from its limited perspective, appeared to be the symptons of self-induced poverty for secondary poverty itself. Thus, while working-class housewives were frequently castigated for their limited culinary knowledge, it was less commonly accepted that those limitations could in their turn be the direct result of the cramping constraints of primary poverty. In part this stemmed from the poor quality of the housing that they were compelled to occupy, for some of the accommodation reserved for the unskilled sectors of the working classes lacked efficient coal ovens or kitchen ranges.[28] Nevertheless even the spread of the gas oven within working-class circles from the 1890s onwards did not by itself remedy this defect, since the high cost of fuel for those at or below the poverty line continued to rule out the systematic preparation of hot meals. Hence the resort to fried fish, and hot pie sellers, and the continued use of the bakehouse by many households.[29] As Mrs. Pember Reeves wrote in 1913, when she scrutinised the feeding habits of the families of Lambeth labourers,

> homes where there is no oven send out to the bakehouse on that occasion [Sunday dinner]. The rest of the week is managed on cold food, or the hard-worked saucepan and frying-pan are brought into play. The centainty of an economical stove or fireplace is out of the reach of the poor. They are often obliged to use old-fashioned and broken ranges and grates which devour coal with as little benefit to the user as possible. They are driven to cook by gas, which ought to be an excellent way of cooking, but under the penny-in-the-slot system it is a way [because of cost] which tends to underdone food.[30]

To turn to the specific level of individual foodstuffs, it was equally wrong to interpret the ingrained preference for the more expensive English bacon as an unmistakable sign of imprudent budgeting. For, in the eyes of the poor, such a purchasing policy conformed to the precepts of buying 'cheap', since 'the fat [in English bacon] did not run out when the bacon was boiled and hence was usually cheaper than the American bacon at half the price.'[31] Lastly, while the reality of secondary poverty must be acknowledged, the narrow and rigid nature of the concept must also be explored. For it not merely assumed a greater degree of control over expenditure than was commonly exercised by the middle class itself; it had also, by very definition, to pay no attention to the palatability of food and to ignore the fact that certain items, if costly in relation to their calorific and protein values, were often accepted as outward signs of social advance. In short, much of middle-class comment upon working-class feeding patterns should not be treated uncritically. By concentrating upon lack of culinary skills and the need for a nutritionally balanced diet, it overlooked some of the principal obstacles to realising the goal of efficient budgeting. Above all, in its most simplistic form, it tends to blur, rather than to clarify, our understanding of primary and secondary poverty.

In the light of this discussion it is clear that it is impossible to chart in a quantifiable form the diets of all those groups who, from whatever cause, lived in a state of poverty. What, at best, can be attempted is to delineate in broad outline, with aid of surveys and qualitative evidence, the eating habits of those families whose adult male head was still in gainful but unskilled employment. But in opting for this course of action it must be remembered that the resultant picture presents an unduly favourable position of urban poverty since it largely omits the unemployed, the elderly who lived alone, the sick and widows with dependants who invariably fared much worse than the household of the employed able-bodied worker.

I

In the pre-1850 era the dietaries of the poorest elements in society were dominated by bread, potatoes and, in urban Scotland and parts of the North of England, oatmeal. Nationally Dr. Salaman, in his pioneering investigation, has succinctly described the pervasive role of potato in society. According to his calculations, daily potato consumption *per capita* rose from 9.40lb. in 1798 to 0.62lb. in 1838 and to 0.70lb. by 1850.[32] Virtually all the extant data, at the microcosmic level of the individual town, underline the plausibility of these global estimates. Gourvish has argued that in Glasgow at the start of the 1830s the family of 'the lowest paid worker', consisting of two adults and two children and spending 9s. per week on necessities, including rent and fuel, consumed 40lb. of potatoes as against 13 lb. of oatmeal and a mere 4.5lb. of household bread.[33] In England a parallel trend can be discerned amongst handloom weavers — the best documented of all lowly paid groups — and other badly remunerated elements in the unskilled labour market. Cotton weavers in the rural parts of North-East Lancashire were tied, in the early 1830s, to a monotonous diet in which the potato always loomed large. 'Their food,' wrote a contemporary chronicler, consisted 'chiefly [of] potatoes, oatmeal porridge, and milk, with the addition of oatcakes in the north of the county; a herring, or a little bacon, is added on Sundays, and the women have a little tea, coffee and bread.'[34] A similar situation obtained in Manchester where in 1840 a complaint was lodged at a meeting, probably representing the interests of calico weavers, that 'potatoes, which constitute the chief part of our diet' were 'now beyond our reach', and among general labourers of Irish birth in Liverpool in the mid-1830s where it was observed that 'persons in this class live on potatoes and stirabout; now and then, perhaps, they may get a herring or a little bacon.'[35] Finally, apart from the testimonies of London-based sweated workers, embedded in the pages of Mayhew's seminal work, Neild's 1841 study of nineteen working-class budgets, drawn from Manchester and Dukinfield, underlined the significance, in terms of bulk intake of foodstuffs, of Cobbett's 'accursed root.' As Professor McKenzie's recent analysis of this survey has demonstrated, the average weekly intake of potatoes was 5.2lb. per head, or, broken down into two distinctive geographical areas, 5.9lb. *per capita* in Manchester and 3.7lb. in Dukinfield.[36]

What is less easy to decipher is whether the potato was used as a supplement to, or substitute for, bread and oatmeal. The fragmentary evidence in this particular sphere is far from unambiguous. At one level fears were expressed in the *Third Report* of the Select Committee on Emigration (1826-7) that the influx of Irish immigrants into Britain could lead to the replacement of the wheaten loaf by the potato, with any savings effected by such a move being devoted to purchasing whisky and beer.[37] Kay was another writer who predicted that the English working classes would fall victims to their own folly by adopting the 'meal and potatoes' diet of the Irish.[38]   But at another level the fragile calculations which have been employed to trace the course of wheat consumption suggest a quite different explanation. Putting upon them the most optimistic gloss, they indicate that at best wheat production kept pace with population growth.[39] In this context, therefore, bread might have been abandoned for the cheaper potato by certain badly paid groups — such as Manchester's calico weavers in 1840 [40] — because of the strength of poverty-inducing exgenous pressure. For, as Professor T.S. Ashton has remarked of price trends between 1790 and 1830 — and the comment was still relevant in the two succeeding decades, — 'there were masses of unskilled or poorly skilled workers — seasonally employed agricultural workers and handloom weavers in particular — whose incomes were almost wholly absorbed in paying for the necessaries of life, the prices of which . . . remained high.'[41] In more general terms, however, substitution could affect a much larger segment of the unskilled on a short-term basis. This would usually occur when an increase in the price of the quartern (4lb. 5oz.) loaf coincided with periods of cyclical unemployment, such as occurred in 1838-9 when in London it touched 10d. and in 1847 when an exceptionally high figure of 11½d. was recorded.[42] In other words, if and when substitution was resorted to, it was more likely to stem from a secular or temporary decline in real earnings than from the indigenous population succumbing *en masse* to the 'contagious example' of the Irish. Indeed, even if the potato diet of the Irish communities in Britain cannot be disputed, it should not automatically be interpreted as a sign of wilful consumer choice. For although heavy whisky drinking was undoubtedly a major feature of immigrant life, briefly interrupted by the success of Father Mathew's temperance campaign in the late 1830s and early 1840s, their firm adherence to the potato was frequently more a manifestation of primary, rather than secondary, poverty among a group which was firmly placed at the foot of the socio-economic ladder.[43]

Substitution, however, has to be kept in perspective since by 1830 the wheaten loaf was as firmly entrenched in the diets of workers living at or slightly below the poverty line in urban England as oatmeal (plus bread) was in urban Scotland.[44] G.R. Porter was one writer who rejoiced at the relatively low price of the quartern loaf in London between 1842 and 1849 — 1847 always excepted — on the grounds that as from one-half to three-quarters of the earnings 'of the most numerous class of the people is expended for this one article, it cannot be held of light importance that a saving of 25 per cent is made in its cost.'[45] (The quartern loaf was retailing at 9½d. in 1842 and at 7d. in 1849.) And if Porter on this occasion palpably over-estimated the proportion of income which was usually spent on this one item, even in the majority of unskilled households, he was largely correct in viewing the price of bread as a sensitive indicator of improvement or deterioration in working-class living standards. As he noted elsewhere, wheat was coming to represent, for the working classes, 'the first necessary of life.'[46] Expressed in a statistical form, the validity of this conclusion was graphically underlined by Neild's Lancastrian budget keepers whose *per capita* intake of bread — 5.4lb. per week — in 1841 rivalled, in terms of weight, their weekly consumption of potatoes. It must, of course, be conceded that this last statistic embraced a much broader spectrum of society than the poor. Indeed, several of the Manchester families 'of sober and industrious habits' who were included in this inquiry belonged to the ranks of the artisan elite. None the less the question of the extent of the commitment of the poor to the wheaten loaf was not completely overlooked. Bread and flour emerged, by a sizable margin, as the largest single source of expenditure amongst those households who, because of family size and/or low earnings, were unmistakably drawn from the impoverished sections of the working classes. In Neild's words,

> as we come down the lists towards the poorer families the per centage [of income spent on bread] rises rapidly and with great regularity; in case No. 12 [a watchman's family of seven with an aggregate weekly income of 21s.] it has risen to the extent of 39.1 per cent [of total expenditure]. The same interesting examplification of the fact that bread forms the staple of the English labourers' food is observed in the seven Dukinfield families. No. 13 with an income of 4s. 9d. per individual expends 17.4 per cent of it on bread; while No. 19, with only 2s. 3d. per individual, expends 32.8 per cent.[47]

In other words, as Burnett has argued, bread, in the first half of the nineteenth century, constituted 'the staple of life for the 80 to 90 per cent of the population that made up the working classes.'[48]

Yet despite the prominent role of bread, oatmeal and potatoes in the dietaries of the poverty stricken, they did not exhaust the range of foodstuffs which, in the pre-1850 decades, were purchased by the urban poor. Tea was acquired by substantial numbers of unskilled workers, albeit usually in relatively small quantities. For example, among handloom weavers in the West of Scotland in the mid-1830s as little as ½oz. per week was expected to meet the needs of the entire family.[49] And while for tea drinkers this lowly figure probably represented an irreducible minimum, it was still rare for the households of the lowly paid to consume more than ¼ to ½lb. of tea in a calendar month. Yet, even taking into account the practice of re-using tea leaves, such an outcome was scarcely surprising since the high rate of duty which was levied — it stood at 2/1d. per lb. in 1841[50] — effectively circumscribed its market. It was precisely for this reason — in Manchester, Birmingham and London four ounces cost between 1s. and 1/9d.

during the 1840s — that coffee, retailing at 8d. to 1s. per ½lb. in the same decade, was accepted as an adequate substitute for, or an invaluable supplement to, tea in certain parts of the country.[51] In Leeds Irish mill-children, according to one authority, largely subsisted in the 1840s upon 'coffee and bread — or tea', while both beverages were employed, on a modest scale, to render more palatable the monotonous diets of plain weavers in rural Lancashire and sweated workers in London.[52]

On the other hand milk, which in many cases meant buttermilk, was consumed by the urban poor in a few areas on a relatively large scale. Thus it was thought that Glasgow's handloom weavers might purchase as much as six quarts of buttermilk in a single week during the 1830.[53] And if this was an exceptionally high figure for the West of Scotland generally, a parallel trend can be discerned amongst the weaving fraternity in parts of Lancashire. Richard Needham, for example, described how a weaver-friend endeavoured to support a wife and five children upon a net income of 4/1½d.:

> When I asked him how he lived, he said, "I buy a pound of meal and make it into porridge, and I buy two quarts of buttermilk, and these amount to 3d., and from that 3d. the whole family breakfasts. . . We get [for dinner] two quarts of buttermilk again, and and as many potatoes as 1½d. will buy; if potatoes are cheap we make a tolerable putting-on for dinner, but if they are dear we are likely to do with less than is sufficient. . . [For the remainder of the day we have] sometimes nothing, and sometimes we muster two quarts of buttermilk again, and one pound of meal.[54]

Again, among the members of four of Neild's Dukinfield household, with incomes ranging from 2/8d. to 3/1½d. *per capita*, milk accounted for between 7.7 per cent and 9.3 per cent, and butter for between 9.4 per cent and 11.4 per cent, of total family expenditure.[55] Assessed overall, however, the admittedly fragmentary and largely qualitative evidence does little to alter the belief that nationally milk was of only marginal significance in the dietaries of the poor. But it is equally important to emphasise that Neild's data did not imply a high level of consumption of butter by this same broad socio-economic grouping. Retailing at between 9d. and 1/1d. per lb. in nearby Manchester during the 1830s,[56] it was rare, when butter appeared in the budgets of the unskilled, for more than one pound per week to be shared amongst the whole household. In this respect it conformed to the general trend, for other supplementary foodstuffs were purchased on an equally sparing scale. While sugar, herring, salted ling, bacon, cheese and fresh vegetables were all mentioned in contemporary accounts of working-class eating patterns, they were at most minor additions to the potato, bread and, to a lesser extent, oatmeal diet of the impoverished. At worst, as with the rural calico weavers of North-East Lancashire, 'butter, beer, and meat are luxuries beyond their reach; even sliced onions, fried with lard, and added as a seasoning to the potatoes, are too dear for common use.'[57]

It does not follow, however, as this last quotation implied, that flesh meat was conspicuous by its absence from the tables of all those who lived at or below the poverty line. Optimistic writers, surveying the living standards of the working classes during the first half of the nineteenth century, have estimated that the average Londoner was consuming more than 30oz. of meat per week by 1850.[58] And although this calculation, resting on relatively insure statistical foundations, applied to London's total population rather than the poor as such, it has still been claimed that 'in the first fifty years of the nineteenth century, the English working class came to expect meat as a part of the normal diet.' [59] Supporting evidence for this thesis, albeit of an indirect nature, has recently been supplied by Alexander's work on the development of retailing in which the growth of butchers' shops and stalls can be interpreted as a positive sign of working-class advance.[60] On the other hand the pessimistic school of thought has reached a very different conclusion, stressing, in E.J. Hobsbawm's words, that 'the figures [for yields of excise on hides and skins] do not indicate a major rise in *per capita* meat consumption.'[61] Yet in relation to the broad issue of poverty, this debate does little to illumine the connection between differing levels of meat consumption and the various strata which collectively comprised the working classes, since the nature of the data effectively preclude any meaningful exercise in comparative quantification. Nevertheless, if the search for precise measurement is a self-defeating undertaking, it is still possible to utilise

Giffen, surveying the 1830s from the vantage point of the mid-1880s, claimed that 'meat fifty years ago was not an article of the workman's diet as it has since become. He had little more concern with its price than the price of diamonds.'[62] This sweeping verdict, with its failure to recognise the nuances of hierarchy which existed within the working classes, cannot, of course, be uncritically endorsed since it is at variance with known fact. Less open to criticism was G.R. Porter's more temperate assessment, delivered in 1850, in which he accepted that 'even in ordinarily prosperous times, there are very many of our fellow subjects who are forced to forego its use.' In this context the numbers of those who were 'thus subjected to privation' were in some measure determined by fluctuations in the price of bread; but 'in large towns . . . few or none are, except in the very dearest times, deprived of the occasional, or perhaps the habitual use, of meat.'[63] Evidence of a similar nature emerged from a variety of contemporaneous surveys which were preoccupied with the plight of those who were subsisting in a state of poverty. Among those who, in the 1830s and 1840s, made either little or no use of flesh meat in their weekly budgets were coarse grade calico weavers in the North of England and the West of Scotland; lower paid factory workers in Manchester who had 'but seldom a little meat' to flavour a dinner 'of boiled potatoes'; Macclesfield silk weavers who in the late 1840s 'didn't eat very much flesh meat. Certainly, as a general thing, not every day'; Irish mill-children in Leeds who ' "never get it" or "sometimes once a week" '; certain grades of sweated workers and the generality of Irish labourers in the towns of Northern England.[64] Elsewhere, and particularly among widows' and labourers' families in St. George's in the East, London, in the mid-1840s,[66] meat might be listed more frequently. But frequency *per se* provides no insight into the quantity consumed and, as in this last instance, gives rise to the suspicion that flesh meat and bacon were sometimes wrongly employed as synonymous terms. Yet notwithstanding such ambiguities they do little, in the last analysis, to alter the principal conclusion to be drawn from the largely qualitative material at the historian's disposal. For although individual exceptions to the rule can be cited, it is clear that the regular consumption of meat on a significant scale remained one of the most meaningful differences between an artisan class which, before 1850, had been the principal beneficiary from the process of economic change within the working classes, and those who, living in a state of poverty, were unable to devote much, or any, of their income to that purpose.

The question that remains to be answered is how far this frugal bill of fare was modified during the course of the second half of the nineteenth century when the real earnings of the bulk of the working classes rose substantially. Since the broader implications of this growth in real income will be examined in the concluding section of this book, it is necessary at this juncture to make only three general points. Firstly, the chronology of this improvement in working-class living standards emphasises the uneven nature of the rate of the advance. Apart from the inevitable checks to growth which occurred at times of dull trade, the 1850s, the early 1860s and a period running roughly from the mid-1870s to the mid-1880s, were years of either stagnant or slowly rising real wages. On the other hand massive gains were recorded during the greatest boom of the entire century — 1868-75 — when real wages rose by thirty per cent. And if after 1886 the process of improvement was of less spectacular dimensions, it is still accurate to speak of a marked rise in real income which was sustained for virtually the next decade and a half and only finally reversed in the bleaker economic climate of the post-Boer War era. Secondly, whereas retail prices and money wages rose on trend during the third quarter of the nineteenth century, this pattern was almost completely reversed from the mid-1870s until the late 1880s when a slight upturn in money income took place. Prices, however, did not resume their upward march until after 1896. Yet within each of these periods the cost of certain basic commodities did not always follow the prevailing trend. Coffee, tea, sugar and tobacco became cheaper during the 1850s and 1860s, primarily as a result of reductions in excise duties, while meat prices, in the post-1875 period, did not effectively fall until the early 1880s. Thirdly, since much of the real wage data that we possess, describe the average experience, they do not provide any direct insights into the position of those who belonged to the poorest elements of working-class society.

Yet in the opening years of this half century this obstacle is more easily circumvented than in the pre-1850 decades because of the pioneering quantitative study of the diets of 'the poorer labouring classes in England', undertaken by Dr. Edward Smith in 1863. Restricting his investigations into urban trades to a broad range of domestic workers — silk weavers, needlewomen, shoemakers, kid glove makers, and stocking weavers, — he opted for a case-study approach to the problem. But at the outset he was acutely aware of the need to select families whose budgets were broadly representative of each of these individual occupational groups. As he wrote, the households whose eating patterns were studied were such 'as in industry, thrift, intelligence, health and capability for labour, and general employment [as] would fairly represent the class of which they are members.'[66] Two further methodological difficulties were faced and at least partially surmounted. Firstly, allowances were made in the final results for the imperfect character of part of the data which had been assembled. Secondly, in the interests of uniformity of treatment, Smith estimated, when he turned to probe the relationship between family size and food consumption, that two persons under ten or one individual over that age were equivalent to an 'average adult.'[67] It is, therefore, against a backcloth of painstaking, scientific inquiry that these results have to be set.

Looking at the picture, embodied in Table 6, in detail, the most striking finding to emerge is the strength of the continuities between the pre- and post-1850 worlds. Judged by these statistics, the central role of the wheaten loaf in the households of the poor had been reinforced rather than weakened by the early 1850s. The same held true of the potato, although the marked fluctuations in intake — between a 'low' of 2lb. per week per adult among silk weavers and a 'high' of 5¼lb. among kid glove makers[68] — scarcely formed the basis for valid inter-trade comparisons since, as Smith acknowledged, these surveys were not all conducted during the same period of the year — and the quantity of potatoes consumed varied according to season.[69] Conversely, despite falls in their price, tea, coffee and sugar were still only acquired by the average family in relatively small quantities, while if fats, which usually meant butter, and meat were purchased on a larger scale than in the 1830s and 1840s, they were scarcely major items in the budgets of many households. In relation to each of these commodities, however, the 'average' concealed the considerable disparities which existed within, as well as between, the various trades. Twenty-eight per cent of the families, for example, bought no milk during the course of the week.[70] Again, the intake of meat was dependent — as among the families of silk weavers in Spitalfields, Bethnal Green, Coventry and Macclesfield — upon the size of aggregate family income and the overall state of the economy:

the use of meat depended much upon the amount of employment obtained [by silk weavers], so that in a family ordinarily well to do [No. 4] the quantity would be 3 lbs. in bad and 7 lbs. in good times weekly. There are also numerous instances in which meat was not obtained every week, but once in two or three weeks, and in such the quantity has been averaged per week. Moreover, when obtained, it was not usually distributed throughout the week, but was provided for Sunday's dinner, and might then be all eaten, or a portion left, which would serve one, two, or three days of the week. In only the most thrifty families conjoined with an approach to sufficiency of income (No. 13) was the meat distributed over all the days of the week.[71]

Yet when such qualifications have been taken into account, the data, considered as a whole, scarcely justify an optimistic assessment of the living standards of any of these socio-economic groupings. For in spite of Smith's stricture that 'as a class they did not spend their money upon food economically'[72] and despite an

Table 6

FOOD INTAKE PER ADULT PER WEEK

	Carbonac-eous Foods	Nitrogen-ous Foods	Bread lb.	Sugar oz.	Fat oz.	Meat oz.	Milk fluid oz.	Tea oz.
	Grains	Grains						
Silk Weavers	27,620	1,151	9½	7½	4½	7¼	22	2/5
Needlewomen	22,900	950	7¾	7¼	4½	15	7	2/5
Kid Glovers	28,623	1,213	8¾	4¼	7	18¼	18¼	.9
Shoemakers	31,700	1,332	11¼	10	5¾	15¾	18	3/4
Stocking Weavers	33,537	1,316	11.9	11	3½	11¾	24¾	2/5
Minimum Subsistence Needs	28,600	1,330						

Source:- *6th Report of the Medical Officer of the Privy Council 1863*, 1864, P.P. [3416] , p.
233; J. Burnett, *Plenty and Want* (1966), p. 153.

undoubted secular rise in the *per capita* consumption of most of the listed food-stuffs compared with the 1840s, the average adult was still, 'with respect to the nitrogen content of food',[73] below the minimum level required for basic subsistence. (See Table 6). In short, the fundamental drawbacks of this diet were in their turn partly responsible for the fact that none of the members of these trades 'exhibited a high degree of health.'

It must, of course, be accepted that the workers covered by this survey belonged to the poorest paid sectors of the labour market. Thus, among shoemakers it was those who were employed upon 'third class' work whose eating habits were scrutinised, while the consumption patterns of their more highly skilled colleagures were ignored. The narrowness of this field of vision, therefore, makes it difficult, on the basis of those findings alone to generalise about the collective experience of other hitherto badly remunerated groups in society. Certainly some occupations whose members usually subsisted at or below the poverty line, fared better in the 1850s and early 1860s than Smith's forlorn domestic workers. For example, returns from several major cities, including Manchester and Glasgow, showed that labourers in the building trades experienced a sizable increase in their money wages during the first five or six years of the 1850s. J. Strang, reporting that 'the rate of wages paid to Common Labourers connected with all matters of house construction' had risen by 'upwards of 40 per cent' — from 12s. to 17s. — in Glasgow between 1850 and 1854, concluded that 'at the present moment' the working classes were 'placed in a more enviable position in the social scale than they were ever formerly in this country', if only they would heed the sound precepts of thrift.[74] Similarly, W. Pollard-Urquhart ended his analysis of Irish dock labourers in the East End of London by expressing his belief that by the early 1860s there were 'few of them who do not eat meat at least once in the day', although given average earnings of between 10s.

and 12s. per week and his acknowledgment of the pervasive influence of seasonal and casual unemployment, there are sound grounds for arguing that for at least part of the year this optimism was wildly misplaced.[75] Yet notwithstanding the recording of gains which were often subsequently reversed — the earnings of builders' labourers were affected by the 1857-8 downturn — underfeeding remained a widespread social phenomenon in the 1860s. In the words of Miss W.A. Mackenzie, assessing the consumption patterns of 1860 from the vantage point of 1921, one-quarter of the population 'appear to have been insufficiently nourished, even when the lower standard of [a food intake] of 3000 calories per man per day is accepted, while about the same proportion managed to attain to the higher standard [of 3500 calories per day].[76]

Unfortunately it is not possible to chart the diets of the poor over the course of the next three decades. On the other hand in the closing twenty-five years of our period when the standard of living of the average member of the working classes was, despite the post-1830 check to the growth of real wages, considerably higher than during the early 1860s, this difficulty is more easily resolved. Growing contemporary concern with the broad issue of social deprivation produced a rich harvest of material, quantitative and qualitative, which illuminates that shadowy area of social history concerned with the budgeting practices of households whose aggregate incomes were slightly above, or fell below Rowntree's primary poverty line of 21/8d. for a family of two adults and three children. The best of this work was embodied in the detailed case-study approach to the poverty question adopted by, among others, Charles Booth in London, Rowntree in York, Paton in Edinburgh, Rathbone in Liverpool, Bell in Middlesborough, and Pember Reeves in Lambeth. And while such data are by no means exhaustive, some of the resultant gaps can be effectively filled by evidence culled from two important ancillary sources of information. In the first place some impression of the consumption patterns of the poorest paid sections of society can be gained from the more descriptive work of such socially concerned writers as Olive Malvery and Robert Sherard whose The White Slaves of England (1897) revealed the extent of social suffering among groups of sweated domestic workers. Secondly, several major government inquiries, including the Royal Commission on Labour (1891-4), the 1904 Memorandum on the Consumption and Cost of Food in Workmen's Families and the 1905-9 Royal Commission on the Poor Laws, contain invaluable comment and statistical data which can be profitably used to evaluate the constraining influence of low pay upon working-class eating habits.

On this occasion it is possible to argue that the evidence, despite its disparate and scattered nature, covering different periods of time and towns of widely divergent socio-economic structure, possesses an underlying thematic unity. For it portrays a group in society whose budgets underwent relatively little diversification over time, still relying heavily for its food upon bread. That the wheaten loaf formed the mainstay of the diets of the impoverished was endorsed by a wide range of contemporary authorities. Charles Booth spoke of its central role among the families of London's poor in the late 1880s, a verdict that was to be repeated in the homes of labourers, working for 17s. to 18s. per week in Chatham's Naval Dockyard in the early 1890s; in the households of Cradley Heath's chain makers in the late 1890s; by Rowntree's Class I budget keepers; and by those unskilled, but regularly employed, hands whose pattern of life was scrutinised by Mrs. Pember Reeves in 1913.[77] Expressed in a quantitative form, those families who were exposed to the debilitating effects of primary poverty, consumed on average around 5½ to 6½ lb. of bread per person per week.[78] But as Table 7, taken from the 1904 survey of the Board of Trade into the spending habits of representative households throughout the United Kingdom, illustrates, there was little difference in this crucial area between those who lived in a state of primary poverty (Column 1) and those who were, in many cases, only marginally removed from it (Column 2). Again, potatoes continued to form the basis of the family dinner, although, because of uncertainties surrounding the returns in some of the 1887-1901 investigations, it is difficult to arrive at an accurate assessment of the weekly *per capita* intake among the working classes generally.[79] For the poverty stricken, however, it is likely that by the early 1900s it averaged around 3 lb. per head per week, but as one moved down the scale, increasing *pari passu* with the reduction or elimination of the meat component in the diet. (See Table 7.)

Partly because of the narrowness of the margins upon which they were operating and partly because of price, other items, in terms of weight, were of much less significance in the budgets of all the victims of primary, and of many of the victims of secondary, poverty. Butter, retailing at 1s. to 1/2d. per lb. in the opening years of this century, was still acquired in relatively small amounts which could fluctuate between ¼lb. to slightly over 1lb. per family per week.[80] Some households, however, unable to afford even this modest outlay, switched to margarine, a course of action which was clearly dictated by economic necessity since for some time after the Butter Substitutes Act of 1887 there was strong consumer resistance to 'cartgrease', as it was unflatteringly called in parts of Kent in the early 1890s.[81] But for the poor it possessed at least one virtue. It was cheap, its price during the years 1900-10 remaining static at 7¼d. per lb., or between 5d. and 6d. less than that of imported or home-produced butter.[82] Furthermore, if it rarely figured in the better known poverty surveys of the period, including Booth's and Rowntree's, scattered references indicate that its use was relatively widespread amongst the impoverished in other parts of the country. One of the female blacksmiths, interviewed by Sherard during his visit to Cradley Heath in the late 1890s, could only aspire to 'a bit of margarine' when trade was good; butter was beyond her reach.[83] Similarly Eleanor Rathbone concluded her 1909 analysis of the budgets of Liverpool's casual labourers by observing that 'the majority of budget-keepers bought nearly always margarine, generally the cheapest quality, rarely butter', while at Chatham during the 1890s margarine featured in the diets of poorly remunerated, but regularly employed, labourers.[84] Yet, as with tea, bought in quantities of ¼ to ½lb. per household

Table 7

Average Weekly Cost and Quantity of Certain Articles of Food Consumed by
Urban Workmen's Families in 1904

Limits of Weekly Income	Column 1 Under 25s	Column 2 25s and under 30s
Number of returns	261	289
	s. d.	s. d.
Average weekly family income	21 4½	26 11¾
Average number of children living at home	3.1	3.3

Cost		
	s. d.	s. d.
Bread and flour	3 0½	3 3¾
Meat (bought by weight)	2 8	3 4¾
Other meat* (including fish)	0 7½	0 8¾
Bacon	0 6¾	0 9
Eggs	0 5¾	0 8½
Fresh milk	0 8	0 11¾
Cheese	0 4¾	0 5½
Butter	1 2	1 7
Potatoes	0 8¾	0 9¾
Vegetables and fruit	0 4¾	0 7
Currants and raisins	0 1½	0 1¾
Rice, tapioca, and oatmeal	0 4½	0 5
Tea	0 9¼	0 11¼
Coffee and cocoa	0 2	0 3¼
Sugar	0 8	0 10
Jam, marmalade, treacle and syrup	0 4¼	0 5¼
Pickles and condiments	0 2	0 2¼
Other items	1 0½	1 3¾
Total expenditure on food	14 4¾	17 10¼

Quantities		
	lbs.	lbs.
Bread and flour	28.44	29.97
Meat (bought by weight)	4.44	5.33
Bacon	0.94	1.11
	pts.	pts.
Fresh milk	5.54	7.72
	lbs.	lbs.
Cheese	0.67	0.70
Butter	1.10	1.50
Potatoes	14.05	15.84
Currants and raisins	0.42	0.50
Rice, tapioca, and oatmeal	2.54	2.64
Tea	0.48	0.55
Coffee and cocoa	0.15	0.18
Sugar	3.87	4.62

*e.g., Sheep's heads, tripe, heart, liver, pig's fry, tinned meats, rabbits.

Source: *Memorandum on the Consumption and Cost of Food in Workmen's Families 1904*,
    P.P. [Cd. 2337] quoted in *Report of an Enquiry of the Board of Trade into Working
    Class Rents, Housing and Retail Prices . . .* 1908, P.P. [Cd. 3864], p. xxvi.

per week, 'the tiny amounts of . . . dripping, butter, jam, sugar and greens [and margarine] may be regarded rather in the light of condiments than of food.'[85]

With little change in emphasis the same conclusion can be applied to the poor's consumption of fresh milk which, in the average home, rarely exceeded 1¼ pints per person per week. In a very limited sense such a trend might have been influenced by purely practical considerations. For as late as 1904 the fresh milk which was sold in many working-class districts was frequently in a putrescent state and badly adulterated. As Mrs. Walter Smyth told the Inter-Departmental Committee on Physical Deterioration — and her testimony was endorsed from other areas, — 'much of the milk consumed in the poorer quarters [of Lambeth] is three or four days old. . . The milk has passed through three or four dealers by each of whom some preservative has been added in order to prevent the actual onset of decomposition.'[86] Nevertheless, a vastly more powerful factor in shaping this pattern of consumption was the working classes' growing preference for condensed milk which was cheaper, at 2d. per half pint, than a pint of fresh milk at the same price since it lasted longer and possessed the additional advantage of reducing a family's outlay upon sugar.[87]

On the other hand there was a limited section of the poor, consisting of households marginally below or slightly above the primary poverty line, who undoubtedly ate more meat in the post-1890 era than at the time of Smith's survey. The enhanced role of meat in the lives of such individuals clearly emerges from the case studies of families belonging to this category which were made in York, Liverpool, Lambeth and Birmingham, and, on a broader canvas, from the Board of Trade inquiry into working-class spending in 1904 (see Table 7). Indeed, in many of these households meat had become either the largest single item of food expenditure or ranked second only to the ubiquitous white loaf.[88] Furthermore, by this point in time the family's weekly supply of meat might be supplemented, as at Lambeth, by purchases of fried fish and bacon or by bacon along.[89] For this economically deprived element, therefore, increasing imports of frozen mutton and beef and falling prices — frozen meat was selling at between 5d. to 7d. per lb. in the early 1900s — were undoubtedly attended with socially beneficial consequences. Even so the size of this advance must not be exaggerated, for at this lowly socio-economic level of society the amount of flesh meat consumed would rarely exceed one pound *per capita* per week. What this meant in practical terms was neatly illustrated by the Middlesborough labourer's household studied by Lady Bell where a weekly meat intake of one pound per person was shown to be equivalent to 'about such a quantity as would last over two meals for the family of the same size who were better off.'[90] Furthermore, as in the earlier decades, flesh meat was a term not simply applied to the chops and steak which figured on the tables of some members of this group. It also covered the cheaper cuts, including ' "block ornaments". as the small pieces of meat that butchers cut from the joint are called'. 'meat bits [or scraps used in Liverpool] for making scouse or stew.; on occasion, sausage and offal, sold in Manchester by 'a lower order of butcher who . . . has for his customers the very poor'.[91] Lastly, meat was usually unevenly distributed between the respective members of the household, with the major share going to the husband. To quote Mrs. Pember Reeves, 'meat is bought for the men, and the chief expenditure is made in preparation for Sunday's dinner, when the man [an unskilled labourer] is at home. It is eaten cold by him the next day. The children get a pound of pieces during the week, and with plenty of potatoes they make a great show with the gravy.'[92]

But this still, of course, left a substantial, albeit unquantifiable, proportion of the poor whose poverty either placed meat beyond their reach or reduced their consumption of it to a bare minimum. Among those who were located in these depressed areas of the unskilled labour market were labourers employed in Chatham's dockyard who, it was claimed in the early 1890s, 'never have any meat except sometimes on a Sunday when they may get a few sheeps' heads, and that is nearly all bone.'[93] And if in this instance this verdict was probably only really applicable to those households where there was no supplementary source of income, there can be little doubt that meatless families abounded among the diminishing number of sweated, and largely female, workers whose conditions were scrutinised by the 1888-90 Select Committee of the House of Lords on the Sweating System. As Mrs. Killick, a London-based trouser finisher, told the inquiry, tea and fish formed the principal ingredients of her family's diet: 'meat I do not expect; I might get meat once in six months.'[94]

Summing up, it is correct to argue that, compared with the 1860s, inderterminate numbers of those living in a state of primary and secondary poverty experienced some improvement in their diets after 1890, although at first glance such a conclusion is difficult to reconcile with Smith's 1863 investigation. Turning to Table 6, for example, is appears that the *per capita* consumption of certain key commodities was higher at the date of Smith's survey than in the quarter century under review. Such a verdict, however, overlooks two important points. Firstly, whereas Smith's data relate to a computed adult — that is, they were adjusted to take account of the reduced food intake of children, — the post-1890 statistics that we have been analysing are largely unweighted *per capita* averages. In that sense direct comparisons are bound to show the 1863 results in an unduly favourable, and the post-1890 data in an unduly gloomy, light. Secondly, for a few items a comparative approach can mislead because of what it excludes. For example, the post-1890 pattern of fresh milk consumption, unlike the situation obtaining in 1863, was to some extent influenced and depressed by the increasing use of condensed milk by the poor. Looking, therefore, at the impoverished in general terms it can be claimed that more meat, sugar and tea were acquired in the post-1890 era than three or four decades earlier and that the range of foodstuffs consumed had over time broadened. Yet such advances need to be kept in perspective. For one thing they did not touch all with an even hand. But what was of even greater significance, they represented at best, in the eyes of their beneficiaries, marginal gains, moving them and their families a trifle nearer to mere subsistence without raising them above the poverty line.

A few qualifications to these lugubrious conclusions must, of course, be entered. Thus, although, because of the imperfect nature of the evidence, it is rarely possible to isolate them as a separate group, some of those who were ill-nourished were the casualties of secondary rather than primary poverty. In this context the pervasive influence of alcohol remained of paramount importance. Indeed, heavy drinking was not only the principal cause of secondary poverty; it also intensified the degree of deprivation which existed among many households already enmeshed in the toils of primary poverty.[95] In addition, as has already been noted, an inadequate diet could stem from imprudent budgeting in a more general sense. It was widely recognised, for example, that excessive reliance upon condensed milk for feeding infants was positively harmful to their physical development.[96] But adults too were denounced for their unwise choice of food-stuffs. In the opening decade of this century came lamentations from Dundee that 'the very poor' were abandoning oatmeal for less nutritious, and more ex-pensive, foods.[97] Similarly the worst managers among the wives of Liverpool's casual labourers 'nearly always buy chops and steaks which, though expensive and wasteful, are not much trouble to cook', while the sufferings of the families of Rowntree's Class I, all of whom fell below his primary poverty line, were exacerbated because of the proportion of income that they devoted to animal foods.[98] (But, if, as Rowntree acknowledged, such individuals ought, on grounds of cost and protein yields, to have opted for an exclusively vegetable diet, he was keenly aware that other factors, including the palatability of such a narrow range of foodstuffs, made the adoption of this course of action a counsel of perfection rather than a practical proposition.)[99] Notwithstanding such qualifications, how-ever, the harsh reality of underfeeding remains.

Poverty, therefore, meant three things. Firstly, it meant that until the 1872 Adulteration of Food, Drink and Drugs Act the health of the poor was adversely affected by the widespread sale of adulterated foodstuffs to the working classes. Secondly, it entailed in some respects a less eligible existence than that enjoyed by the indoor pauper. Rowntree, for example, who defined a primary poverty line which was 'less generous than the Local Government Board would require for able-bodied paupers in workhouses' — meat was excluded from the projected pattern of expenditure — had no difficulty in demonstrating that all labouring households in York, in which the husband was the sole wage-earner, fell below this grim minimum.[100] But this situation was not unique to the 1890s, since its antecedents can be traced back to the opening decade of our period. Moreover, it was not confined to the English Poor Law, for by the 1860s at the latest whole groups of workers, employed in the unskilled sectors of the labour market, ate less well than institutionally fed prisoners.[101] Thirdly, malnutrition, a prom-inent feature in all these households, hit hardest those able-bodied families where the children contributed little or nothing to aggregate family income. In 1863 Dr. Edward Smith discussed this point at length, drawing attention to the deficiencies in the diets of the young children of 'the very poor' and the grinding monotony of the wife's meals.

> On Sundays she generally obtains a moderately good dinner, but on other days the food
> consists mainly of bread with a little butter or dripping, a plain pudding, and vegetables
> for dinner or supper, and weak tea. She may obtain a little bacon at dinner once, twice
> or thrice a week; but more commonly she does not obtain it.[102]

The validity of this analysis was subsequently confirmed by Rowntree who calculated that in 1899 one-third of York's population under one year of age, 31.91
per cent of those between one and five, and 37.58 per cent of children between
five and fifteen subsisted 'in poverty', and by the less precise evidence, submitted
to the 1904 Inter-Departmental Committee on Physical Deterioration, which
stressed that the underfeeding of school children was a major social problem
among the poorer elements of society in London, Manchester, Edinburgh and
the Potteries.[103] Finally, in 1913 Bowley and Burnett-Hurst discovered that
seventeen per cent of the children under the age of five who belonged to the
families of their sample of Northampton's population, fell below the primary
poverty line. The comparable results for Warrington, Reading and Stanley were
22.5 per cent, 45 per cent and 5.5 per cent respectively.[104] In other words,
translating this litany of stark statistics into social terms, parents under the pressures of primary or secondary poverty — for the social sequel was the same, —
would tend to produce children of 'puny size and damaged health', underweight,
threatened by rickets, the classic disease of malnutrition, and, in the lottery of
life itself, more likely to die at an early age than the offspring of any other socio-
economic group.[105]

II

The deprivations to which the urban poor were subjected cannot, however, be
completely understood within this restricted framework of reference. For, in the
eyes of many contemporary writers, it was impossible to divorce the question of
underfeeding from other quantifiable hallmarks of urban poverty, including bad
housing. Housing, in fact, formed a central issue in all discussions of the nature
of the poverty problem. To a minority the poor quality of accommodation
which sheltered the unskilled elements of the working classes was an outward
sign of an unregenerate race that was prepared to sacrifice household comforts
for alcohol.[106] Overcrowding and the existence of slum property were thus
defined as moral problems which possessed an economic dimension, for the
private developer, according to this thesis, would only contemplate providing
new housing for this class it is first showed itself capable of handling its finances
wisely. There was, of course, a small element of truth in this argument since
some of those who rented furnished rooms had effectively penalised their families
through their own improvidence.[107] But as a total explanation of the accom-

modation difficulties which confronted those living below the poverty line, it must be rejected, primarily because it ignores the reality of exogenous economic constraints. In particular it fails to explore the relationship between rent and earnings and the impact of the increasingly strict building codes which were adopted by many local authorities in the second half of the nineteenth century, upon the cost structure of small speculators in the housing market. Most important of all, it does not start to answer the question of whether perfect sobriety would have been sufficient to have persuaded private developers to cater, on a significant scale, for those whose feet were placed on the lowest rungs of the economic ladder. Not surprisingly, informed contemporary opinion came over time to reject this moralistic analysis for an approach which stressed the sturdy links between bad housing and the economic causes of social deprevation. As F.W. Lawrence observed, 'to a great extent the Housing Problem for this class [Booth's Classes A and B and part of his Class C] is merely a part of the general problem of poverty; and only when the vital causes which lie at the root of their poverty are removed, is there any hope that the evils of their housing will be overcome.'[108] Simply put, 'the condition of the houses of the poor, far from being a quaint expression of their own debased tastes — a view widely held among the ruling classes of Victorian England — was a reflex of the allocation of political power and economic resources in society at large.'[109]

The type of urban housing which was the special preserve of the poor did not, however, conform to a monolithic model. In the industrial areas of Scotland, for instance, the single apartment was widely accepted as the prerogative of occupational groups which were exposed to the debilitating rhythms of primary poverty. Yet while both the 1902-3 Glasgow Municipal Commission on Working-Class Housing and the 1904 investigations of the Charity Organisation Society in Edinburgh provided evidence to support this conclusion, they at the same time showed that the social composition of the inhabitants of the classic 'single end' embraced a far broader range of individuals than those whose lives were tinged with poverty.[110] This kind of social 'mix' was much less common in single-room dwellings in the major industrial towns and cities of England. But in a sense this was inevitable since, outside those few areas of the North-East of England which were influenced by the Scottish style of tenement construction, the English single apartment differed in one crucial aspect from its Scottish equivalent. For whereas the Scottish 'single end' had been specifically designed for the exclusive use of one family, the average English single apartment was located in either a middle-class house which had been subsequently divided into a series of smaller units or a working-class cottage which had been sublet to 'a still more needy class.' (Such sub-division clearly took place in urban Scotland, but it still does not obscure the essential difference between this form of accommodation in the two countries.) In England, therefore, the inhabitants of such dwellings possessed a much greater degree of social and economic homogeneity, being for the most part drawn from a background — the sweated trades, casual work and the poorest paid sectors of the unskilled — which was unmistakably associated with poverty.

As Dr. H.J. Hunter wrote of the occupants of single rooms in Hull in 1865 in terms which, with only minor changes of emphasis, were equally applicable to other parts of the country and to any year within our period of study, 'these lodgings are sometimes furnished with a few shillings' worth of goods, when a high price was asked. A good deal of misery was seen. The rooms were in very poor condition, and the people very destitute.'[111]

The cellar dwelling was also designed to serve as a home for individuals belonging to these same humble socio-economic groups, the multitude of Irish immigrants, hawkers, domestic workers and casual labourers who, as in the Bank District of Leeds in the early 1840s, existed, 'with incomes of a few shillings a week, derived from the labour of half-starved children, or the more precarious earnings of casual employment, . . . from hour to hour, under every kind of privation and distress.'[112] Yet while such dwellings were to be found in every British city — in the Inner Ward of St. George's, Hanover Square, London, 'many families' in 1842 inhabited 'miserable little garrets and front and back cellers in confined situations, at a rent of 1/6 or 2/- a week',[113] — it is possible, in this specific sphere to speak of marked divergences between the experience of different regions. Compared with any other part of Britain, the cellar achieved its firmest foothold in the North of England, although even here the picture was patchy, with relatively few such dwellings in Hull, a sizable number in the poorest districts of Bradford and Leeds, and the most extensive use of this basic form of accommodation occurring in Manchester, Salford and Liverpool.[114] In the early 1840s more than ten percent of Liverpool's total population was to be found in 'these dark and miserable abodes',[115] while the global result for Manchester was probably only marginally less. After 1850, however, the significance of the cellar dwelling in the lives of the working classes slowly declined as it increasingly came under the surveillance and control of local authorities which recognised it as a threat to public health.

But there were also, of course, strong similarities between the housing experience of those who collectively comprised the poor. The households of casual hands, for instance, invariably gravitated towards the central parts of the large towns and the riverside areas of ports where the worst, but by no means cheapest, property was located but where casual labour possessed its best chance of securing employment. Again, the mean and insanitary courts and 'back' houses, many of them erected by speculators in the pre-1850 era; the closely packed rows of two- and three-storeyed front 'cottages', usually bereft of all basic amenities, and decayed back-to-back houses in Leeds and 'backland' tenements in Glasgow were all eagerly sought after by the poor because, whatever their social drawbacks, they had much to commend them on cost grounds. The same concern with economy informed the actions of those men and women, drawn from the single, widowed, deserted and peripatetic elements of society who used, on a nightly or weekly basis, the common and model lodging houses and night shelters of Britain's conurbations. But in this field the points of contacts between those living in primary and secondary poverty were more widely based than this modest inventory implies.

For one thing many who fell below the poverty line were compelled to submit to overcrowded conditions. In the opening years of our period overcrowding was endemic in common lodging houses where proprietors, free from the constraints of compulsory licensing, endeavoured to maximise their returns by cramming as many lodgers into their beds and 'wretched filthy pallets of straw' as possible.[116] Such a policy was carried furthest in the double cellars which were used for this purpose in such towns as Liverpool where they were alleged to present 'in miniature a picture of the Black Hole of Calcutta.'[117] A fundamentally similar pattern, although on a less spectacular scale, was reproduced in private houses, rented by the poor, in different parts of the country. Thus, a Britstol survey of 5981 families, conducted in 1839, revealed that 9.3 per cent of that total occupied only part of a room, 37.5 per cent aspired to a single apartment, and 24.1 per cent could afford to rent two rooms.[118] Employing the conventional overcrowding index of more than two persons per room and assuming an average-sized family of two adults and three children, almost all these households lived in a chronically cramped environment. Equally lugubrious conclusions can be drawn from the inquiry which was mounted in St. George's in the East, London, in the mid-1840s, for one of its principal findings was that the average householder, living in one or two room apartments.[119] Finally, in the Liverpool of the early 1840s, some of the most notoriously overcrowded districts — Lace Street with 13.15, Crosbie Street with 11.27, and North Street with 10, persons per inhabited house — were the strongholds of unskilled Irish labourers whose weak economic position made it difficult for them to resist the temptation to sublet rented accommodation.[120]

It is difficult to decide how far the dimensions of this social problem diminished after 1850 and more especially in the post-1870 decades. Certainly, whether overcrowding is viewed at a national or a local level signs of amelioration can be discerned; for if a few blackspots remained — in London, Scotland and the North-East of England — the general trend meant that the average family was living in more spacious accommodation than hitherto. For example, whereas in Glasgow 30.4 per cent of the city's population occupied one room in 1871, by 1891 the comparable percentage was 18.0.[121] Again, while 40.78 per cent of Gateshead's, 35.08 per cent of Newcastle-upon-Tyne's, 32.85 per cent of Sunderland's, 26.27 per cent of Plymouth's and 21.31 per cent of Halifax's population were living in overcrowded conditions in 1891,[122] marked improvements, on the whole to be sustained until 1911, had occurred in other major urban areas during the course of the previous two decades. Yet, as we have seen in a variety of different contexts, such averages, far from encapsulating the experience of the impoverished sections of the working classes, often confuse the issue. Indeed, there are concrete grounds for believing that after 1850, and in a few areas before that date, the position of the poverty stricken was adversely affected by two inter-related developments. In the first place the construction of freight termini and stations by the major railway companies often entailed the destruction of their existing homes without any fresh accommodation being provided for them. Thus A. Ransome and W. Royston claimed in 1866 that railway clearances had hit hardest the poor in the affected districts of Manchester and Salford who 'cling to the old localities and are thus driven to herd more and more closely together, and greatly to overcrowd the houses which remain.'[123] An identical complaint was voiced in Plymouth in 1865 where the combined activities of railway developers and the local corporation had, it was alleged, destroyed 'the residences of thousands of persons.'[124] But what was even more disastrous to their short-term interests was the intervention of local authorities in the housing field.

Such intervention was, of course, only slowly mounted in the 1850s and even under the impulse of the civic gospel in the 1870s was far from a uniform process, with many town councils content to keep down the rates rather than to embark upon ambitious schemes of urban renewal. Nevertheless, whenever calls for environmental improvement were acted upon, they were attended with deleterious results. For instance, when Liverpool in the early 1840s tried to close down certain categories of cellar dwellings, it was castigated for its lack of foresight by Lyon Playfair:

> the effect produced by the adoption of this measure . . . has been, up to the present time, one of physical inconvenience and of moral injury. The labouring classes who have been ejected from the cellars have, so far as can be ascertained, been driven into other inferior and ill-conditioned dwellings, and have suffered great inconvenience from the change without deriving any sanatory [sic] benefits.[125]

As Aspinall expressed it more succinctly, transferred overcrowding was the inevitable sequel, with 'three or four, or five families' going 'into a house, where only one or two families were before.'[126] Inevitably, as slum clearance programmes became more ambitious in their scope after 1870, whether they were mounted under privately sponsored acts such as that which established the City of Glasgow Improvement Trust in 1866 or under such national statutes as the widely quoted Cross Act of 1875, they threatened the poor in a more fundamental fashion. For while their poverty prevented them from generating an effective demand for new housing, a local authority's destruction of their existing homes simply moved them on to overcrowd the cheapest, and invariably the nearest, accommodation which remained open to them. In the words of the Medical Officer of Health for Bermondsey, 'as they are all poor and cannot afford to occupy more than a single room, they would but go into some other locality equally objectionable.'[127] The accuracy of these observations in a London context has been underlined by the researches of Stedman Jones who has argued that overcrowding in Central London, a principal target for the improvers and a stronghold of casual and sweated labour, tended to increase between 1850 and 1880. Even as late as 1891 between thirty and forty per cent of the people in this area lived in overcrowded conditions as against 19.7 per cent for the capital as a whole.[128] On the other hand, in some medium-sized towns which had been untroubled by extensive slum clearance schemes, the poor might to some extent share in the progressive post-1870 decline in the incidence of overcrowding. This was true of York where only 6.4 per cent of the total population were overcrowded in 1899, although twenty-eight per cent 'are in poverty either "primary" or "secondary".'[129] Yet if, as these two examples suggest, it is not possible to speak of a uniform trend, there is little in the evidence to justify a glowingly optimistic assessment of the overcrowding problem which faced the poverty stricken. While in a a few places some social gains accrued to them in the wake of the general post-1870 trend towards less crowded accommodation, they came belatedly and were always on a small scale. And they have to be balanced against the substantial worsening of the position of the urban poor in the short and longer-term in every locality that was committed to a vigorous assault on the urban slum.

'Smallness of income' guaranteed, of course, that such families were inherently more likely to be exposed to overcrowded conditions than any other section of society.[130] Their poverty, however, affected them in two further ways. Firstly, it meant that in the majority of cases their dwellings were sparsely furnished, although some improvement in this sphere could be expected when children became wage-earners. Scarcely surprisingly, the paucity of their material possessions formed one of the major themes which was raised in all the important social inquiries of the 1830s and 1840s, primarily because this was one way of measuring the extent of their distress. The very brevity, for instance, of the inventory of goods listed in the households of handloom weavers was correctly interpreted as proof of widespread deprevation. And this applied not only to coarse-grade calico weavers who were among the first groups to be threatened by the power loom but also to websters who were engaged upon fabrics which were only slowly affected by mechanisation. For example, the description of the impoverished homes of Leeds' linen weaving community in the late 1830s was equally valid for other areas and other branches of the domestic textile industry. To quote S. Keyser's words,

> scarcely any furniture, or necessary culinary or other utensils; the very ragged state of their clothing, and particularly that of their children; their scanty supply of bedding, and general want of every comfort, afford abundant proof of their great distress, more particularly in families where there are many young children not yet able to assist in obtaining a wretched livelihood.[131]

The provision of bedding was, in fact, often little more than a token gesture. In some parts of Leeds the term itself was a euphemism for 'corded bedstocks' serving as 'beds, and sacking for bed-clothing', while at a still lower level Aberdeen's linen weavers 'lay upon straw like dogs.'[132] But in the pre-1850 period such scenes were not confined to the weaving community. They were repeated, with a few alterations in points of detail, among Mayhew's sweated workers in the needlework, tailoring, and shoemaking trades; among the households of unskilled Irish labourers in Liverpool; and among the victims of typhus fever in Manchester in the late 1830s. As one observer commented in relation to this last group, 'a table, a chair, or a stool, a few, and very few, articles of culinary apparatus, some shavings, or a little straw in a corner, with a scanty piece or two of filthy bed-covering, constitute the whole furniture of numerous habitations in this town, and numbers may be found where even this meagre catalogue is far from being complete.'[133]

Some changes for the better, a reflection of shifts in the social composition of the poor and, for many groups, of a modest rise in real income, clearly occurred in this field after 1850. Yet, as the work of Sherwell, examining the West End of London in the late 1890s and Mrs. Pember Reeves analysing labourers' budgets in Lambeth in 1913, indicate, the links between the pre- and post-1850 worlds in London remained strong. According to Pember Reeves, the homes of the unskilled were still characterised by few chairs, limited table space, no wardrobes, unsatisfactory cooking utensils — a kettle, a frying pan and two saucepans 'both burnt are often the complete outfit,' and an inadequate supply of beds, including, under this heading, the ubiquitous 'banana-crate cot'.[134] Typical of those Lambeth house-holders who conformed to this pattern was her 'Case Three', consisting of a family of husband, wife and six children and occupying four rooms:

> one double bed for four people in a very small room, crossing the window; cot in corner by bed. One single bed for two people (girls aged 13 and 10 years) in smaller room, eight feet by ten feet . . . One sofa for boy aged 11 years in front downstairs room . . . The kitchen, which is at the back, has the copper in it, and is too small for a bed, or even a sofa to stand anywhere.[135]

But London was in one sense untypical of other areas. Despite being a high-wage city, its high rents could have squeezed the incomes of whole sectors of its unskilled labour force to such effect that it made it difficult for them to have devoted more than small sums towards basic furnishings. Certainly, a more favourable picture emerged from Rowntree's Class I budget keepers, some of whose homes contained items — a chest of drawers, an easy chair — which were largely absent in Lambeth, although it is impossible to determine how far this experience in York was in its turn representative of Britain's poor.[136] It can, however, reasonably be argued, that it probably reflected the trend in those medium-sized towns which were relatively unscathed by the twin evils of sweated and casual labour. But wherever these last two problems existed on any scale, inside and outside London, there can be little doubt that the material possessions of the poverty stricken were of much more modest proportions than Pember Reeves' regularly employed, but poorly remunerated, labourers.

Secondly, the nature of the locality in which the housing of the poor was set, frequently militated against their best interests. As the major sanitary inquiries of 1842 and 1844-5 demonstrated, those groups in Britain's cities and large towns that lacked specific skills were the main victims of blind urban growth, much of which had occurred in the late eighteenth and early nineteenth centuries, and of a strongly entrenched preoccupation with civic economy. For whether the historian turns to the central wynds of Glasgow, Exchange Ward in Liverpool, Little Ireland and Angel Meadow in Manchester, or the Bank

District of Leeds, the overwhelming impression is of an environment which, in the 1830s and 1840s, posed severe threats to the health of its inhabitants and lacked all the amenities necessary for civilised life. Furthermore, while it must be conceded that these were the most notorious 'plague spots' in these cities, they were not in any way unique. For they not only had parallels elsewhere; they also represented, in their own localities, only the extreme end of the spectrum of neglect.

The salient features of that pattern can be defined in precise terms. Firstly, the water supply was deficient in almost every area where the urban poor were congregated. In a few cases, as in parts of Glasgow, water to serve their needs came from polluted wells; but more usually it was drawn from either common stand-pipes or taps in their own homes. Supplies from this last source might also be contaminated, but they possessed one further drawback: they tended to be provided by private companies on an intermittent basis, often for as little as one hour to three hours on alternate days and posing for the poor the fundamental problem of storage. Secondly, in some districts, such as the courts of Liverpool, communal privies were expected to cater for between ten to twenty persons. Thirdly, many courts, tenements and undedicated streets lacked even the most rudimentary form of drainage and were rarely or never visited by the municipal scavenging services. The sequel to such indifference was simply to add to the already formidable social problems created by an insanitary environment. Dunghills and middens were formed 'as places of deposit for refuse from all the houses [in a court] ', while 'surface water and fluid refuse of every kind' stagnated 'in the street and add, especially in hot weather, their pestilential influence to that of more solid filth.'[137]

By the late 1840s the growing public awareness of the high social and economic costs of an insanitary environment prompted central government and a small number of local authorities to try to remedy some of the worst aspects of this legacy from the past. At its most ambitious this programme of reform entailed, among other things, the municipalisation of water supplies; the paving and draining of streets; the licensing of lodging houses; the appointment of Medical Officers of Health which was in itself an open acknowledgement of the utility of social medicine to a community; and the exercise of a measure of control over the activities of housebuilders. Before the 1870s, however, the permissive character of government legislation — the prime reason why the Public Health Act of 1848 promised much more than it actually achieved — and the apathy of most town halls guaranteed that the implementation of the doctrine of urban renewal on this scale would be confined to a few, narrowly circumscribed parts of the country. On the other hand, under the aegis of a more actively interventionist state and the impact of the civic gospel, enunciated by Joseph Chamberlain in Birmingham, the pace of environmental advance quickened perceptibly from the mid-1870s onwards, bringing in its wake tangible gains, including the removal of some forms of nuisances, more regular and purer water supplies, improved sanitary facilities, an expanded cleansing service, and a saving of human life.

Nevertheless, if a balanced appraisal of the effect of these post-1875 changes is to be obtained, two other factors have to be considered. First, to emphasise a point that has already been made, wherever the implementation of the sanitary gospel was equated with the wholesale demolition of slum property, the social sequel to such intervention was far from favourable to those who lived below the poverty line. Second, apart from the question of slum clearance, the most impoverished areas in some cities derived only modest benefits from these reforms. But this conclusion applied not simply to the great cities, London, Liverpool, and Glasgow among them, but to areas of more gentle demographic growth such as Norwich where a vigorous attack upon the insanitary problems posed by its courts and court yards was only finally mounted in 1898, and York.[130] In this context the graphic picture which Rowntree drew of York's worst housing is worth quoting at length, because while it is specifically concerned with a limited geographical area, it also conveys the nature of the general problem.

> Overcrowding and insanitary conditions of all kinds abound in the slums, and back-to-back houses, in which through ventilation is impossible are common in them. The water-supply is very inadequate, one tap being often the sole supply for a large number of houses. In some cases the tap which supplies the drinking water is fixed in the wall of the water-closet. Pantries and water-closets are sometimes separated by a wall only one brick in thickness. Many of the ashpits are overflowing, and heaps of all kinds of rubbish are distributed promiscuously over the yard or court . . . Midden privies are usual, and these, like the water-taps, are in many cases shared by several houses. They are particularly offensive in these over-populated and under-ventilated districts. A number of slaughter-houses situated in the midst of the slum district form another unsatisfactory feature. . . . From the point of view of public health there is no doubt that midden privies are unsatisfactory even when they are frequently cleansed. Until January 1901, however, the Corporation made a charge of about 1s. each time an ashpit or midden privy was cleared, thus giving the householder a strong inducement to allow refuse to accumulate for as long a time as possible. . . . In many cases the water-taps are at a considerable distance from some of the houses which they serve . . . this circumstance militates against the free use of water for washing and other domestic purposes. The grates under many of those water-taps which are shared by several houses are in a filthy condition.[139]

Despite such drawbacks, cleanliness could, of course, still be practised within the home itself. In the vast majority of cases, however, the tenantry succumbed to the depressing external environment and abandoned the uneven struggle. As Rowntree wrote,

> inside the rooms are often dark and damp, and almost always dirty. Many of the floors are of red bricks, or of bricks that would be red if they were washed. They are often uneven and much broken, having been laid on to the earth with no concrete or other foundations. On washing-days pools of water collect which gradually percolate through to the damp and unsavoury soil below.[140]

But notwithstanding the poor quality of the accommodation reserved for the urban poor, rent always absorbed a sizable percentage of their income, simply because the tendency was for rents of all types of urban property to rise throughout the period with which this book is concerned.[141] It thus formed one of the main exceptions to the general downward movement in prices during the last quarter of the nineteenth century, with the average working-class rent in London increasing from an index figure of eighty-seven in 1880 to one hundred in 1900.[142] Similarly in Glasgow a rise of 17.5 per cent was recorded between 1870 and 1902, most of it occurring in the 1890s.[143] None the less the rate of increase and absolute levels of rent varied quite considerably from area to area. For example, rentals in urban Scotland appear on trend to have been lower than those in urban England, a reflection of corresponding differentials in average earnings and of the major role played by the cheaper tenement in Scottish working-class society. But within England itself fundamental differences in regional experience also persisted until 1914 and beyond. Between 1830 and 1914 London remained the most expensive place in which to live. In the early 1840s, for instance, a double cellar could be rented in Liverpool for as little as 1s. per week; in the Inner Ward of St. George's Parish, Hanover Square, London, identical accommodation cost from 1/6d. to 2s.[144] Again, while the averate rent for an unfurnished room in Bristol was 1/3¾d. in 1839, complaints were made in St. George's Parish about 'extremely high rents, 4/3 being the average sum . . . ; 4/6 and 5/- were the usual sums paid for an unfurnished room on the second or third floor, while in the parishes of St. Margaret and St. John, Westminster the average amount of rent paid by the working classes is only 2/11¼'.[145] The same theme was echoed in the early 1900s, when a single apartment in the inner zone of the capital cost 5s. and two rooms 6/6d.[146] And if cheaper accommodation than this could be found elsewhere in the capital, the savings were still at best only marginal. As Steel-Maitland and Squire observed, 'two shillings for the smallest unfurnished "slip" rooms overlooking the back court and little more extensive than a cupboard, 3/-, 3/6, 4/- and even more, for a single unfurnished room of moderate size are prices not at all uncommon [in London in 1909].'[147] On the other hand, workers in other parts of the country, including Birmingham, Leeds, Blackburn, and Coventry, could expect to obtain, in 1905, a three room house for a weekly outlay of between 3/6d. and 5s.[148]

The consequences of this secular trend for those who fell below the poverty line were twofold. In the first place the upward movement of rents in London in the post-1870 era offset many of the advantages which were gained from cheaper foodstuffs.[149] But in a more general sense it penalised the poor by establishing, in many areas, an inequitable correlation between income and rent. Simply put, the poorer the family, the higher the percentage of its income which it tended to devote to the hiring of accommodation. In faint outline evidence to support this thesis can be found in the pages of the local reports of the 1842 inquiry into the Sanitary Conditions of the Labouring Population, where it was argued that while the 'poorest description of persons' in the cotton towns of Lancashire frequently spent one-quarter of their income upon the 'lowest class' of housing, 'the better class of labourer' expended only one-sixth of his earnings for a superior dwelling.[150] For if these data must be treated as estimates rather than precise calculations, they still conform to a pattern whose contours can be more clearly perceived in the closing twenty years of our period, when Rowntree demonstrated that house rent in York in 1899 'abosrbs no less than 29% of the total income of the very poor, whose family earnings are under 18s. weekly.' For the next group, with an aggregate income of 18s. to under 20s. per week, the corresponding statistic was eighteen per cent, but for 'the few exceptionally well-to-do working-class families, earning as much as, or more than 60s. a week', it fell to nine per cent.[151] Mrs. Pember Reeves referred in 1913 to the existence of the same problem in even more trenchant terms:

> the London poor are driven to pay ane third of their income for dark, damp rooms which are too small and too few in houses which are ill built and over-crowded. Even if the food which can be provided out of 22s. a week, after 7s. or 8s. has been taken for rent, were of first rate quality and sufficient in quantity, the night spent in such beds in such houses would devitalise the children.[152]

There were, of course, several exceptions to this trend. In some cases outlay on rent was reduced at a stroke by tenants following the well-established practice of subletting property. Again, the high percentage of income allocated to rent was an English, rather than a Scottish, phenomenon. For as J.W. Warrington's analysis of his sample of labourers and carters, registered with Glasgow's Corporation Employment Bureau in 1902, illustrated, a single apartment in the West of Scotland could be secured for as little as eleven to thirteen per cent of the earnings of these casual and unskilled elements of the local labour force.[153] Nevertheless, when due allowance has been made for these factors, they do little to alter a picture of a housing market which was shaped by exogenous forces largely inimical to the interests of the poor.

III

The cost of food and accommodation absorbed such a large percentage of an impoverished family's income that little remained with which to purchase other basic necessities. Fuel and lighting, which accounted for a mere nine per cent of the average total expenditure of Rowntree's Class I households,[154] were invariably acquired on a relatively small scale and could disappear completely from such budgets at times of seasonal and cyclical unemployment. But the acquisition of sufficient supplies of clothing was another problem which war rarely satisfactorily resolved. At the start of our period descriptions abound of the deprivations suffered in this area of need by outworkers and labourers. In Scotland the earnings of many hand-loom weavers' families were too low during the years 1830-50 to leave much margin for footwear and dress, a situation which had exact parallels among sections of Bolton's cotton weaving community in the mid-1820s who 'in consequence of not getting a remunerative price, are so ill clothed, that they are not able to attend divine service' and among worsted weavers in Yorkshire who 'clothe themselves when bread is cheap.'[155] Similarly, the bulk of the children of Liverpool's Irish-born general labourers went about barefoot for much of the year,[156] although in March 1843, in the wake of the 1842 depression, destitution manifested itself in a more acute form. As the *Liverpool Mercury* commented, 'such . . . is the extreme wretchedness reigning in many parts of their district that the children have not actually clothing to show themselves in the streets, much less to attend the Schools.'[157]

It was, in fact, only after 1870, under the triple influence of rising real wages, an expansion in the number of clothing charities, and the proliferation of boot and clothing clubs, that it becomes possible to speak of some improvement in this specific field. Even then the gains that were recorded were strictly limited, for, according to Rowntree, only 6.3 per cent of the average total expenditure of his Class I families was devoted to clothes.[158] Moreover, at least part of that outlay was spent on second-hand garments.

The vital role played by the second-hand shop, the clothing hawker and the rag-man can be illustrated from a variety of sources. It was captured, at the micro-economic level of the individual household, in the evidence of 'Mrs. Smith', a York housewife whose family experienced the harsh consequences of primary poverty.

> One new dress, Mrs. Smith tells us, will last for years. For everyday wear she buys some old dress at a jumble sale for a few shillings. Old garments, cast off by some wealthier family, are sometimes bought from the ragman for a few coppers; or perhaps they are not paid for in cash, but some older rags and a few bones are given in exchange for them. Garments so purchased are carefully taken to pieces, washed, and made up into clothes for the children.[159]

At a more extended level, the budgets kept by Lambeth labourers in 1913 underlined both the paucity of the poor supply of clothing and their reliance upon a flourishing second-hand market.

> In the poor budgets items for clothes appear at extraordinarily distant intervals, when, it is to be supposed, they can no longer be done without . . . any clothes which are bought seem to be not only second-hand, but in many instances fourth- or fifth-hand. In the course of fifteen months' visiting, one family on 23s. a week spent £3-5-5½ on clothes for the mother and six children. Half the sum was spent on boots, so that the clothes other than the boots of seven people cost 32/9 in fifteen months — an average of 4/8 per head.[160]

Moreover, the acquisition of the most basic items of dress and footwear taxed the ingenuity and the resources of the poor to the limit. For some it entailed making considerable sacrifices in other areas of household expenditure; for others it involved the careful husbanding of the extra earnings which occasional overtime brought in; and for yet others it meant reliance upon public bodies and philanthropic agencies.[161] And for an indeterminate number of households, supplies of new clothing depended in part upon the proceeds realised from the sale of goods which had outlived their usefulness, although, as 'Mrs. K', a Lambeth housewife, supporting a family of eight upon an income of 22/6d., acknowledged, the gains which accrued from this source were small: 'sole old pram for 3s, it was to litle. Bourt boots for Siddy for 2/11½d. Made a apeny.'[162] But, as this testimony makes clear, there was little hope, for all those who lived below the poverty line, or relief from the social penalties of poverty, even when they attained some of the modest clothing targets which they set themselves. Simply put, inadequate clothing was, in the early years of the twentieth century, yet another hallmark of poverty.[163]

Conclusion

Between 1830 and 1914 Britain underwent a major social revolution. It became, what it is today, an urban society. The early stages of that transformation were inevitably accompanied by social dislocation and hardship, as the market mechanism, attuned to economic rather than social stimuli, sought to cope with the rapid growth of urban numbers. Nevertheless, assessing the period as a whole, it is clear that for the bulk of the working classes the quality of urban life underwent a series of modest, but cumulatively significant, improvements. Hours of work were shortened; the conditions under which the factory-hand worked, were increasingly subject to the Factory Inspectorate as the Factory Acts were extended to cover a broader range of economic activity; and the exploitative relationship, inherent in the truck system, was reduced to a residual problem by the early 1890s. Again, from the 1870s onwards much less use was made of juvenile labour in a whole host of industries, a development that owed much to the increased emphasis which was placed upon working-class education in the wake of the 1870 Forster Act and the 1872 Scottish Education Act. But ameliorative influences were not exclusively confined to the work situation. Within the home itself over-crowding tended to diminish and water supplies were improved. Externally the urban environment also slowly changed for the better as local authorities, sometimes at the behest of the State, accepted social burdens in the post-1870 era which many ratepayers would have strenuously resisted a generation earlier. Partly as a result of this kind of interventionism and partly as a result of rising real wages, life expectancy itself increased, with the crude death rate falling on trend from the mid-1870s onwards and the infant mortality rate from the early 1900s. Finally, the Liberal welfare reforms of 1905-14, covering such areas as the provision of school meals for necessitous children, old-age pensions, sickness and unemployment insurance, and the attempt, embodied in the 1909 Trade Boards Act, to protect the weak bargaining position of the sweated worker, marked the commencement of a process designed to remove some of the insecurity which, for the working classes, was indelibly associated with the ordinary contingencies of life.

But what was equally important, urbanisation and industrialisation produced a substantial, long-term rise in the standard of living, although in this particular field it is difficult to isolate the movement of the real income of the urban worker, from the national trend since most of the published estimates make no distinction between the urban and rural experience. In view of the fact, however, that rural wages consistently lagged behind their urban equivalent and that agriculture over time played a diminishing role as an employer of labour, it is reasonable to argue that the national trend encapsulates accurately enough the broad dimensions of the economic advance which was made by the 'average' urban-hand. That advance was not, of course, consistently maintained. Thus, real wages grew relatively slowly from 1830 to 1850 and from the mid-1870s to the mid-1880s, while they actually fell by around three per cent, between 1900 and 1909.[1] Yet overall the size of the improvement remains impressive. G.H. Wood, for instance, has argued that among those who did not change their job, a rise of fifty per cent in their real wages was recorded between 1850-4 and 1900-2. This, however, was a minimum figure, for, taking into account the shift in the occupational structure which took place during that half century from less, to more, skilled employment, the 'average' worker experienced a gain of eighty per cent.[2] Similarly, Bowley, examining trends between 1882 and 1902, concluded that whereas the average increase in money wages during those two decades would have been fifteen per cent if no alteration in the social structure of British society had occurred, the 'very considerable flow from low-paid to better-paid trades' raised this statistic to thirty per cent.[3] The findings of the social statistician were underlined by the qualitative testimonies of informed commentators on the early Edwardian social scene. From Glasgow came the claim that between the mid-1880s and the mid-1900s the economic fortunes of the skilled and the 'upper stratum of the unskilled' had undergone a profound transformation: 'people now get food and comforts that they did not have and would never had thought of having.'[4] As Dr. Alexander Scott put it in 1904, 'the social condition of the working man is very much better. He gets far more, and if he would not drink whisky he would be far better off; and the food is cheaper, in fact they get more food.'[5] That verdict was to be endorsed in other major towns and cities, such as Manchester, where Dr. Niven, the local Medical Officer of Health, drew attention, in the same year, to the better physique of school children and young adults.[6]

And yet amidst this process of advance, widespread poverty continued to exist in urban society. According to Charles Booth, 30.7 per cent of London's total population lived in a state of poverty in the early 1890s. Almost a decade later Rowntree, surveying the incidence of poverty in the city of York, arrived at a statistic — 27.84 per cent — which diverged little from that of his mentor.[7] In one sense, of course, these results are not strictly comparable since the methodologies utilised by the two investigators were markedly different. Booth was largely concerned with examining the amount of social suffering amongst those households with families of school age and, on the basis of these data, making assumptions about the size of the poverty problem in London as a whole. Moreover, his pioneering definition of the poverty line lacked the precision of that of Rowntree, while his classification of the poor was to some extent blurred by his failure to elicit reliable information on aggregate family income. Rowntree, on the other hand, examined every working-class family in York, relied on family earnings alone to break the population down into composite groups, and invoked the aid of the dietician when he defined the minimum subsistence needs of an average-sized household. Finally, and what was perhaps the most crucial development of all, he drew attention to the existence of two distinct types of poverty. Primary poverty, which accounted for 9.91 per cent of York's population, denoted an aggregate family income which was insufficient to maintain the members of the household in a condition of physical efficiency. Secondary poverty, embracing 17.93 per cent of the city's population, arose in those households where earnings enabled the family to reach this basic minimum but where the family penalised itself by disbursing its income in an unscientific manner.[8] None the less, as Rowntree pointed out, imprudent budgeting did not simply relate to expenditure, upon drink, although drink itself was the largest single cause of secondary poverty.[9]

> . . . let us clearly understand what "merely physical efficiency" means. A family living upon the scale allowed for in this estimate [that is, on the poverty line] must never spend a penny on railway fare or omnibus. They must never go into the country unless they walk. They must never purchase a halfpenny newspaper or spend a penny to buy a ticket for a popular concert. They must write no letters to absent children, for they cannot afford to pay the postage. They must never contribute anything to their church or chapel, or give any help to a neighbour which costs them money. They cannot save, nor can they join sick club or Trade Union, because they cannot pay the necessary subscriptions. The children must have no pocket money for dolls, marbles, or sweets. The father must smoke no tobacco, and must drink no beer. The mother must never buy any pretty clothes for herself or for her children, the character of the family wardrobe as for the family diet being governed by the regulation, "Nothing must be bought but that which is absolutely necessary for the maintenance of physical health, and what is bought must be of the plainest and most economical description." Should a child fall ill, it must be attended by the parish doctor; should it die, it must be buried by the parish. Finally, thw wage-earner must never be absent from his work for a single day.[10]

Paradoxically enough, therefore, as this inventory makes plain, those households whose incomes were marginally above Rowntree's poverty level of 21/8d. for an average-sized family, could be plunged into secondary poverty through the practice of thrift.

But apart from the differences in methodology which tend to rule out any direct comparison of Booth's and Rowntree's data, doubts have also been expressed about how far social conditions in York and London mirrored those of urban society as a whole. London, at the time of Booth's inquiry, was still the city of the small workshop, while York lacked those major units of production which were the hallmark of the staple industries. The problem, when presented in this form, cannot be completely resolved since we lack any parallel survey using *all* the techniques employed by either Booth or Rowntree. Yet there are indicators from other sources that their conclusions were more representative than their critics maintained. Bowley and Burnett-Hurst, for example, were concerned with measuring the incidence of primary — but not secondary — poverty in three towns of widely different socio-economic structure in 1913, a year which, like 1899, the date of Rowntree's initial investigations, was characterised by relatively full employment. Using Rowntree's criterion, they discovered that 6.4 per cent of Northampton's, 11.5 per cent of Warrington's, and 15.3 per cent of Reading's households subsisted in a state of primary poverty, statistics which were reasonably close to the 9.91 per cent result for York.[11] Again, Lady Bell's less rigorous survey of 900 families in the iron and steel town of Middlesborough in the opening years of this century, found that

> 125, in round numbers, were found to be absolutely poor. The people living in them never have enough to spend on food to keep themselves sufficiently nourished, enough to spend on clothes to be able to protect their bodies adequately, enough to spend on their house, to acquire a moderate degree of comfort.

Furthermore, another 175 'were so near the poverty line that they are constantly passing over it.'[12] Lastly, although admittedly evidence of an indirect nature, it was still true that as late as 1900 one in five in England and Wales could expect a pauper's funeral, with all that that entailed in the form of the stigma which was attached to the surviving members of the family.[13] When this sombre backcloth of material deprivation is related to the firm, but slowly diminishing, hold which the drink trade exercised over working-class consumers, it is possible to accept that Rowntree's considered judgment that between twenty-five and thirty per cent of Britain's urban dwellers subsisted in either primary or secondary poverty,[14] did not widely exaggerate the extent of poverty at the turn of the twentieth century.

But if that was the situation obtaining at the end of a long period of working-class advance, how great was the volume of poverty in the pre-1890 decades? Unfortunately no exact statistical answer can be given to this question since there is no major work by a social statistician to enable us to chart the parameters of the poverty problem. Nevertheless, notwithstanding this drawback, most of the available indices, qualitative as well as quantitative, suggest that primary poverty was more deeply entrenched and of wider dimensions and that the amount of secondary poverty was on no less a scale than by the time Booth and Rowntree had turned their attention to what, for them, was the burning social issue of the day. It was greater partly because many low-paid, and/or casually employed, groups which, by the 1890s, had either disappeared completely or existed in a much diminished form, represented, in the early years of our period, an important segment of the total occupied population. In 1830 there were a quarter of a million handloom weavers engaged in the manufacture of cotton fabrics alone, while the sweated outwork trades remained an important outlet for working-class employment both in the pre-1850 era and in the ensuing two or three decades. Another, more general factor, contributing to the impoverishment of the working classes was the movement of prices and money wages in the pre-1870 decade, for in general terms the wages of the unskilled were lower, and retail prices higher, in that period than subsequently.

After 1840, however, economic change started to affect the social structure of the poor in a more positive fashion. After that date the numbers of handloom weavers and woolcombers underwent rapid contraction; by 1870 the framework knitter was being superseded by the hosiery factory; and by the late 1880s whole areas of the sweated trades were passing from the domestic hearth and the small workshop to larger, mechanised units of production. Furthermore, in certain areas of economic activity casual labour, after 1890, became of diminishing significance. But even if the amount of primary poverty was reduced over time, it still remained, before and after Rowntree, a fundamental social problem which neither Poor Law nor philanthropy could eradicate. As more than one social critic noted, to be poor in this basic sense — to lack, that is, sufficient income for a subsistence standard of existence — was to be condemned to a life in which material deprivation was present on the grand scale.[15]

Sources and References

Introduction

1. E.P. Thompson and E. Yeo (eds.), *The Unknown Mayhew* (1973), p. 565.
2. J. Ruskin, *Unto This Last* (Cassell and Co., n.d.), p. 77.
3. W.H.B. Court, *British Economic History 1870-1914. Commentary and Documents* (1965), p. 373.
4. G.R. Porter, On the self imposed Taxation of the Working Classes in the United Kingdom, *Journal of the Royal Statistical Society*, Vol. XIII (1850), p. 364.
5. J.H. Clapham, *An Economic History of Modern Britain, Vol. II 1850-86* (1963), p. 451.
6. T. Wright, *Our New Masters* (1873), p. 43.
7. *Minutes of Evidence taken before the Glasgow Municipal Commission on Housing* (1902-3), q. 13273 A.
8. *Ibid.*, q. 13300.
9. *Report of the Select Committee on Manufacturers, Commerce and Shipping, P.P.*, 1933 (690), vi, q. 3972.
10. S. Rowntree, *Poverty A Study of Town Life* (2nd ed., 1902), p. 55.
11. *Ibid.*, p. 281.
12. D. Thompson (ed.), *The Early Chartists* (1971), p. 185.
13. W.H.B. Court *op. cit.*, p. 291.
14. S. Rowntree *op. cit.*, p. X.
15. *Ibid.*
16. *The Report of the Industrial Remuneration Conference 1885* (1885) (Paper by Edith Simcox), p. 90.

Chapter 1

1. Much of this paragraph is based upon *Report of an Enquiry of the Board of Trade into Working Class Rents, Housing and Retail Prices together with the Standard Rate of Wages Prevailing in certain occupations in the Principal Industrial Towns of the United Kingdom, P.P.*, [Cd. 3864], 1908. [Henceforth cited *Board of Trade Inquiry*, 1908].
2. J. Saville, *Royal Depopulation in England and Wales 1851-1911* (1957), pp. 47-8.
3. M. Gray, Scottish Emigration: The Social Impact of Agrarian Change in the Rural Lowlands 1775-1875, *Perspectives in American History*, Vol. VII (1973), pp. 158, 162.
4. B.R. Mitchell and P. Deane, *Abstract of British Historical Statistics* (1962), pp. 21-3.
5. G. Best, *Mid Victorian Britain 1851-75* (1971), p. 6.
6. L. Levi, *Wages and Earnings of the Working Classes* (1885), pp. 30, 55.
7. W.H.B. Court *op. cit.*, p. 287.
8. *The Report of the Industrial Remuneration Conference 1885* (1885), p. 20.
9. H. Perkin, *The Origins of Modern English Society* (1969), p. 414.
10. *Royal Commission on the Poor Laws and Relief Distress. Appendix Vol. XIX A. Report by the Rev. J.C. Pringle on The Effects of Employment or Assistance given to the 'Unemployed' since 1886 as a means of Relieving Distress outside the Poor Law in Scotland, P.P.*, [Cd. 5073], 1910, p. 5. [Henceforth quoted as *Pringle Report*.]
11. C. Booth, *Life and Labour of the People of London*, Vol. I (1892), pp. 48-50;

S. Rowntree *op. cit.*, p. 120

12. A.L. Bowley and A.R. Burnett-Hurst, *Livelihood and Poverty* (1915), pp. 41-2. The fourth town in their survey was not of course York but the coal-mining community of Stanley.
13. L. Faucher, *Manchester in 1844* (Cars Reprint 1969), p. 29.
14. *Manchester Times* 4 January 1840.
15. E.P. Thompson and E. Yeo (eds.) *op. cit.*, pp. 311-2.
16. *Morning Chronicle* 22 January 1850.
17. J. Foster, *Class Struggle and the Industrial Revolution* (1974), p. 96.
18. Quoted in M. Anderson, *Family Structure in Nineteenth Century Lancashire* (1974), p. 30.
19. *Ibid.*, p. 31.
20. N. Murray, *A Social History of the Scottish Handloom Weavers 1790-1850* (University of Strathclyde Ph.D., 1977), p. 206. This study is to be published by John Donald in 1978.
21. J. Foster *op. cit.*, p. 257; Anderson, *op. cit.*, p. 30.
22. M. Anderson *op. cit.*, p. 30.
23. A.L. Bowley, Wages in the Worsted and Woollen Manufactures of the West Riding of Yorkshire, *Journal of the Royal Statistical Society*, Vol. 65 (1902), p. 103.
24. N. Murray, *op. cit.*, pp. 102, 140-1; J. Prest, *The Industrial Revolution in Coventry* (1960), p. 72.
25. *Royal Commission on Labour, Group C*, Vol. II, *P.P.*, (C.6795 – II), 1892-3, q. 17631, Appendix XXX.
26. N.B. Dearle, *Problems of Unemployment in the London Building Trades* (1908), p. 99.
27. C.P. Griffin, The Standard of Living in the Black Country in the Nineteenth Century: a Comment, *Economic History Review*, Vol. xxxvi (1973), p. 512; J. H. Treble, The Navvies, *Journal of the Scottish Labour History Society*, No. 5 (1972), pp. 49-50.
28. S. Rowntree *op. cit.*, pp. 132-3.
29. A.L. Bowley and A.R. Burnett-Hurst *op. cit.*, p. 35.
30. *Glasgow Municipal Commission on Housing*, (1902-3) [Henceforth cited as *Glasgow Commission*], qq. 12794, 12857.
31. G. Barnsby, The Standard of Living in the Black Country during the Nineteenth Century, *Economic History Review*, Vol. xxiv (1971), p. 233.
32. H. Bosanquet (ed.), *Social Conditions in Provincial Towns* (1912), p. 24.
33. *Royal Commission on the Condition of the Poorer Classes in Ireland, Appendix G, State of the Irish Poor in Great Britain, P.P.*, 1836, [40], p. ix. [Henceforce cited as Appendix G Irish Poor].
34. *Journal of the Royal Statistical Society*, Vols. XXI (1858), p. 424; and XXIII (1860), p. 12.
35. *Board of Trade Inquiry* 1908, *P.P.*, [Cd. 3864], pp. 83, 258, 514 and 549; *Glasgow Commission*, q. 12059.
36. *Journal of the Royal Statistical Society*, pp. 110-1, 376-81; *Glasgow Commission*, qq. 12059, 13492-4.
37. *Report of the Select Committee on Home Work, P.P.*, 1907, (290), q. 2115.
38. *Minutes of Evidence taken before the Lords Committee to consider of the Poor Laws, P.P.*, 1818, [400], p. 167; *Second Report of the Minutes of Evidence taken before the Committee appointed to consider of the Several Petitions relating to the Ribbon Weavers*, 1818, *P.P.*, [211 and 278], p. 89.
39. *Report from the Select Committee on Handloom Weavers' Petitions*, 1835, *P.P.*, (341), p. 230.
40. *Ibid.*, q. 2428; *Report from the Select Committee on Handloom Weavers' Petition*, 1834, *P.P.*, (556), q. 6659.
41. *Scottish Patriot* 23 May 1840.
42. *Manchester Guardian* 21 August 1841.
43. N. Murray *op. cit.*, pp. 43-4.
44. R. Church, *Economic and Social Change in a Midland Town* (1966), pp. 20-1, 43.
45. *Morning Chronicle* 22 January 1850.
46. *Report from the Select Committee on Handloom Weavers' Petitions, P.P.*, 1835, (341),

p. XIII.
47. *Appendix G Irish Poor*, p. ix.
48. *Assistant Commissioners' Reports upon Handloom Weavers, Part III, P.P.*, 1840.
    (43 — I), pp. 475, 484.
49. N. Murray *op. cit.*, p. 156.
50. *Report from the Select Committee on the Silk Trade, P.P.*, 1831-2, (678), q. 11664.
51. *Ibid., passim; Report from the Select Committee on Handloom Weavers' Petitions,
    P.P.*, 1835, (341), q. 2409.
52. *Reports from Assistant Handloom Weavers' Commissioners, P.P.*, Part III, 1840,
    (43 — I), p. 491.
53. This Summary of the Coventry silk trade is based upon J. Prest, *The Industrial
    Revolution in Coventry* (1960).
54. This discussion of wage trends in the worsted industry is based upon E.M. Sigsworth,
    Black Dyke Mills (1961), pp. 7-38; A.L. Bowley, Wages in the Worsted and Woollen
    Manufactures of the West Riding, *Journal of the Royal Statistical Society*, Vol. 65
    (1902), espec. pp. 102-123; *Report from the Select Committee on Handloom Weavers'
    Petitions, P.P.*, 1835, (341), p. 229.
55. *Reports from Assistant Handloom Weavers' Commissioners, Part III, P.P.*, 1840,
    (43 — II), p. 564
56. *Ibid.*, pp. 535, 538.
57. N. Murray *op. cit.*, pp. 131-2, 157.
58. *Journal of the Royal Statistical Society*, Vol. 65 (1902), p. 114.
59. *Reports from Assistant Handloom Weavers' Commissioners, Part III, P.P.*, 1840,
    (43 — II), p. 535.
60. N. Murray *op. cit.*, p. 149.
61. *Reports from Assistant Handloom Weavers' Commissioners, Part V, P.P.*, 1840, [220],
    p. 585.
62. *Ibid.*, Part III, *P.P.*, 1840, (43 — I), p. 490.
63. N. Murray *op. cit.*, p. 152.
64. *Manchester Guardian* 21 August 1841. The words are those of Edward Curran, one of
    the leading spokesmen of the handloom weaving community in Manchester; N. Murray,
    op. cit., pp. 90-1, 96, 102.
65. N. Murray *op. cit.*, pp. 96-7, 154.
66. *Royal Commission on the Poor Laws, Report A Part I, Assistant Commissioners Reports*,
    1834, *P.P.*, (44), p. 909A.
67. N. Murray *op. cit.*, p. 39.
68. *Select Committee on Poor Law Removal, P.P.*, 1854, (396), q. 6332.
69. N. Murray *op. cit.*, p. 36.
70. G.R. Porter, *The Progress of the Nation* (1851), p. 456; R. Church, *op. cit.*, pp. 261-5.
71. L.P. Gartner, *The Jewish Immigrant in England 1870-1914* (1960), pp. 81-95.
72. E.P. Thompson and Eileen Yeo (eds.) *op. cit.*, pp. 471, 543.
73. This discussion of female involvement in the clothing trades is based upon M. Stewart
    and L. Hunter, *The Needle Is Threaded* (1964), p. 115; P.G. Hall, *The Industries of
    London since 1861* (1962), p. 60; A. Sherwell, *Life in West London* (1897), p. 106.
74. E.P. Thompson and Eileen Yeo (eds.) *op. cit.*, pp. 461-4; P.G. Hall *op. cit.*, pp. 85-9.
75. L.P. Gartner *op. cit.*, p. 81; C. B. Hawkins, *Norwith A Social Study* (1910), pp. 23-34.
76. *Royal Commission on Labour, The Employment of Women, P.P.*, 1893, (Cd. 6894 —
    XXIII), p. 266.
77. S.J. Chapman, *Work and Wages, Vol. III Social Betterment* (1914), pp. 288-291.
78. *Ibid.*
79. E.P. Thompson and Eileen Yeo (eds.) *op. cit.*, p. 318.
80. J. Foster *op. cit.*, p. 94.
81. *Sixth Report of the Medical Officer of the Privy Council 1863, P.P.*, 1864, (3416),
    p. 230.
82. *Royal Commission on the Poor Laws, Report by Miss Constance Williams and Mr
    Thomas Jones on The Effect of Outdoor Relief on Wages and the Conditions of
    Employment, P.P.*, 1909, (Cd. 4690), p. 247. [Henceforth cited as Williams and Jones
    Report.]

83. *Poor Law Inquiry (Scotland)*, Appendix, Part I, *P.P.*, 1844, [563], qq. 323, 1532-3.
84. E.P. Thompson and Eileen Yeo (eds.) *op. cit.*, pp. 142-3, 214-5.
85. *Journal of the Royal Statistical Society*, Vol. XI (1848), pp. 206-7.
86. E.P. Thompson and Eileen Yeo (eds.) *op. cit.*, p. 143.
87. *Ibid.*, p. 149.
88. *Journal of the Royal Statistical Society*, Vol. XXI (1858), p. 466.
89. *Sixth Report of the Medical Officer of the Privy Council 1963, P.P.*, 1864, [3416], pp. 224-5.
90. *Fifth Report. Sweating System. (House of Lords), P.P.*, 1890, (169), p. xv.
91. C. Booth, *Life and Labour of the People of London*, Vol. IV (1983), pp. 259-60.
92. *Report from the Select Committee on Home Work, P.P.*, 1907, (290), qq. 2112, 2123.
93. W.H.B. Court *op. cit.*, p. 391.
94. S.J. Chapman *op. cit.*, p. 290.
95. *Ibid.*, pp. 290-1.
96. E.P. Thompson and Eileen Yeo (eds.) *op. cit.*, p. 141.
97. *Ibid.*, p. 158.
98. *4th Report of the House of Lords Committee on the Sweating System, P.P.*, 1889, (331), q. 25634.
99. *Ibid.*, qq. 25758-9.
100. *Ibid.*, qq. 26088, 26091.
101. Charles Booth *op. cit.*, Vol. IV, pp. 50-2.
102. *Ibid.*, Vol. I, p. 56.
103. *Royal Commission on the Poor Laws. Report by A.D. Steel-Maitland and Miss Rose E. Squire on The Relations of Industrial and Sanitary Conditions to Pauperism, P.P.*, 1909, [Cd. 4653], 1909, p. 22. [Henceforth cited as *Steel-Maitland and Squire Report*]
104. *C. Booth op. cit.*, Vol. IV, pp. 62-3.
105. C. Booth *op. cit.*, Vol. IV, pp. 62-3.
106. *Royal Commission on Labour, The Employment of Women*, 1893, *P.P.*, (C.6894 – xxiii), p. 273.
107. *Steel-Maitland and Squire Report*, p. 72.
108. C. Booth *op. cit.*, Vol. IV, pp. 50-2.
109. A. Sherwell *op. cit.*, pp. 107-8.
110. *Royal Commission on Labour. The Employment of Women*, 1893, *P.P.*, (C.6894 – xxiii), pp. 266-7.
111. C. Booth *op. cit.*, Vol. IV, pp. 52, 54.
112. *Royal Commission on Labour. The Employment of Women* 1893, *P.P.*, (C.6894 – xxiii), p. 266.
113. M. Stewart and L. Hunter *op. cit.*, pp. 145, 148.
114. J. Foster *op. cit.*, pp. 86-7.
115. R.Q. Gray, *The Labour Aristocracy in Victorian Edinburgh* (1976), pp. 70-1.
116. E.P. Thompson and Eileen Yeo (eds.) *op. cit.*, pp. 322-3, 333.
117. *Sixth Report of the Medical Officer of the Privy Council 1863*, 1864, *P.P.*, (3416), pp. 229-30.
118. R.Q. Gray *op. cit.*, p. 71.
119. This discussion on the East End boot trade in the 1890s is based upon D.F. Schloss, Bootmaking, C. Booth *op. cit.*, Vol. IV, especially pp. 69-118. The quotation is taken from page 114.
120. *Steel-Maitland and Squire Report*, p. 23.
121. C.B. Hawkins *op. cit.*, pp. 31-3.
122. C. Booth *op. cit.*, Vol. IV, p. 280.
123. *Steel-Maitland and Squire Report*, p. 25.
124. C. Booth *op. cit.*, Vol. IV, pp. 277, 299.
125. E. Cadbury, M. Cecile Matheson and G. Shann, *Women's Work and Wages* (1906), p. 149, 158.
126. S. Pollard, *A History of Labour in Sheffield* (1959), pp. 54-5, 61, 125-33; *5th Report Sweating System (House of Lords), P.P.*, 1890, (169), pp. xxxiv-v.
127. *Ibid.*, p. xxxvi.
128. S. Pollard *op. cit.*, pp. 202-10.

129 *Steel-Maitland and Squire Report*, pp. 133-6.
130. *Ibid.*, pp. 135-6; S. Pollard *op. cit.*, p. 208.
131. J. H. Clapham, *An Economic History of Modern Britain*, Vol. II (1963), p. 98; Vol. III (1963), p. 472.
132. *Ibid.*, Vol. III, p. 472; W.H.B. Court *op. cit.*, p. 387.
133. E. Hopkins, Small Town Aristocrats of Labour and Their Standard of Living 1840-1914, *Economic History Review*, Vol. xxviii (1975), p. 231. The Coventry statistic is taken from G. Drage, *The Problem of the Aged Poor* (1895), p. 41.
134. *5th Report Sweating System (House of Lords)*, 1890, *P.P.*, (169), p. xxix; P. Keating (ed.), *Into Unknown England 1866-1913* (1976), p. 183.
135. *Ibid.*, p. 179.
136. *Ibid.*, pp. 175-7, 181.
137. *5th Report Sweating System (House of Lords)*, 1890, *P.P.*, (169), p. xxv.
138. Cadbury, Matheson and Shann *op. cit.*, pp. 210-11.
139. *Poor Law Inquiry (Scotland)*, Appendix, Part I, 1844, *P.P.*, (563), qq. 318-9, 321, 1532-3.
140. *Journal of the Royal Statistical Society*, Vol. XI (1848) pp. 206-7
141. *Ibid.*, Vol. lxi (1898), p. 225.
142. *Steel-Maitland and Squire Report*, p. 28.
143. *Ibid.*, p. 73; *Williams and Jones Report*, p. 240; *Glasgow Commission*, q. 11336.
144. *Ibid.*
145. *Steel-Maitland and Squire Report*, pp. 28, 73.
146. *Williams and Jones Report*, p. 273.
147. *Journal of the Royal Statistical Society*, Vol. lxi (1898), p. 224.
148. *Annual Report of the Chief Inspector of Factories and Workshops for the Year 1900*, 1901, *P.P.*, [Cd. 668], pp. 381-2.
149. *Williams and Jones Report*, p. 273.
150. R. Samuel (ed.), *Village Life and Labour* (1975), pp. 177, 179-183.
151. *Williams and Jones Report*, pp. 263, 329.
152. C. Booth *op. cit.*, Vol. IV, p. 295.
153. Cadbury, Matheson and Shann *op. cit.*, pp. 189, 191.
154. *Ibid.*, pp. 121, 232-4.
155. *Steel-Maitland and Squire Report*, p. 92.
156. *Ibid.*, pp. 99-100.
157. *Ibid.*, p. 72.
158. *Ibid.*, pp. 17, 30-1; C. Booth *op. cit.*, Vol. IV, pp. 289-290; O.C. Malvery, *The Soul Market* (6th ed., n.d.), pp. 73-4.
159. *Transactions of the National Association for the Promotion of Social Science for 1862* (1963), p. 747.
160. Robert Roberts, *The Classic Slum* (Pelican Books, 1973).
161. *Ibid.*, pp. 82-3.
162. *Poor Law Inquiry (Scotland)*, Appendix, Part I, 1844, *P.P.*, (563), q. 317.
163. *Journal of the Royal Statistical Society*, Vol. xi (1848), p. 207.
164. *Appendix G Irish Poor*, p. 89.
165. *Report from the Select Committee on Building Regulations and Improvement of Boroughs*, 1842, *P.P.*, (372), qq. 1535-6, 1553.
166. *Appendix G Irish Poor*, p. viii.
167. P. Quennell (ed.), *Mayhew's London* (1969), p. 121.
168. D. Alexander, *Retailing in England during the Industrial Revolution* (1970), pp. 70-1.
169. *Ibid.*, p. 62.
170. *Ibid.*, p. 71; *Morning Chronicle* 4, 18, 22, and 25 January 1850.
171. D. Alexander *op. cit.*, pp. 234-8; L.P. Gartner *op. cit.*, pp. 59-60.
172. C. Booth *op. cit.*, Vol. I, pp. 57-9.
173. Cadbury, Matheson and Shann *op. cit.*, pp. 179-80.
174. C. Booth *op. cit.*, Vol. I, p. 48.
175. *Forward* 12 August 1911.

Chapter 2

1. W.P. Alison, *Observations on the Management of the Poor in Scotland* (wnd ed., 1840), pp. 3, 12, 38-9.
2. *Select Committee on Manufactures, Commerce and Shipping,* 1833, *P.P.,* (690), q. 4774.
3. G. Drage, *The Unemployed* (1894), p. 84.
4. *Pringle Report,* p. 9.
5. J. Brown, Charles Booth and Labour Colonies, *Economic History Review,* 2nd Series Vol. xxi (1968).
6. W.H.B. Court *op. cit.,* pp. 292-3.
7. J. Harris, *Unemployment and Politics* (1972), pp. 7-20.
8. B.S. Rowntree and Bruno Lasker, *Unemployment a Social Study* (1911).
9. *Report from the Select Committee on Distress from Want of Employment,* 1896, *P.P.,* (321), p. iv.
10. R. Dudley Baxter, *National Income. The United Kingdom* (1868), pp. 41-2, 47.
11. Charles Booth *op. cit.,* Vol. I, pp. 146-7.
12. Seebohm Rowntree *op. cit.,* p. 120.
13. B.S. Rowntree and Bruno Lasker *op. cit.,* pp. viii-ix.
14. *Williams and Jones Report,* p. 373.
15. *Ibid.*
16. *Glasgow Herald* 28 February 1907.
17. G. Stedman Jones, *Outcast London* (1971), p. 81.
18. *Royal Commission on the Poor Laws,* Vol. ix, *Minutes of Evidence,* 1910, *P.P.,* [Cd. 5068], q. 96625; *Minutes of Evidence taken before the Inter-Departmental Committee on Physical Deterioration,* 1904, *P.P.,* [Cd. 2210], qq. 6016-7.
19. *Ibid.,* qq. 6287-9.
20. A.V. Woodworth, *Report on an Inquiry into the Condition of the Unemployed conducted under the Toynbee Trustee Winter 1895-6* (1897), p. 54. This quotation applied to the unskilled unemployed generally, but it seems to me to relate, with particular force, to the casual worker.
21. *Glasgow Herald* 20 November 1909.
22. *Minutes of Evidence taken before the Inter-Departmental Committee on Physical Deterioration,* 1904, *P.P.,* [Cd. 2210], q. 6017.
23. *Glasgow Municipal Commission,* qq. 818-9, 6633.
24. *Ibid.,* qq. 818-9.
25. *Appendix G Irish Poor,* p. 22.
26. G. Stedman Jones *op. cit.,* p. 53.
27. *Transactions of the National Association for the Promotion of Social Science for 1862* (1863), pp. 745-6.
28. *Liverpool Mercury* 16 February 1838.
29. *Transactions of the National Association for the Promotion of Social Science for 1862* (1863), p. 745.
30. G. Stedman Jones *op. cit.,* pp. 120.2.
31. *Royal Commission on the Poor Laws,* Vol. ix, *Minutes of Evidence,* 1910, *P.P.,* [Cd. 5068], q. 89615.
32. *Ibid.,* p. iiii. Evidence of W.S. Workman.
33. *Ibid.,* qq. 89791, 89871.
34. *Ibid.,* p. 1098.
35. quoted in W.H.B. Court *op. cit.,* p. 305.
36. *Steel-Maitland and Squire Report,* p. 36.
37. G. Stedman Jones *op. cit.,* p. 122.
38. *Minutes of Evidence before the Royal Commission on Labour,* Group B, Vo. II, 1892, *P.P.,* [C.6895 − V], q. 12817.
39. G. Stedman Jones *op. cit.,* pp. 73, 76, 79.
40. *Ibid.,* pp. 67-79; *Steel-Maitland and Squire Report,* p. 81.
41. G. Stedman Jones *op. cit.,* pp. 317-21.
42. *Steel-Maitland and Squire Report,* pp. 35-7.
43. G. Stedman Jones *op. cit.,* p. 319.

44. E.G. Howarth and Mona Wilson, *West Ham* (1907), pp. 191-4.
45. *Steel-Maitland and Squire Report*, pp. 35-7.
46. *Organised Help* May 1914, pp. 91-3.
47. E.G. Howarth and Mona Wilson *op. cit.*, p. 345.
48. W.H.B. Court *op. cit.*, p. 310.
49. *Royal Commission on the Poor Laws*, Vol. ix, *Minutes of Evidence*, 1910, P.P., [Cd. 5068], q. 89615.
50. *Ibid.*
51. W.H.B. Court *op. cit.*, p. 310.
52. *Appendix G Irish Poor*, p. 31.
53. *Manchester Guardian* 17 June 1840; C.B. Hawkins *op. cit.*, pp. 65-6, 70.
54. Charles Booth *op. cit.*, Vol. I, pp. 200-2, 211.
55. *Steel-Maitland and Squire Report*, pp. 98-9; *Organised Help* May 1913, pp. 57-8; B.S. Rowntree and Bruno Lasker *op. cit.*, p. 131.
56. G. Stedman Jones *op. cit.*, p. 58.
57. *Steel-Maitland and Squire Report*, p. 67.
58. *Glasgow Herald* 26 May 1909.
59. *Royal Commission on Labour. Answers to the Schedule of Questions* Group B., 1892, P.P., [C. 6795 – VIII], No. 328, Horsemen's Union, Glasgow.
60. Angela Tuckett, *The Scottish Carter* (1967), p. 46.
61. M. Anderson *op. cit.*, p. 24.
62. *Royal Commission on the Poor Laws*, Appendix Vol. xi, *Miscellaneous*, 1911, P.P., [Cd. 5072], pp. 55-6; *Steel-Maitland and Squire Report*, p. 147.
63. *Pringle Report*, pp. 60-1.
64. C.B. Hawkins *op. cit.*, pp. 65-6, 69-70.
65. *Royal Commission on the Poor Laws*, Vol. ix, *Minutes of Evidence*, 1910, P.P., [Cd. 5068], q. 89977; *Pringle Report*, pp. 192-3.
66. *Glasgow Herald* 23 January 1907.
67. *Royal Commission on the Poor Laws*, Vol. ix, *Minutes of Evidence*, 1910, P.P., [Cd. 5068], p. 331.
68. N.B. Dearle, *Problems of Unemployment in the London Building Trades* (1908), p. 98.
69. B.S. Rowntree and Bruno Lasker *op. cit.*, p. 132.
70. N.B. Dearle *op. cit.*, pp. 99-100.
71. *Ibid.*, pp. 92-5, 94-5; *Royal Commission on the Poor Laws*, Vol. ix, *Minutes of Evidence*, 1910, P.P., [Cd. 5068], p. 331.
72. R. Dudley Baxter *op. cit.*, p. 43.
73. N.B. Dearle *op. cit.*, pp. 128-9.
74. *Royal Commission on Labour. Answers to the Schedules of Questions* Group C, 1892, P.P., [C. 6795 – ix], No. 418, National Federal Union of Operative Bakers of Scotland.
75. *Steel-Maitland and Squire Report*, p. 20.
76. *Royal Commission on the Poor Laws*, Vol. ix, *Minutes of Evidence*, 1910, P.P., [Cd. 5068], p. 1086. Evidence of James MacFarlane of Messrs. MacFarlane, Lang and Co.
77. *Minutes of Evidence Taken Before the Departmental Committee on the Hours and Conditions of Employment of Van Boys and Warehouse Boys*, 1913, P.P., [Cd. 6887], qq. 5484-5.
78. *Steel-Maitland and Squire Report*, p. 17.
79. *Second Report of Minutes of Evidence taken before the Committee appointed to consider of the Several Petitions relating to Ribbon Weavers*, 1818, P.P., [211 and 278], p. 103.
80. *Report from the Select Committee on the Silk Trade*, 1831-2, P.P., (678), q. 11462.
81. J. Prest *op. cit.*, p. 44.
82. D. Bythell *op. cit.*, pp. 60-1; N. Murray *op. cit.*, p. 52.
83. *Report from the Select Committee on Handloom Weavers' Petitions*, 1834, P.P., (556), q. 469; *Assistant Commissioners' Report upon Handloom Weavers*, Part III, 1840, P.P., (43 – I), pp. 534-6.
84. *Report from the Select Committee on Handloom Weavers' Petitions*, 1835, P.P., (341), qq. 2504-5.
85. *Assistant Commissioners' Reports upon Handloom Weavers*, Part II, 1840, P.P., (43 –

I), p. 478.

86. E.P. Thompson and Eileen Yeo (eds.) *op. cit.*, p. 224.

87. *Ibid.*, pp. 229-33.

88. *Ibid.*, pp. 321-2.

89. I.P. Gartner *op. cit.*, p. 71.

90. *4th Report of the House of Lords Committee on the Sweating System*, 1889, *P.P.*, (331), qq. 25678-80.

91. Charles Booth *op. cit.*, Vol. IV, pp. 96-9, 103-8.

92. C.B Hawkins *op. cit.*, pp. 31-3.

93. D. Alexander *op. cit.*, p. 62; S. Pollard *op. cit.*, pp. 55-7; *5th Report Sweating System House of Lords*, 1890, *P.P.*, (169), pp. xxxiv-vi.

94. Charles Booth *op. cit.*, Vol. V (1895), p. 131.

95. *Organised Help* March 1910, pp. 553-4; H.J. Dyos and M. Wolff (eds.), *The Victorian City*, Vol. I (1976), pp. 127, 149-150; *Royal Commission on the Poor Laws*, Vol. ix, *Minutes of Evidence*, 1910, *P.P.*, [Cd. 5068], q. 90345; Charles Booth *op. cit.*, Vol. I, p. 211.

96. H. Bosanquet (ed.) *op. cit.*, p. 25.

97. *Journal of the Royal Statistical Society*, Vol. 54 (1891), p. 613.

98. General William Booth, *In Darkest England and the Way Out* (1890), pp. 27-9.

99. *Ibid.*, p. 28.

100. *Organised Help* March 1910, pp. 552-4; *4th Report of the House of Lords Committee on the Sweating System*, 1889, *P.P.*, (331), q. 25622; Charles Booth *op. cit.*, Vol. IV, p. 281.

101. *Ibid.*, p. 289.

102. *Steel-Maitland and Squire Report*, p. 17.

103. *Ibid.*, p. 16.

104. *Ibid.*, pp. 70, 73 for casual female hawkers in the centre of Liverpool in 1907.

105. *Report from the Select Committee on Home Work*, 1907, *P.P.*, (207), q. 2222.

106. E.G. Howarth and Mona Wilson *op. cit.*, p. 255.

107. *Steel-Maitland and Squire Report*, p. 31.

108. H. Bosanquet (ed.) *op. cit.*, p. 25.

109. Charles Booth *op. cit.*, Vol. 1, p. 50.

110. *Williams and Jones Report*, p. 240.

111. *Steel-Maitland and Squire Report*, p. 69.

112. G. Stedman Jones *op. cit.*, p. 56.

113. *Journal of the Royal Statistical Society*, Vol. III (1840-1), p. 221.

114. *Ibid.*; W.P. Alison *op. cit.*, p. 3.

115. *Poor Law Inquiry (Scotland)*, Appendix, Part I, 1844, *P.P.*, (563), q. 5681.

116. *Journal of the Royal Statistical Society*, Vol. IV, p. 18.

117. J.H. Treble, The Seasonal Demand for Labour in Glasgow 1890-1914, *Social History*, Vol. III (January 1978).

118. Charles Booth *op. cit.*, Vol. V (1895), pp. 115-6.

119. Strathclyde Regional Archives DTC 8/65, J.V. Stevenson, Chief Constable of Glasgow to John Lindsay, 26 February 1903.

120. Charles Booth *op. cit.*, Vol. V (1895), p. 116; *Royal Commission on Labour. Answers to the Schedule of Questions*, Group C, 1895, *P.P.*, [C. 6795 — ix], No. 566, Society of Scottish United Paviors.

121. J.H. Treble, The Seasonal Demand for Adult Labour in Glasgow 1890-1914, *Social History*, Vol. III (January 1978).

122. N.B. Dearle *op. cit.*, p. 74.

123. *Royal Commission on the Poor Laws*, Vol. xi, *Miscellaneous*, 1911, *P.P.*, [Cd. 5072], p. 56.

124. See above.

125. Quoted in G. Stedman Jones *op. cit.*, p. 47.

126. *Ibid.*, pp. 44-6. The quotation is taken from *Reynolds News* 25 February 1855.

127. P. Quennell (ed.) *op. cit.*, p. 564.

128. See above.

129. *Pringle Report*, p. 58; *Steel-Maitland and Squire Report*, p. 80; H.J. Dyos and M.

Wolff (eds.) *op. cit.*, Vol. I, p. 147.

130. *Steel-Maitland and Squire Report*, p. 83.
131. *Pringle Report*, p. 2; J.H. Treble, The Seasonal Demand for Labour in Glasgow 1890-1914, *Social History*, Vol. III (January 1978); G. Stedman Jones *op cit.*, p. 36.
132. Charles Booth *op. cit.*, Vol. I (L892), pp. 200-1.
133. *Steel-Maitland and Squire Report*, p. 98.
134. N. Murray *op. cit.*, pp. 102, 105.
135. J. Prest *op. cit.*, p. 44; N. Murray *op. cit.*, p. 44; *Leeds Mercury* 15 March 1834.
136. E.P. Thompson and E. Yeo (eds.) *op. cit.*, p. 228.
137. *4th Report of the House of Lords Committee on the Sweating System, P.P.*, 1889, (331), q. 25554.
138. *Ibid.*, qq. 25885-7, 25903.
139. Charles Booth *op. cit.*, Vol. IV, p. 53.
140. C.B. Hawkins *op. cit.*, pp. 47-8; *Steel-Maitland and Squire Report*, p. 100.
141. A. Sherwell *op. cit.*, pp. 83-4.
142. C.B. Hawkins *op. cit.*, p. 48.
143. Charles Booth *op. cit.*, Vol. IV, pp. 74-6, 106, 117, 274, 277.
144. W.P. Alison *op. cit.*, p. 3; J.H. Treble *art. cit.*; H. Bosanquet (ed.) *op. cit.*, pp. 24-5, *Poor Law Inquiry (Scotland)*, Appendix, Part I, 1844, *P.P.*, (563), q. 1531; H.J. Dyos and M. Wolff (eds.) *op. cit.*, p. 135.
145. *Steel-Maitland and Squire Report*, p. 97.
146. *Ibid.*, p. 92.
147. G. Stedman Jones *op. cit.*, pp. 34-5; A. Sherwell *op. cit.*, p. 66; *Royal Commission on Labour. Answers to Schedules*, 1892, *P. P.*, [C.6795 − ix], No. 509, Alliance Cabinet Makers' Association, Glasgow and District Branch.
148. G. Stedman Jones *op. cit.*, pp. 35-6; J.H. Treble *art. cit.*
149. J.H. Treble *art. cit.*
150. *Ibid.*
151. N. Murray *op. cit.*, p. 44; D. Bythell *op. cit.*, p. 59.
152. J.H. Treble *art. cit.*; G. Stedman Jones *op. cit.*, p. 40; *Pringle Report*, p. 61.
153. J.H. Treble *art. cit.*; H.J. Dyos and M. Wolff (eds.) *op. cit.*, p. 132.
154. *Steel-Maitland and Squire Report*, p. 17; H. Bosanquet (ed.) *op. cit.*, pp. 24-5.
155. G. Stedman Jones *op. cit.*, p. 37-8; J.H. Treble *art. cit.*
156. C. B. Hawkins *op. cit.*, pp. 22-3; *Williams and Jones Report*, p. 376.
157. See above
158. Charles Booth *op. cit.*, Vol. IV, p. 277.
159. *Ibid.*, p. 117; *4th Report of the House of Lords Committee on the Sweating System*, 1889, *P.P.*, (331), qq. 25887, 25903.
160. G. Stedman Jones *op. cit.*, p. 43.
161. A. Sherwell *op. cit.*, p. 146.
162. Charles Booth *op. cit.*, Vol. I, p. 153.
163. S. and B. Webb, *Industrial Democracy* (1902 (ed.), Part II, Chapter VIII, *passim*.
164. *Royal Commission on Labour. Minutes of Evidence.* Group A, Vol. III, 1893, *P.P.*, [C. 6894 − vii], p. 497.
165. K. Burgess, *The Origins of British Industrial Relations* (1975), pp. 49-71.
166. R.A. Church *op. cit.*, p. 268.
167. *Ibid.*, pp. 235-6.
168. *Select Committee on Handloom Weavers' Petitions, P.P.*, 1834, (556), q. 6248; *Bradford Observer* 4 October 1838 quoted in E.M. Sigsworth *op. cit.*, p. 36.
169. N. Murray *op. cit.*, p. 134.
170. Quoted in E.M. Sigsworth *op. cit.*, p. 41.
171. *Ibid.*, pp. 41.2.
172. *Select Committee on Handloom Weavers' Petitions, P.P.*, 1834, (556), qq. 6248, 6251.
173. *The Morning Chronicle* 1 January 1850.
174. J.H. Clapham *op. cit.*, Vol. II, p. 459.
175. *Williams and Jones Report*, p. 246.
176. J.A. Schmiechen, State Reform and the Local Economy, *Economic History Review*,

Vol. xxviii (1975), pp. 418-22.
177. S. and B. Webb *op. cit.*, pp. 396-7, 417-20.
178. C.B. Hawkins *op. cit.*, pp. 23-4, 33-4; *Steel-Maitland and Squire Report*, p. 105.
179. *Ibid.*
180. The problem of changes in the laundry industry was discussed above. For the other references, see *Williams and Jones Report*, p. 246; *Royal Commission on Labour. Answers to the Schedules of Questions* Group B, 1892, *P.P.*, [C. 6795 – viii], No. 341, National Union of Dock Labourers, Glasgow Branch; *Steel-Maitland and Squire Report*, pp. 35-6; *Forward* 14 May 1910.
181. *Forward* 14 May 1910.
182. *Report from the Select Committee on Home Work, P.P.*, 1907, (290), qq. 2926-7.
183. G. Stedman Jones *op. cit.*, pp. 105-6.
184. *Royal Commission on Labour*, Group B, Volume II, 1892, *P.P.*, [C. 6795 – v], qq. 14348, 14351.
185. *Ibid.*, Group C, Volume II, 1892, *P.P.*, [C. 6795 – II], qq. 17806-8.
186. Strathclyde Regional Archives G3 36(1) Lord Provost's Relief Fund 1907-9. Letter of G. Lyon, 50 Kinning Street, Kingston, 14 October 1908.
187. *Royal Commission on Labour*, Group A, Vol. II, 1892, [C. 6795 – iv], qq, 15977, 16226.
188. *Glasgow United Trades' Council Report for 1884-5* (1995), p. 7; *Forward* 11 September 1909.
189. *Royal Commission on the Poor Laws*, Vol. ix, *Minutes of Evidence*, 1910, *P.P.*, [Cd. 5068], q. 89905.
190. *Ibid.*, p. 332.
191. *Ibid.*, q. 96633.
192. J.H. Trebble, Unemployment and Unemployment Policies in Glasgow 1890-1905, in P. Thane (ed.) *The Origins of British Social Policy*, (1978).
193. J. Foster *op. cit.*, p. 96.
194. *Royal Commission on the Poor Laws*, Vol. ix, *Minutes of Evidence*, 1910, *P.P.*, [Cd. 5068], q. 89905.
195. *Journal of the Royal Statistical Society*, Vol. I (1838-9), p. 167.
196. *Glasgow Evening Post* 22 April 1837.
197. *Glasgow Argus* 6 April 1837.
198. *Ibid.*, 10 August 1837.
199. D. Bythell *op. cit.*, p. 106; R.A. Chruch *op. cit.*, pp. 106-7; *Journal of the Royal Statistical Society*, Vol. I (1838-9), pp. 86-8.
200. J. Adshead, *Distress in Manchester Evidence (tabular and otherwise) of the State of the Labouring Classes in 1840-2* (1842), pp. 19-20.
201. *Leeds Times* 29 February 1840.
202. *Poor Law Inquiry (Scotland)*, Appendix, Part I, 1844, *P.P.*, (563), q. 5681.
203. *Manchester Times* 28 May 1842.
204. *Journal of the Royal Statistical Society*, Vol. V (1842), p. 75; *Supplement to The Glasgow Argus* 17 January 1842.
205. Quoted in P. Dunkley, The 'Hungry Forties' and the New Poor Law: A Case Study, *The Historical Journal*, Vol. xviii (1974), p. 332.
206. *Journal of the Royal Statistical Society*, Vol. V (1842), p. 75; *Poor Law Inquiry (Scotland)*, Appendix, Part I, 1844, *P.P.*, (563), q. 6761.
207. *Liverpool Mercury* 21 January 1842.
208. *Ibid.*, 14 January 1842.
209. Quoted in W.O. Henderson, *The Lancashire Cotton Famine 1861-1865* (1934), p. 99.
210. Strathclyde Regional Archives G3 36(1) Lord Provost's Relief Fund 1907-9. Letters of Alfred Dailkin, 54 Scott Street, [Port] Dundas, 12 October 1908; Mrs. Hugh Quinn, 202 Rockvilla off Possil Road, n.d.; J. Chalmer, 56 Cedar Street, 13 October 1908.

Chapter 3

1. B.S. Rowntree *op. cit.*, p. 120.
2. Lady Bell, *At The Works* (Nelson, n.d.), p. 80.
3. B.S. Rowntree *op. cit.*, p. 54.
4. E.P. Thompson and Eileen Yeo (eds.) *op. cit.*, p. 259.
5. M.E. Rose, *The Relief of Poverty 1834-1914* (1972), p. 18.
6. D. Fraser (ed.), *The New Poor Law in the Nineteenth Century* (1976), p. 135.
7. *Ibid.*, p. 55. This paragraph is based upon M.W. Flinn, Medical Services under the New Poor Law, *ibid*.
8. *Poor Law Inquiry (Scotland)*, Appendix, Part I, 1844, *P.P.*, [563], q. 31.
9. *Ibid.*, qq. 5924-5.
10. *Journal of the Royal Statistical Society*, Vol. III (1840-1), p. 219.
11. W.P. Alison *op. cit.*, pp. 33-4.
12. *Poor Law Inquiry(Scotland)*, Appendix, Part I, 1844, *P.P.*, [563], q. 48.
13. *Journal of the Royal Statistical Society*, Vol. 72 (1909), p. 213.
14. *Williams and Jones Report*, p. 200.
15. Alice Albert, Working Class Women in Glasgow c. 1890-1914, p. 9 (University of Strathclyde Dissertation for B.A. Honours Degree in Economic History 1977).
16. E. Cadbury, M. Cecile Matheson and G. Shann *op. cit.*, p. 147.
17. M. Anderson *op. cit.*, p. 141.
18. M.E. Rose *op. cit.*, p. 19.
19. *Poor Law Inquiry (Scotland)*, Appendix, Part I, 1844, *P.P.*, [563], p. 41-4.
20. *Ibid.*, q. 5796.
21. S.G. and E.O. Checkland (eds.), *The Poor Law Report of 1834* (1974), p. 114.
22. *Morning Chronicle* 22 January 1850.
23. This discussion of Longley's findings is taken from *Williams and Jones Report*, pp. 356-9.
24. *Ibid.*, p. 335. On 1st January 1907 33,644 able-bodied widows were in receipt of outdoor relief in England and Wales.
25. *Royal Commission on the Poor Laws*, Appendix Vol. XXIII, 1910, *P.P.*, [Cd. 5075], p. 29.
26. *Ibid.*, pp. 14, 16, 29. For a discussion of the treatment of women paupers in Glasgow, see Margaret Fleming, Attitudes and Policies to Pauper Women and Children in Glasgow 1900-14 (University of Strathclyde B.A. Honours Dissertation in Economic History 1975).
27. *Ibid.*, p. 17; *Williams and Jones Report*, p. 353.
28. *Journal of the Royal Statistical Society*, Vol. II (1839), p. 370, 374-5.
29. *Ibid.*, Vol. XI (1848), p. 207. There were 54 needlewomen.
30. E.P. Thompson and Eileen Yeo (eds.) *op. cit.*, p. 159.
31. Charles Booth *op. cit.*, Vol. IV (1893), pp. 259, 295 and 301.
32. E. Cadbury, M. Cecile Matheson and G. Shann *op. cit.*, pp. 147, 210, 213-4.
33. *Royal Commission on the Poor Laws*, Appendix Vol. xxiii, *P.P.*, [Cd. 5075], p. 46.
34. *Journal of the Royal Statistical Society*, Vol. 72 (1909), p. 217.
35. Strathclyde Regional Archives G3 36(1). Lord Provost's Relief Fund 1907-9. Letter of Mrs. E. Conway, 48a Maitland Street, Cowcaddens, Glasgow, n.d.
36. *Morning Chronicle* 22 January 1850.
37. E.P. Thompson and Eileen Yeo (eds.) *op. cit.*, p. 166.
38. *Journal of the Royal Statistical Society*, Vol. xi (1848), pp. 201, 211-3.
39. A. Sherwell *op. cit.*, pp. 9-10.
40. H.J. Dyos, The Slums of Victorian London, *Victorian Studies*, Vol. II (1967-8), pp. 29-33.
41. Charles Booth *op. cit.*, Vol. I (1892), p. 254.
42. *Williams and Jones Report*, pp. 247-8.
43. B.S. Rowntree *op. cit.*, p. 33.
44. General William Booth *op. cit.*, p. 27.
45. *Return of Boards of Guardians (Persons in Receipt of Relief)* 1904, *P.P.*, (113), pp. iii-iv.

46. *Journal of the Royal Statistical Society*, Vol. 72 (1909), p. 208.
47. *Steel-Maitland and Squire Report*, p. 142.
48. *Glasgow Echo* 19 December 1894.
49. P. Quinnell (ed.) *op. cit.*, p. 557.
50. P.E. Razzell and R.W. Wainwright (eds.), *The Victorian Working Class* (1973), p. 232.
51. Charles Booth, *The Aged Poor in England and Wales*, (1894), p. 218.
52. *Steel-Maitland and Squire Report*, p. 97.
53. *Ibid.*, p. 92.
54. *Report of the Second Annual Conference of the Labour Representation Committee February 20, 21, 22, 1902*, (n.d.), p. 17.
55. *Return of Boards of Guardians (Persons in Receipt of Relief)* 1904, *P.P.*, (113), p. v.
56. *Journal of the Royal Statistical Society*, Vol. 61 (1898), p. 362.
57. *Ibid.*, Vol. 54 (1891), p. 631.
58. Charles Booth, *The Aged Poor in England and Wales* (1894), pp. 420, 424.
59. *Journal of the Royal Statistical Society*, Vol. 69 (1906), p. 292.
60. *Ibid.*, pp. 290-2.
61. C.S. Loch, *Old Age Pensions and Pauperism* (1892), p. 23.
62. Charles Booth, *The Aged Poor in England and Wales* (1894), p. 330.
63. *Poor Law Inquiry (Scotland)*, Appendix, Part I, 1844, *P.P.*, [563], qq. 5761, 5763; *Journal of the Royal Statistical Society*, Vol. 61 (1898), p. 323.
64. B.S. Rowntree *op. cit.*, p. 382.
65. *Return of Boards of Guardians (Persons in Receipt of Relief)* 1904, *P.P.*, (113), p. iv.
66. Pat Thane, Old Age Pensions 1878-1908, in Pat Thane (ed.) *op. cit.*
67. M. Anderson *op. cit.*, p. 137.
68. *Steel-Maitland and Squire Report*, p. 31.
69. E.P. Thompson and Eileen Yeo (eds.) *op. cit.*, p. 149.
70. W.H.B. Court *op. cit.*, p. 34.
71. Charles Booth, *The Aged Poor in England and Wales* (1894), pp. 220-1.
72. *Poor Law Inquiry (Scotland)*, Appendix, Part I, 1844, *P.P.*, [563], q. 395.
73. Charles Booth, *The Aged Poor in England and Wales* (1894), pp. 219-20; P.E. Razzell and R.W. Wainwright (eds.) *op. cit.*, p. 237.
74. *Poor Law Inquiry (Scotland)*, Appendix, Part II, 1844, *P.P.*, [564], pp. 30, 182-3.
75. *Ibid.*, Appendix, Part I, 1844, *P.P.*, [563], q. 5763.
76. G. Drage, *The Problem of the Aged Poor* (1895), pp. 60-76; G. Stedman Jones *op. cit.*, pp. 275-6.
77. Charles Booth, *The Aged Poor in England and Wales*, (1894), pp. 325-6.
78. *Ibid.*, p. 326 for this practice in relation to outdoor relief.
79. M. Anderson *op. cit.*, p. 139.
80. P.E. Razzell and R.W. Wainwright (eds.) *op. cit.*, p. 232.
81. See, for example, the case study of the Huddersfield mill-worker's family in *Morning Chronicle Supplement* 18 January 1850, Letter xiv.
82. *Ibid.*, M. Anderson *op. cit.*, p. 164.
83. I am greatly indebted to Dr. Norman Murray for bringing this song — 'Old Age Pensions' — to my attention and for his literal translation of it from the Gaelic. Only those verses which relate to old age pensions have been quoted here.
84. *Glasgow Echo* 19 December 1894. The speaker was John Cronin.
85. J.R. Poynter, *Society and Pauperism* (1969), pp. 22-3.
86. *Ibid.*, pp. 201.2.
87. *Transactions of the National Association for the Promotion of Social Science for 1866* (1867), p. 311.
88. Quoted G. Stedman Jones *op. cit.*, p. 244. This account of the residuum draws heavily on Stedman Jones's work.
89. quoted *ibid.*, p. 246.
90. *Report by the Board of Supervision on the Measures taken by the Local Authorities of the Principal Centres of Population in Scotland for the Relief of the Ablebodied Unemployed during the Winter of 1893-4*, 1894, *P.P.*, [C. 7410], p. 6.
91. G. Drage, *The Unemployed* (1894), p. 154.
92. Such statements abound in the minutes of evidence, particularly among the testimonies

of employers of labour and of full-time Poor Law officials.
93. quoted G. Stedman Jones *op. cit.*, pp. 288-9.
94. Charles Booth, *Life and Labour of the People in London*, Vol. I (1892), pp. 42-3, 149, 154.
95. quoted W.H.B. Court *op. cit.*, pp. 301.2.
96. T.M. Devine, 'The rise and fall of illicit whisky-making in Scotland, c. 1780-1840', *Scottish Historical Review*, LIV (1975), pp. 155-177.
97. W. B. Neale, *Juvenile Delinquency in Manchester: its Causes and History and some suggestions concerning its cure* (1840) p. 62. For brief discussion of the Irish illicit whisky trade, see J.H. Treble, The Place of the Irish Catholics in the Social Life of the North of England 1829-51. (University of Leeds Ph.D. thesis, 1969), pp. 117-9.
98. *Liverpool Mercury* 6 December 1839.
99. For heavy female drinking, see, among other sources, O.C. Malvery, *The Soul Market* (6th ed., n.d.), pp. 48, 87; Charles Booth, *Life and Labour of the People of London* Vol. IV (1893), pp. 323-4.
100. E.P. Thompson and Eileen Yeo (eds.) *op. cit.*, pp. 231-2; P. Quennell (ed.) *op. cit.*, pp. 554-5.
101. *Report from the Select Committee on Railway Labourers, 1846, P.P., XIII, q 1078; Glasgow Municipal Commission on Working-Class Housing* (1902-3), q. 7274.
102. E.P. Thompson and Eileen Yeo (eds.) *op. cit.*, p. 538.
103. *Ibid.*, p. 233.
104. B. Harrison, *Drink and the Victorians* (1971), pp. 37, 43, 47-9.
105. *Ibid.*, pp. 300-3, 326, 331, 334-5; D.J. Oddy and D.S. Miller (eds.), *The Making of the Modern British Diet* (1976), pp. 127-30.
106. G.B. Wilson, *Alcohol and the Nation* (1940), pp. 229-71.
107. Lady Bell *op. cit.*, p. 351; O.C. Malvery *op. cit.*, pp. 73-4; S. B. Rowntree *op. cit.*, pp. 142-3.
108. *Royal Commission on the Poor Laws*, Vol. ix, *Minutes of Evidence*, 1910, P.P., [Cd. 5068], q. 90112.
109. I. Archer, *The Jags* (1976), pp. 30-2.
110. J. Burnett, *Plenty and Want* (1966), p. 155.
111. S.B. Rowntree *op. cit.*, pp. 142-3.
112. quoted in J. Brown, The Pig or The Stye: Drink and Poverty in late Victorian England, *International Review of Social History*, Vol. xviii (1973), pp. 387-9.
113. Charles Booth, *Life and Labour of the People of London*, Vol. I. (1892), pp. 146-7.
114. S.B. Rowntree *op. cit.*, pp. 140, 142.
115. N. Murray *op. cit.*, pp. 207-8.
116. *Report from the Select Committee on the Poor Law (Scotland)*, 1870, P.P., q. 2587. The speaker was James Moir, the former Chartist leader in Glasgow and at this moment in time a Town Councillor.
117. P. Quennell (ed.) *op. cit.*, pp. 554-5; Charles Booth, *Life and Labour of the People of London*, Vol. I (1892), pp. 42-4.
118. *Minutes of Evidence taken before the Inter-Departmental Committee on Physical Deterioration*, 1904, P.P., [Cd. 2210], q. 6297.
119. General William Booth *op. cit.*, p. 48.
120. S.B. Rowntree *op. cit.*, p. 144.
121. *Liverpool Mercury* 29 July 1842.
122. M. Loane, *The Queen's Poor* (1910), pp. 136-9, 151, 153; Mrs. B. Bosanquet, *Rich and Poor* (2nd ed., 1898), pp. 90-2.
123. M. Anderson *op. cit.*, pp. 72-4; E. Cadbury, M. Cecile Matheson and G. Shann *op. cit.*, pp. 213-6.
124. W.H.B. Court *op. cit.*, pp. 294, 310-11.
125. S.B. Rowntree *op. cit.*
126. Mrs. B. Bosanquet, *Rich and Poor* (2nd ed., 1898), p. 99.
127. M.S. Pember Reeves, *Round About a Pound a Week* (1913), p. 145.
128. *Ibid.*, pp. 56, 59, 145.
129. *Ibid.*, p. 145.

Chapter 4

1. *Report of the Inter-Departmental Committee on Physical Deterioration*, Vol. I, 1904, *P.P.*, [Cd. 2715], p. 126.
2. *4th Report of the House of Lords Committee on the Sweating System*, 1889, *P.P.*, (331), q. 26, 282.
3. *Forward* 21 May 1910.
4. *Williams and Jones Report*, p. 248.
5. Charles Booth, *Life and Labour of the People of London*, Vol. I (1892), p. 43.
6. E. Cadbury, M.C. Matheson and G. Shann *op. cit.*, pp. 211-16; W.H.B. Court *op. cit.*, p. 307; *Williams and Jones Report*, pp. 248-50.
7. M. Anderson *op. cit.*, pp. 72-3.
8. *Report of the Inter-Departmental Committee on Physical Deterioration*, Vol. I, 1904, *P.P.*, [Cd. 2175], p. 125.
9. *Ibid.*, p. 118.
10. *Ibid.*, p. 125.
11. D. Bythell *op. cit.*, pp. 60-2; N. Murray *op. cit.*, pp. 51-2.
12. *Reports of the Inspectors of Factories for the Half-Year ending 31st. December 1843*, 1844, *P.P.*, p. 4.
13. Leeds Diocesan Archives. Packet W131. Letter of James M'Donnell to Canon James Harrison, 19 September 1854.
14. Lynn Lees, Mid-Victorian Migration and the Irish Family Economy, *Victorian Studies*, Vol. xx (1976), pp. 36-7; T.M. Marshall, General Report on Roman Catholic Schools for the Year 1849, *Minutes of the Committee of Council on Education 1848-50*, Vol. II, p. 525.
15. *Appendix G Irish Poor*, p. 15.
16. *Minutes of the Committee of Council on Education 1850-1*, p. 965.
17. *Transactions of the National Association for the Promotion of Social Science for 1870* (1871), p. 347.
18. *Organised Help* March 1910, pp. 552-3.
19. *Minutes of Evidence taken before the Inter-Departmental Committee on Physical Deterioration*, Vol. II, 1904, *P.P.*, [Cd. 2210], qq. 1922, 1925.
20. *Annual Report of the Chief Inspector of Factories and Workshops for the year 1902*, 1903, *P.P.*, [Cd. 1610], pp. 137-8. This loophole, however, was not widely exploited under 300 exemptions being granted in the whole of Scotland in 1902.
21. S.B. Rowntree *op. cit.*, p. 74.
22. quoted in David Kynaston, *King Labour* (1976), p. 103.
23. *Forward* 5 March 1910.
24. *Journal of the Royal Statistical Society*, Vol. xi (1848), pp. 200-1.
25. M. Anderson *op. cit.*, pp. 72-3.
26. Reports from Assistant Handloom Weavers' Commissioners, Part III, 1840, *P.P.*, (43 – II), pp. 565-7; Lynn Lees *art. cit.*, *Victorian Studies*, Vol. xx (1976), pp. 35-7.
27. S.B. Rowntree *op. cit.*, pp. 54, 71.
28. *Forward* 23 April 1910.
29. *Report of Handloom Weavers' Commissioners*, 1841, *P.P.*, [x], pp. 4-5; S.B. Rowntree *op. cit.*, pp. 135-8.
30. *Ibid.*, pp. 136-7.
31. M. Anderson *op. cit.*, p. 127.
32. *Ibid.*, pp. 124, 129.
33. Charles Booth, *Life and Labour of the People in London*, Vol. I (1892), p. 43.
34. *Morning Chronicle* Supplement 22 January 1850.
35. Lynn Lees *art. cit.*, *Victorian Studies*, Vol. xx (1976), p. 37.
36. *Transactions of the National Association for the Promotion of Social Science for 1861* (1862), p. 626.
37. Mrs. B. Bosanquet, *Rich and Poor* (2nd. ed., 1898), p. 99.
38. Charles Booth, *Life and Labour of the People in London*, Vol. IV (1893), p. 27.
39. *Poor Law Inquiry (Scotland)*, Appendix, Part I, *P.P.*, 1844, [563], q. 5681.
40. *Report from the Select Committee on Pawnbrokers*, *P.P.*, 1870, (377), q. 1381.

41. Lady Bell *op. cit.*, p. 347; L. Faucher *op. cit.*, p. 50.
42. *Report from the Select Committee on Pawnbrokers, P.P.*, 1870, (377), q. 226. Evidence of Alfred Hardaker, Secretary of Liverpool Pawnbrokers' Association.
43. *Journal of the Royal Statistical Society*, Vol. vi (1843), p. 18; N.B. Dearle *op. cit.*, pp. 140-1.
44. Lady Bell *op. cit.*, p. 127.
45. J. Adshead, *Distress in Manchester, Evidence (tabular and otherwise) of the State of the Labouring Classes in 1840-42*, (1842), pp. 22-3.
46. *Report from the Select Committee on Pawnbrokers, P.P.*, 1870, (377), q. 963.
47. *Ibid.*, q. 1124.
48. *Ibid.*, q. 963.
49. S.B. Rowntree *op. cit.*, p. 59.
50. *Report from the Select Committee on Pawnbrokers, P.P.*, 1870, (377), qq. 316, 4404.
51. *Ibid.*, q. 4402; Norman Murray *op. cit.*, p. 191.
52. Norman Murray *op. cit.*, pp. 190-1.
53. W.H.B. Court *op. cit.*, p. 308.
54. *Ibid.* M.S. Pember Reeves *op. cit.*, p. 73
55. W.H.B. Court *op. cit.*, p. 308.
56. *Ibid.*
57. O.C. Malvery *op. cit.*, p. 69.
58. *Select Committee on Handloom Weavers' Petition, P.P.*, 1834, (556), qq. 6465-5.
59. *How the Labourer Lives. Report of the Liverpool Joint Research Committee on the Domestic Condition and Expenditure of the Families of the Liverpool Labourers* (1909), p. xxii.
60. D. Alexander *op. cit.*, pp. 82-3.
61. Lady Bell *op. cit.*, p. 111.
62. *Ibid.*, pp. 110-11.
63. *Transactions of the National Association for the Promotion of Social Science for 1860* (1861), p. 746.
64. Charles Booth, *Life and Labour of the People in London*, Vol. I (1892), p. 112; E. Cadbury, M. Cecile Matheson and G. Shann *op. cit.*, p. 238.
65. *How the Casual Labourer Lives. Report of the Liverpool Joint Research Committee on the Domestic Condition and Expenditure of the Families of the Liverpool Labourers* (1909), p. xv.
66. E. G. Howarth and Mona Wilson *op. cit.*, pp. 66-7, 113-8. The quotation is taken from p. 67.
67. *Assistant Commissioners' Handloom Weavers Report*, Part III, *P.P.*, 1840, 42 – II, p. 538.
68. E.P. Thompson and Eileen Yeo (eds.) *op. cit.*, p. 199.
69. E.G. Howarth and Mona Wilson *op. cit.*, p. 117.
70. *Supplement to the Glasgow Argus* 17 January 1842.
71. S.D. Chapman (ed.), *The History of Working Class Housing* (1971), pp. 76-8.
72. E.P. Thompson and Eileen Yeo (eds.) *op. cit.*, p. 252.
73. *Report from the Select Committee on Pawnbrokers, P.P.*, 1870, (377), q. 1023.
74. O.C. Malvery *op. cit.*, p. 69.
75. A. Sherwell *op. cit.*, p. 111 footnote.
76. S.B. Rowntree *op. cit.*, p. 281.
77. *Glasgow Argus* 17 January 1842.
78. *Transactions of the National Association for the Promotion of Social Science for 1860* (1861), p. 747.
79. Chaper 3 *passim*.
80. S. and B. Webb, *English Local Government*, Vol. 10 *English Poor Law Policy* (1963), p. 28.
81. D. Fraser (ed.) *op. cit.*, p. 178; *Journal of the Royal Statistical Society*, Vol. 61 (1898), p. 326.
82. *Royal Commision on the Poor Laws. Report on Scotland, P.P.*, 1909, [Cd. 4922], pp. 166-7.
83. S. and B. Webb, *English Local Government. Vol. 10 English Poor Law Policy* (1963),

pp. 22-3; M.E. Rose *op. cit.*, p. 14.

84. M.A. Crowther, The Later Years of the Workhouse 1890-1929 in Pat Thane (ed.) *op. cit.*

85. S. and B. Webb, *English Local Government. Vol. 10 English Poor Law Policy* (1963), pp. 26-7.

86. *Ibid.*, pp. 90-1.

87. D. Fraser (ed.) *op. cit.*, p. 5.

88. P. Dunkley *art. cit.*, *The Historical Journal*, Vol. xviii (1974), p. 335; D. Fraser (ed.) *op. cit.*, pp. 137-8; G. Stedman Jones *op. cit.*, p. 274.

89. S. and B. Webb, *English Local Government. Vol. 10 English Poor Law Policy* (1963), pp. 155-8.

90. *Ibid.*, pp. 159-64.

91. Jose Harris *op. cit.*, p. 148.

92. *Ibid.*, p. 373.

93. *Ibid.*, p. 148; S. and B. Webb, *English Local Government. Vol. 9 English Poor Law History* (1963), pp. 367-8.

94. *Manchester Guardian* 5 April 1848.

95. S. and B. Webb, *English Local Government. Vol. 8 English Poor Law Policy* (1963), pp. 368, 375.

96. *Ibid.*, p. 375; M.E. Rose *op. cit.*, p. 17.

97. S. and B. Webb, *English Local Government. Vol. 8 English Poor Law History* (1963), p. 373.

98. J. Adshead *op. cit.*, p. 31.

99. *Leeds Times* 13 February 1841.

100. *Appendix G Irish Poor*, pp. 12, 45.

101. *Report of the Select Committee on Poor Law Removals, P.P.*, 1854, (396), q. 5118.

102. D. Fraser (ed.) *op. cit.*, pp. 29-31.

103. *Leeds Times* 13 November 1841; *Manchester Times* 28 May 1842.

104. J. Adshead *op. cit.*, pp. 10-11; *Third Report of the Select Committee on Distress from Want of Employment, P.P.*, 1895, (365), p. 520.

105. N. Murray *op. cit.*, p. 236.

106. G. Stedman Jones *op. cit.*, p. 278.

107. Jose Harris *op. cit.*, p. 78.

108. *Poor Law Inquiry (Scotland)*, Appendix, Part I, *P.P.*, 1844, [563], q. 7010.

109. *Report on the Administration of the Glasgow Unemployed Relief Fund 1878-9* (1879), pp. 34-5; *Glasgow Herald* 9 June 1908.

110. *Anti-Bread Tax Circular* 5 May 1842; *Leeds Mercury* 22 February 1843; R.J. Morris, The Voluntary Society — A Response to Urbanism 1780-1850, p. 6 (Unpublished Paper presented to the Urban History Group Conference 1973).

111. J. H. Treble *art. cit.*, in Pat Thorne (ed.) *op. cit.*

112. *Glasgow Chronicle* 17 April 1829 quoted in N. Murray *op. cit.*, p. 231.

113. *Third Report of the Select Committee on Distress from Want of Employment, P.P.*, 1895, (365), q. 8629.

114. *Ibid.*, q. 8316. For the work of the Charity Organisation Society in the city see Garrick M. Fraser, The Glasgow Charity Organisation Society 1905-14 (Unpublished B.A. Honours Dissertation in Economic History, University of Strathclyde 1977).

115 Margaret Simey, *Charitable Effort in Liverpool in the Nineteenth Century* (1951). These details are taken from the chapter entitled Slumming 1885-1900.

Chapter 5

1. N. Murray *op. cit.*, p. 168.

2. B.S. Rowntree *op. cit.*, p. 235.

3. See, for example, Miss W.A. Mackenzie, Changes in the Standard of Living in the United Kingdom 1860-1914, *Economica*, Vol. I (1921), p. 226; D.J. Oddy and D.S. Miller (eds.), *The Making of the Modern British Diet* (1976), p. 216.

4. *Board of Trade Inquiry*, 1908, pp. 516, 521, 529.
5. quoted by W.H. Chaloner, Trends in British Fish Consumption in the Eighteenth and Nineteenth Centuries, in T.C. Barker, J.C. McKenzie and J. Yudkin (eds.), *Our Changing Fare* (1966); *Sixth Report of the Medical Officer of the Privy Council, P.P.*, 1864, [3416] *passim*.
6. Elizabeth Roberts, Working-Class Standards of Living in Barrow and Lancaster 1890-1914, *Economic History Review*, Vol. xxx (1977), pp. 313-4.
7. T.R. Gourvish, The Cost of Living in Glasgow in the Early Nineteenth Century, *Economic History Review*, Vol. xxv (1972), pp. 73-8.
8. R. Perren, The Meat and Livestock Trade in Britain 1850-70, *Economic History Review*, Vol. xxviii (1975), p. 396.
9. *Board of Trade Inquiry*, 1908, p. xxxviii.
10. quoted in M. Anderson *op. cit.*, p. 30.
11. T. Wright *op. cit.*, p. 368.
12. quoted in W.H.B. Court *op. cit.*, pp. 309-10.
13. quoted in E.P. Thompson, *The Making of the English Working Class* (Pelican ed., 1968), p. 349.
14. *Morning Chronicle* 18 January 1850.
15. E. Cadbury, M. Cecile Matheson and G. Shann *op. cit.*, pp. 234-5.
16. *Foresters' Miscellany* December 1891, p. 271.
17. W.H.B. Court *op. cit.*, pp. 311-2.
18. The attempt of a Committee of the Royal Statistical Society to calculate the annual meat consumption *per capita* in the United Kingdom in 1904 produced a figure of 86lb. for labourers, but it acknowledged that the smallness of the sample deprived this calculation of much validity. *Journal of the Royal Statistical Society*, Vol. 67 (1904), p. 382.
19. *Ibid.*, Vol. 55 (1892) pp. 267, 271.
20. *Ibid.*, Vol. 67 (1904) p. 391.
21. *Ibid.*, p. 392.
22. *How the Labourer Lives. Report of the Liverpool Joint Research Committee on the Domestic Condition and Expenditure of the Families of the Liverpool Labourers* (1909), p. xxv.
23. *Sixth Report of the Medical Officer of the Privy Council*, 1864, *P.P.*, [3416], p. 224.
24. S.J. Chapman *op. cit.*, pp. 159-160.
25. *Report from the Select Committee on Handloom Weavers' Petitions*, 1834, *P.P.*, (556), qq. 6458-9, 6467, 6705.
26. B.S. Rowntree *op. cit.*, p. 237.
27. *How the Labourer Lives. Report of the Liverpool Joint Research Committee on the Domestic Conditions and Expenditure of the Families of the Liverpool Labourers* (1909), pp. x-xi.
28. M.S. Pember Reeves *op. cit.*, p. 59; M. Loane *op. cit.*, p. 138.
29. T.C. Barker, Nineteenth Century Diet: Some Twentieth Century Questions, in T.C. Barker, J.C. McKenzie and J. Yudkin (eds.) *op. cit.*
30. Mrs. M.S. Pember Reeves *op. cit.*, p. 59.
31. *Sixth Report of the Medical Officer of the Privy Council*, 1864, *P.P.*, [3416], p. 230.
32. R.M. Hartwell, The Rising Standard of Living in England 1800-50, in A.J. Taylor (ed.), *The Standard of Living in Britain in the Industrial Revolution* (1975), p. iii; B.R. Mitchell and P. Deane *op. cit.*, p. 358.
33. T.R. Gourvish *art. cit.*, p. 71.
34. *Royal Commission on the Poor Laws. Report A Part I Assistant Commissioners' Report*, 1834, *P.P.*, (44), p. 909A.
35. *Manchester Times* 18 July 1840; *Appendix G Irish Poor*, p. x.
36. J.C. McKenzie, Past Dietary Trends as an Aid to Prediction, in T.C. Barker, J.C. McKenzie and J. Yudkin (eds.) *op. cit.*
37. *Third Report of the Select Committee on Emigration*, 1826-7, *P.P.*, (550), p. 7.
38. J.P. Kay, *The Moral and Physical Condition of the Working Classes in Manchester in 1832* (2nd. ed., 1832), pp. 20-2.
39. A.J. Taylor (ed.) *op. cit.*, p. xxxii.

40. *Manchester Times* 18 July 1840.
41. T.S. Ashton, The Standard of Life of the Workers in England 1790-1830, in A.J. Taylor (ed.) *op. cit.*, p. 57.
42. B.R. Mitchell and P. Deane, *Abstract of British Historical Statistics* (1962), p. 498.
43. J.H. Treble *thesis cit.*, Chapter 11 *passim.*
44. For oatmeal in the Scottish diet, see T.R. Gourvish *art. cit.*, and R.H. Campbell, Diet in Scotland: An Example of Regional Variation, in T.C. Barker, J.C. Mckenzie and J. Judkin (eds.) *op. cit.*
45. G.R. Porter, On a Comparative Statement of Prices and Wages during the Years from 1842-9, *Journal of the Royal Statistical Society*, Vol. xiii (1850), p. 211.
46. G.R. Porter, *The Progress of the Nation* (1851), p. 452.
47. *Journal of the Royal Statistical Society*, Vol. iv (1842), pp. 321-2; J.C. McKenzie *art. cit.*
48. J. Burnett, Bread and Social Change in Britain 1815-1965, in T.C. Barker, J.C. McKenzie and J. Yudkin (eds.) *op. cit.*
49. T.C. Gourvish *art. cit.*, p. 71 footnote 6.
50. D.J. Oddy and D.S. Miller (eds.) *op. cit.*, p. 92.
51. *Journal of the Royal Statistical Society*, Vol. XIII (1850), p. 212; XXIII (1860), p. 35.
52. *Sanitary Conditions of the Labouring Population 1842, P.P.*, (H.L.), p. 392; E.P. Thompson and E. Yeo (eds.) *op. cit.*, pp. 585-6.
53. T.R. Courvish *art. cit.*, pp. 70-1.
54. *Report of the Select Committee on Manufactures, Commerce and Shipping*, 1833, *P.P.*, (690), q. 11747.
55. *Journal of the Royal Statistical Society*, Vol. IV (1842), pp. 330-1.
56. *Report from the Select Committee on Handloom Weavers' Petitions 1834, P.P.*, (556), q. 6459; *Journal of the Royal Statistical Society*, Vol. XXIII (1850), p. 35.
57. *Royal Commission on the Poor Laws. Report A. Part I Assistant Commissioners' Reports*, 1834, *P.P.*, (44), q. 909A.
58. R.M. Hartwell, The Rising Standard of Living in England 1800-50, in A.J. Taylor (ed.) *op. cit.*, p. 116.
59. *Ibid.*, pp. 112-3.
60. D. Alexander *op. cit.*, pp. 42-3.
61. E.J. Hobshawm, The British Standard of Living 1790-1850, in A.J. Taylor (ed.) *op. cit.*, p. 78.
62. R. Giffen, *The Progress of the Nation in the Last Half Century* (1884), p. 11.
63. *Journal of the Royal Statistical Society*, Vol. XIII (1850), p. 211.
64. *Manchester Times* 18 July 1840; *Report from the Select Committee on Handloom Weavers' Petitions*, 1834, *P.P.*, (556), q. 6459; N. Murray *op. cit.*, p. 205; J.P. Kay *op. cit.*, p. 23; P.E. Razzell and R.W. Wainwright (eds.) *op. cit.*, pp. 195-6; *Sanitary Conditions of the Labouring Population*, 1842, *P.P.*, (H.L.), p. 392; E.P. Thompson and Eileen Yeo (eds.) *op. cit.*, *passim*; J.H. Treble *thesis cit.*, Chapter II, *passim; Appendix G. Irish Poor, passim.*
65. *Journal of the Royal Statistical Society*, Vol. XI (1848), p. 213. 330-1.
66. *Sixth Report of the Medical Officer of the Privy Council*, 1863, *P.P.*, [3416], p. 216.
67. *Ibid.*, pp. 217-8.
68. *Ibid.*, p. 232.
69. *Ibid.*
70. *Ibid.*
71. *Ibid.*, p. 221.
72. *Ibid.*, p. 233.
73. J. Burnett, *Plenty and Want* (1966), p. 153.
74. *Journal of the Royal Statistical Society*, Vol. XX (1857), p. 311-2.
75. *Transactions of the National Association for the Promotion of Social Science for 1862* (1863), p. 748.
76. Miss W.A. Mackenzie *art. cit.*, p. 225.
77. D.J. Oddy, Working-Class Diets in Nineteenth Century Britian, *Economic History Review*, Vol. xxiii (1970), p. 321; *Royal Commission on Labour. Minutes of Evidence Group A. Vol. III*, 1893, *P.P.*, [C.6984 — vii], q. 24,010; S.B. Rowntree *op. cit.*,

pp. 231-4, 263-84; M.S. Pember Reeves *op. cit.*, pp. 94-7.
78. See Table 7.
79. D.J. Oddy and D.S. Miller (eds.) *op. cit.*, p. 222.
80. A.R. Prest assisted by A. Adams, *Consumers' Expenditure in the United Kingdom 1900-19* (1954), p. 40; Table 7 of this text; B.S. Rowntree *op. cit.*, pp. 408-23.
81. *Royal Commission on Labour. Minutes of Evidence*, Group A, Vol. III, 1893, *P.P.*, [C.6984 – vii], q. 24,010.
81. A.R. Prest *op. cit.*, p. 47.
83. Quoted in P. Keating (ed.) *op. cit.*, p. 175.
84. *How the Casual Labourer Lives. Report of the Liverpool Joint Committee on the Domestic Conditions and Expenditure of the Families of the Liverpool Labourers*, (1909), p. xxi; *Royal Commission on Labour. Minutes of Evidence*, Group A, Vol. III, 1893, *P.P.*, [C. 6984 – vii], q. 24,010.
85. M.S. Pember Reeves *op. cit.*, p. 103.
86. *Report of the Inter-Departmental Committee on Physical Deterioration*, 1904, *P.P.*, [Cd. 2175], p. 53. Mrs. Smyth was quoting the views of Dr. Priestly, Medical Officer of Health for Lambeth.
87. *Ibid.*, p. 51.
88. Table 7; B.S. Rowntree *op. cit.*, pp. 408-23; M.S. Pember Reeves *op. cit.*, p. 96.
89. *Ibid.*, p. 103; Lady Bell *op. cit.*, pp. 92-7.
90. *Ibid.*, p. 99.
91. O.C. Malvery *op. cit.*, p. 70; *How the Casual Labourer Lives. Report of the Liverpool Joint Committee . . .*, (1909), p. xxi; *Board of Trade Inquiry 1908*, p. 304.
92. M.S. Pember Reeves *op. cit.*, p. 97.
93. *Royal Commission on Labour. Minutes of Evidence*, Group A, Vol. III, 1893, *P.P.*, [C. 6984 – vii], q. 24,010. The labourers' representatives giving evidence were W.J. Lewington and R.S. Gordon.
94. *Fifth Report. Sweating System (House of Lords)*, 1890, *P.P.*, (169), p. v.
95. See Chapter 3 for a discussion of this point.
96. *Report of the Inter-Departmental Committee on Physical Deterioration*, 1904, *P.P.*, [Cd. 2175], p. 51.
97. *Minutes of Evidence taken before the Inter-Departmental Committee on Physical Deterioration*, 1904, *P.P.*, [Cd. 2210], qq. 2046-7.
98. *How the Labourer Lives. Report of the Liverpool Joint Committee . . .*, (1909), p. xxi; B. S. Rowntree *op. cit.*, pp. 240-1.
99. *Ibid.*, pp. 241-2.
100. *Ibid.*, pp. 106, 132-3.
101. W.A. Gray, On sufficient and insufficient dietaries, with especial reference to the dietaries of prisoners, *Journal of the Royal Statistical Society*, Vol. xxvi (1863), especially pp. 244-80.
102. quoted in J. Burnett, *Plenty and Want* (1966), pp. 143-4.
103. B.S. Rowntree *op. cit.*, p. 382; *Report of the Inter-Departmental Committee on Physical Deterioration* 1904, *P.P.*, [Cd. 2175], pp. 66-7.
104. A.L. Bowley and A.R. Burnett-Hurst *op. cit.*, p. 44.
105. M.S. Pember Reeves *op. cit.*, pp. 176-95 (the quotation is taken from p. 193); B.S. Rowntree *op. cit.*, pp. 205-16.
106. See, for instance, the evidence of several witnesses who appeared before the *Glasgow Municipal Commission on Working-Class Housing* (1902-3), including Miss M.B. Blackie, Secretary of the Housing Branch of the Kyrle Society.
107. S.D. Chapman (ed.) *op. cit.*, p. 77.
108. F.G. Masterman, *The Heart of the Empire* (reissued 1973 by Harvester Press), p. 95.
109. H.J. Dyos *art. cit.*, p. 27.
110. *Glasgow Municipal Commission* (1902-3), q. 691; R.Q. Gray *op. cit.*, pp. 96-7.
111. *8th Report to the Medical Officer of the Privy Council for 1865*, (1866), p. 137.
112. *Sanitary Conditions of the Labouring Population. Local Reports*, 1842, *P.P.*, (H.L.), p. 361.
113. *Journal of the Royal Statistical Society*, Vol. vi (1843), p. 17.
114. *8th Report of the Medical Officer of the Privy Council for 1865*, (1866), pp. 111,

137-8; *Sanitary Conditions of the Labouring Population. Local Reports*, 1842, *P.P.*, (H.L.), p. 361; S.D. Chapman (ed.) *op. cit.*, pp. 178-9.

115. *Ibid.*

116. *Ibid.*, pp. 181-4.

117. quoted in *Ibid.*, p. 179.

118. *Journal of the Royal Statistical Society*, Vol. II (1839), pp. 370-1.

119. *Ibid.*, Vol. XI (1848), p. 211.

120. S.D. Chapman (ed.) *op. cit.*, p. 174.

121. *Journal of the Royal Statistical Society*, Vol. 64 (1901), p. 213.

122. *Ibid.*, p. 215.

123. *Transactions of the National Association for the Promotion of Social Science for 1866* (1967), p. 464.

124. *8th Report of The Medical Officer of the Privy Council for 1865*, (1866), p. 169.

125. quoted in S.D. Chapman (ed.) *op. cit.*, p. 196.

126. quoted in *ibid.*

127. quoted in H.J. Dyos and M. Wolff (eds.) *op. cit.*, Vol. II (1973), p. 614.

128. G. Stedman Jones *op. cit.*, pp. 174-7, 219.

129. S.B. Rowntree *op. cit.*, pp. 170, 177.

130. *Ibid.*, pp. 176-8.

131. *Assistant Commissioners' Report upon Handloom Weavers* Part II, *P.P.*, 1840, (43 — I), p. 475.

132. *Sanitary Condition of the Labouring Population. Local Reports*, 1842, *P.P.*, (H.L.), p. 361; quoted in N. Murray *op. cit.*, p. 265.

133. *Sanitary Condition of the Labouring Population. Local Reports*, 1842, *P.P.*, (H.L.), p. 306.

134. M.S. Pember Reeves *op. cit.*, pp. 49, 52, 56.

135. *Ibid.*, p. 49.

136. B.S. Rowntree *op. cit.*, pp. 279, 282.

137. quoted in S.D. Chapman (ed.) *op. cit.*, p. 185.

138. C.B. Hawkins *op. cit.*, p. 174.

139. B.S. Rowntree *op. cit.*, pp. 153, 188.

140. *Ibid.*, p. 154.

141. For short-lived exceptions see, for instance, *Journal of the Royal Statistical Society*, Vol. IV (1842), p. 320.

142. S.D. Chapman (ed.) *op. cit.*, p. 26.

143. *Ibid.*, p. 75.

144. *Journal of the Royal Statistical Society*, Vol. VI (1843), p. 17.

145. *Ibid.*, Vol. II (1839), p. 372; *ibid.*, Vol. IV (1843) , p.17.

146. S.D. Chapman (ed.) *op. cit.*, p. 37.

147. *Steel-Maitland and Squire Report*, p. 51.

148. *Board of Trade Inquiry*, 1908, pp. 86, 94, 161, 259.

149. S.D. Chapman (ed.) *op. cit.*, p. 26.

150. *Sanitary Condition of the Labouring Population. Local Reports.*, 1842, *P.P.*, (H.L.), p. 247.

151. B.S. Rowntree *op. cit.*, p. 165.

152. M.S. Pember Reeves *op. cit.*, pp. 41-2.

153. S. D. Chapman (ed.) *op. cit.*, p. 82.

154. B.S. Rowntree *op. cit.*, p. 244.

155. N. Murray *op. cit.*, pp. 172, 188; *5th Report from Select Committee on Artizans and Machinery*, *P.P.*, 1824, [51], p. 397; Report from *Assistant Handloom Weavers' Commissioners*, *P.P.*, 1840, Part III, (43 — II), p. 577.

156. *Appendix G Irish Poor*, p. 24.

157. *Liverpool Mercury* 24 March 1843.

158. B.S. Rowntree *op. cit.*, p. 244.

159. *Ibid.*, pp. 55-6.

160. M.S. Pember Reeves *op. cit.*, p. 62.

161. *Ibid.*, pp. 62, 83; Garrick Fraser *dissertation cit.*, pp. 70, 73; Mrs. H. Bosanquet, *Rich and Poor* (2nd ed., 1898), p. 84; E.G. Howarth and Mona Wilson *op. cit.*, pp.

pp. 332-3.
162. M.S. Pember Reeves *op. cit.*, p. 83.
163. *Ibid.*, pp. 62-4; B.S. Rowntree *op. cit.*, pp. 44-5.

Conclusion

1. *Journal of the Royal Statistical Society*, Vol. 72 (1909), p. 99; B.R. Mitchell and P. Deane *op. cit.*, pp. 344-5.
2. *Journal of the Royal Statistical Society*, Vol. 72 (1909), p. 99.
3. A.L. Bowley *Statistical Studies Relating to National Progress in Wealth and Trade since 1882* (1904), p. 11.
4. *Royal Commission on the Poor Laws*, Vol. ix, *Minutes of Evidence*, 1910, P.P., [Cd. 5068], q. 90112.
5. *Minutes of Evidence taken before the Inter-Departmental Committee on Physical Deterioration*, 1904, P.P., [Cd. 2210], q. 1773
6. *Ibid.*, q. 6373
7. B.S. Rowntree *op. cit.*, p. 117.
8. *Ibid.*, pp. 86-7, 111 and 117.
9. *Ibid.*, p. 142.
10. *Ibid.*, pp. 133-4.
11. A.L. Bowley and A.R. Burnett-Hurst *op. cit.*, p. 38.
12. Lady Bell *op. cit.*, pp. 85-6.
13. J. Burnett, *Plenty and Want* (1966), p. 94.
14. B.S. Rowntree *op. cit.*, p. 301.
15. *Ibid.*, passim.

Index